Racism and Sexism in Corporate Life

Racism and Sexism in Corporate Life

Changing Values in American Business

John P. Fernandez

LexingtonBooks
D.C. Heath and Company
Lexington, Massachusetts
Toronto

Library of Congress Cataloging in Publication Data

Fernandez, John P., 1941-
   Racism and sexism in corporate life.

   1. Minority executives—United States. 2. Women executives—United
States. 3. Discimination in employment—United States. 4. Corporations—
United States—Personnel management. I. Title.
HF5500.3.U54F474   658.3′041   80-8945
ISBN 0-669-04477-6   AACR2

Third printing, June 1982

Published simultaneously in Canada

Printed in the United States of America

Casebound International Standard Book Number: 0-669-04477-6

Paperbound International Standard Book Number: 0-669-05891-2

Library of Congress Catalog Card Number: 80-8945

This book is dedicated to the following white men who have played a crucial role in my surviving the corporate environment:

George Denend,

Bill Ebsworth,

Jim Franz,

Ed Gilligan,

Martin Griglak,

Ed Henle,

Jim Howard,

Norm Johnson,

Lou O'Leary,

Frank Lupinacci,

Gene Kofke,

Dick McCormick,

John Read,

Don Smith,

Bob Tobin.

Not only have they been fantastic corporate subordinates, peers, and bosses but also good people. If corporations had more white men like these, many corporate employee problems would be easily and readily solved.

Contents

Contents

List of Figures

List of Tables

Preface

Three factors stand out as I review the time between now and 1975 when my first book, *Black Managers in White Corporations*, was published: (1) my realization that little has changed in the situation and treatment of minority and female managers, (2) my acute awareness of the stress under which minorities and women are placed as they become isolated in middle- and upper-management levels, and (3) my conviction that some fundamental managerial-employment problems are very detrimental to employees regardless of race and sex.

These three factors are underscored directly and indirectly by the data collected for this book. Corporate organizations clearly should begin to provide healthy and supportive environments in which important consideration is given not to conformity and its resultant mediocrity of performance but to individual responsibility and the recognition of excellent performance.

I hope that the attitudes and opinions of the 4,209 native-American, Asian, black, Hispanic, and white male and female managers who participated in this study will more-clearly delineate the complex race, sex, and value problems confronting corporations in the 1980s.

I hope that those white men who are the power group in the corporate world do not dismiss the opinions and attitudes of minority and female managers because they find some of those opinions and attitudes disturbing and offensive. To ignore these managers' concerns will not only be costly to the white male managers themselves but also to the efficient functioning of the corporation.

Minorities and women who read this book must recognize that even before they were allowed to become corporate managers, the corporate-employment processes were unfair. Thus they must carefully distinguish between racist and sexist acts of the corporate-employment system and the general unfairness of the system. This book should help make these distinctions clearer. In addition, it will assist them in understanding, coping, and overcoming their oppression.

For all managers, regardless of race and sex, I have presented a managerial-employment system that, if properly implemented, will go a long way toward solving the race, sex, and value-system problems that will confront corporations in the 1980s.

Acknowledgments

Sincerity needs no embellishment. Briefly, I express my great appreciation to the management of the twelve companies whose total cooperation made this book possible. To protect the anonymity of their companies, I cannot name the managers who were my coordinators and advisers. However, I would be remiss if I did not mention that they all went well beyond their normal duties.

Dr. David Nasatir, George Mapp, Mindy Printz, Joan Wicks, Judy David, and Pamela Steen not only assisted me in understanding the uses and misuses of statistics but also in reviewing the manuscript. Ms. Steen, in particular, greatly influenced the analysis of all the data and the basic direction of the book.

Eva Kaplan, Anne Gaudio, Janet Sherwood, Bill Ebsworth, Renee Ebsworth, Don Smith, Ed Gilligan, Betty Roberts, and Shirley Risoldi were very helpful in editing the various drafts of the manuscript and in suggesting substantive changes.

Because of the large amount of data, three different drafts of the manuscript needed to be typed. For this I am greatly indebted to Margaret Georges, Carol Schaefers, Mary Ann Nardina, Rita Fagan, and Betsy Schweppe.

John Read, a friend for twelve years, encouraged me to finish the book and helped me obtain financial assistance.

I am grateful to Philip Hallen of the Maurice Falk Medical Foundation for financial assistance. In addition, partial support for this research was received from the U.S. Department of Labor, Employment Standards Administration. However, the opinions expressed herein are solely mine and do not necessarily reflect those of the U.S. Department of Labor. I am also grateful to Peggy Albert and Art Edmunds of the Urban League, and Ted Adams of the Department of Labor for assistance in finding a publisher.

During the preparation of the manuscript, Carolyn Boardman served as editor, researcher, proofreader, and did many other chores, but most of all she provided moral support and was a friend.

The third printing and the paperback printing of this book would never have been achieved if it were not for the skills, talent, and cooperation of Kathy Benn and Pam Walch.

Finally, my daughters Michele, Eleni, and Sevgi once again tolerated their father's ups and downs while he was writing a book.

Part I
Race and Sex Problems of the 1980s

1

What Is Happening in the Heterogeneous Corporations?

A 45-year-old white male, a middle-level manager with a college degree, told an interviewer that he is seriously considering early retirement. He said that he is frustrated with his job and lack of advancement opportunities, and he expressed grave concern that "things aren't like they used to be" in his company. These days women supervise men, minorities get all the opportunities, and many new young managers question work methods and authority. He believes that standards have shifted and that the work atmosphere has become more difficult. He said:

> Hard work, ability, and merit are no longer of value. The minorities and women are promoted regardless of qualifications. White males, especially older ones, have no opportunities for advancement. We are now discriminated against. The government is running this company and my life. This company does not have the courage to tell the government where to go. When I get the minimum amount of time in and if I can afford it, I shall retire—I am fed up.

A 28-year-old college-educated Hispanic woman at a lower level of management is frequently mistaken for a black because of her dark skin and coarse hair. She feels rewards for ability, merit, and hard work are only a reality for white men. In her opinion, her race, sex, and black appearance are limiting her advancement opportunities. She feels the company does not respect employees as human beings but views them instead as objects. Minorities and women are, in her mind, excluded from informal work groups by whites. They are told directly and indirectly that they got their jobs because of quotas, not because of their abilities. She believes her job is boring and that it does not allow her to use her skills in mathematics. She is a personnel specialist who plans to leave the company in the near future unless drastic changes occur in her work situation. In her words:

> As a Hispanic female who happens to look black, I get it from all directions—my race, ethnic origin, and sex. You would think I have it made from all the propaganda about the opportunities for women and minorities, but that is not true. The white males have the power, and they promote white males 95 percent of the time. The equal-employment laws are easily circumvented. Not only are women and minorities not promoted but they are usually put in boring staff jobs with little power. In addition, this company does not like new, creative ideas. It is conservative and authori-

3

tarian. I want to have a challenging job. I want to be listened to. This isn't the military, or at least I thought it wasn't. I probably will be gone in six months.

A 32-year-old white man, a middle-level manager with an MBA in finance, is very concerned about his career. He entered the company on a fast-track program, but he is now experiencing conflicts between his style of management and that of his bosses. He believes that his company holds conformity at a premium as opposed to creativity and innovation. As he notes:

> My concern is not with minorities and women, it's with the old-style-management ideas. My first boss in the company was open minded and liked my style. However, my past two bosses are very threatened by any new ideas, whether it has to do with running the mechanics of the job, managing people, or managing one's personal life. All they know how to say is, "We've never done things that way." If they wanted a robot, why didn't they say so? If the company's inflexible attitudes change, I have a future. If they can't, I don't—and I'm not optimistic.

These three managers see little or no future for themselves in the corporate structure. One sees affirmative action as a threat, diluting the quality of the work force and jeopardizing his own chances for advancement. Another sees affirmative action as ineffectual. She views her sex and her minority status as handicaps in what is still essentially a white-male-dominated world. The third discounts affirmative action as a major problem. To him, the real problem is the failure of management to respond to new ideas and new styles.

All three, however, express a strong dissatisfaction with the job and the corporate-management style. All are representative of the more-heterogeneous management teams that comprise today's corporate management. Their complaints are indicative of the problems corporations must resolve if they are to sustain a reasonable degree of stability in personnel and productivity for the future.

Background

The conflict between the needs and aspirations of the individual and the goals and requirements of the organization has always been present. In the past, as Douglas T. Hall and Francine S. Hale noted, the outcome was that the organization socialized the person into accepting its goals. This usually stifled creativity and suppressed individuality. Today, however, many employees are beginning to try to make the organization more human. They are gaining an increased sense of identity and power that reduces the odds against them and against possible change.[1]

Two major forces have combined in the past fifteen years to produce an impact upon the American-employee body and workplace as significant as that of the Industrial Revolution and its concomitant technological developments. One of these forces is the changing value system of our society. The other force is the combined effect of Equal-Employment-Opportunity legislation and Affirmative-Action Programs (EEO/AAP) that have created a more-heterogeneous corporate-employee body. Together, these forces could surpass technology's role as an agent of change.

The shifting composition of the labor force has created new types of conflict and stress. Large numbers of people in the managerial work force who were raised during the Depression era of the 1930s and the war era of the 1940s are being replaced by a succession of management cohorts who grew up in the affluent 1950s, the socially conscious 1960s, and the so-called me decade of the 1970s. Many of these younger managers tend to display a different value system. As they make up a larger and larger part of the corporate work force, and as they move up the corporate ladder, their attitudes and expectations will begin to influence the traditional group of managers. The resultant shift in values has been stimulated not only by a younger work force but also by a better-educated managerial force. Educated people tend to expect more. They also ask more "why," "hows," and "whens" of their corporate bosses.

Values are further influenced by changes in economic conditions that permit more income to be directed toward interests or concerns beyond the basics of food and shelter. The "new-breed" managers, in contrast to their elders, are no longer satisfied simply because they have a stable job and receive a regular paycheck. These managers increasingly express a concern that their work must be a source of self-respect and other nonmaterial rewards such as challenge, growth, personal fulfillment, and the opportunity to advance and accumulate. These managers' values have moved well beyond the "day's work for a day's pay" and "what the boss says goes" adages.

These new-breed employees represent more than half of the adult Americans. Daniel Yankelovich described this group as ". . . those who feel that their aspirations for self-fulfillment can no longer be wholly satisfied through conventional success. . . ." He went on to point out the conflict in values:

> Not surprisingly the younger, better-educated, and more-affluent parts of the population are disproportionately represented in the new breed, whereas the older, poorer, less-well-educated segments of the population cling more tenaciously to the old value system and to traditional success symbols.[2]

The present mood and its impact on the orgnization are aptly summed up by Hall and Hale who perceived what is commonly called a *generation gap* as being a *value/perception* gap.

All these moves toward greater personal choice represent a significant change in the norms and internal environment of the organization. Increasingly, organizations and administrators will not be permitted the "luxury" of overlooking the impact of their actions upon the personal life and careers of their employees. Much of what is thought to be a generation gap today is more accurately called a value/perception gap. Part of the difference between younger and older people is that they tend to value things differently, and part of the difference is that they perceive things differently.[3]

An example is the difference that exists between how older people estimate the younger generation's support of the work ethic and what the younger generation believes. Although older people today do not think that the younger generation espouses the work ethic, a study by Rogene Buckholz showed an inverse relationship between age and the presence of work ethic—that is, the older the workers the lower the manifest strength of the work ethic.[4] One possible explanation for this is that young people, who initially tend to believe hard work and good performance lead to jobs that are interesting and challenging as well as to promotional opportunities, fair treatment, and other rewards, become aware that their hard work and good performance on the job do not necessarily lead to such rewards. Thus, they become less work oriented in later years as the realities of the corporate structure become more apparent.

Another example is the great turmoil and uneasiness that young managers create among older managers when they ask simple questions about such areas as their job performance, potential evaluations, and career plans. Many of the older managers believe that these questions show aggressiveness and lack of tact. Others believe they show a lack of faith in the company, and some even interpret such questions as a sign of disloyalty to the company. In short, younger managers believe they have a right to ask these questions so they can make their own decisions about their careers and life directions. However, many older managers do not concur with this view.

Attitudes and opinions about the changing "success and fulfillment ethics" were sought in a study conducted by the American Management Associations (AMA). The AMA studied 2,800 U.S. businesspeople and found that half of the managers had considered changing their occupational field, while over one-third have seriously considered such a change, believing another field would be much more satisfying than their present one. Forty percent of middle-level managers and 52 percent of lower-level managers were dissatisfied with their present work. More than half of the participants believed that the pressures to conform to organizational standards were either increasing or were the same as in the past. Finally, nearly 30 percent of the managers believed that the pressures and stress of their job requirements had adversely affected their health at one time or another during the past five years.[5]

Similarly disturbing findings emerged from a series of polls of American workers conducted over the past twenty-five years by the Opinion Research Corporation. One-third of all hourly employees and one-half of all clerical employees felt they were "treated with respect as individuals" for the period 1975-1977. Managers' attitudes about their treatment were almost as discouraging. Whereas 84 percent of the group surveyed prior to 1960 felt they were treated fairly, only 47 percent felt favorably about their treatment in 1977. The figure decreased by almost 50 percent when the managers were asked whether the company was willing to listen to their problems and complaints. Less than one-third of the hourly employees and only 38 percent of the clerical employees responded affirmatively. Only half of the managers seemed to be satisfied in this regard. In terms of perceived inequity, as of 1977 only about 20 percent of the hourly and clerical employees and 50 percent of the managers believed that their company selected the best person for the job.[6]

Although many of the problems just discussed are caused primarily by the creation of a younger, more-affluent, and better-educated work force, another set of factors—race and sex—also has made an impact on the conflicts and stresses of the corporate workplace. Corporations are changing from homogeneous organizations dominated by white men to heterogeneous organizations, a fact that is very slowly forcing the dominant group to share its positions and power with minorities and women

Many minorities and women have been socialized differently. They have diverse cultural backgrounds, different value systems, and different expectations than do the white males who presently dominate these corporations. The coming together of these people of diverse backgrounds, in some cases for the first time and in others for the first time in the corporate setting, has created great tension for everyone.

Not only has the clashing of different backgrounds created tensions but also the new competition from women and minorities. In the past, white men dominated 95 percent of the corporate-management ranks, while representing only 37 percent of the population. Now, they must compete with 63 percent of the population with whom they have never had to compete. Thus, many of these white males now believe that they are treated unfairly and that reverse discrimination is a common occurrence. However, large numbers of minorities and women believe that even after fifteen years of equal-employment-opportunity progress, white men are still the preferred race/sex group by far. This phenomenon of perception can be attributed largely to the differences between the people who have been accustomed to having almost all of the power in the corporate hierarchy and the people who have had almost none. Any loss from exclusivity is viewed as great, while small gains from exclusion are not viewed as being important.

It is important to understand that the conflict is not exclusively white men versus women and minorities. Conflict exists between minorities and white women, between the various minority groups, and between the different sexes of the same minority group. Numerous accusations fly among these groups as to who is getting all the opportunities and who is being treated fairest of them all.

The AAP hiring promotional programs present interesting changes in traditional authority relationships. Young educated women are supervising older, less-educated men; older workers are subordinates of younger managers; and minority employees are supervising whites, many of whom have never had previous contact with minorities. These new relationships are in many cases like all new relationships: difficult, stressful, and full of conflicts.

Kathryn Welds expertly noted the ultimate destructive effect of these new conflicts if they are not dealt with in an effective and honest manner:

> Many unanticipated conflicts may occur overtly, but there are also more-subtle, self-destructive displacements when conflict is ignored altogether. Besides decreasing an organization's potential for an open, creative, and friendly atmosphere, hidden conflict can also be reflected in tardiness and absenteeism; high turnover and production errors; increased accidents, grievances, and transfer requests; plus decreased productivity. In addition, there are stress-related physical symptoms: insomnia; headache; hypertension; asthma and cardiac irregularities; weight changes; ulcers and colitis; uncontrolled use of drugs, cigarettes, or food; anxiety; and depression. These all suggest unresolved conflict in the workplace and add to occupational burnout.[7]

In short, the new value systems created by affluence, education, youth, sex, and race, in combination with the changing makeup of the corporate work force, are creating new conflicts and stresses that could be a time bomb if ignored.

The time for appealing to corporate beneficence is long past. The question is no longer one of a moral responsibility to be fair and equitable in the hiring and advancement of employees. It is no longer even a simple question of adhering to federal fair-employment laws. It is also no longer a question of corporations determining what is right and good for their employees. The new breed of employee will not tolerate unfair treatment or put up with such authoritarian paternalism. Facing the problems of today's corporate structure is, purely and simply, a matter of survival. Corporations must begin to listen to their employees' concerns about the work environment and the work itself.

The Study

This book presents the results of a study undertaken to address the problems that have just been introduced. It was originally designed to determine whether minorities and women needed special training to become effective managers in corporations. Responses to an initial investigation, however, indicated that the study should be expanded to look at (1) the overall effect of employment policies and practices on managerial utilization and (2) the overall atmosphere in which managers perceive they currently work.

The book is directed toward helping corporate managers, students of business, government officials, and others interested in better understanding the problems and their solutions. In addition, various employment policies and practices are illustrated, discussed, and critically analyzed to aid corporations in the alleviation of these new problems.

Characteristics of Participating Companies

Twelve large companies participated in this study at various stages. All have been very active in striving for equal-employment opportunities over the past ten years. Their combined managerial force exceeds 125,000 people. The participating companies were selected on the basis of their geographic location, their numbers of minority and female managers, and the corporate levels of these managers. The study included representatives from all sections of the country.

All parties involved in this study felt it was important to include members of all races. Numerous other studies have discussed overall work experiences and attitudes of managers. An increasing number of studies relate to minorities, almost exclusively blacks. Other studies about women in management focus almost exclusively on white women. This, however, is the first study to analyze the views and attitudes of native Americans, Asians, blacks, Hispanics, and whites—both male and female—at all levels of management. To date, this is also the only study to attempt this comprehensive overview of contemporary corporate management.

A total of 4,202 managers, stratified by race, sex, and managerial level, were randomly selected from ten companies. Sample size enabled the data to be generalized to each specific race/sex/level group, with a 90 percent accuracy rate. This means that if this study were done one hundred times, at least 90 percent of the time similar results would occur with small percentage deviations in either direction of the present findings. Where there were only a few managers at any level, all of the managers participated in the study. For example, where only twelve black men from these companies were at the fourth level and above, all participated. Table 1-1 gives the race/sex/level breakdown of the participating managers.

Two major findings arose from the study: (1) some basic managerial needs and concerns are common to all employees, regardless of age, race, and sex, and (2) substantial race and sex differences exist among managers' views regarding EEO/AAP and the present overall situation and treatment of white-male, minority, and female managers in the participating companies.

Table 1-1
Study Participants

Race	Women					Men						
	First Level[a]	Second Level[b]	Third Level[c]	Fourth Level[d]	Subtotal	First Level[a]	Second Level[b]	Third Level[c]	Fourth Level[d]	Fifth Level[e]	Subtotal	Total
Native Americans	87	16	0	1	104	73	49	16	4	2	144	248
Asians	115	20	0	0	135	89	31	2	0	0	122	257
Blacks	264	153	16	0	433	231	176	55	8	4	474	907
Hispanics	212	68	7	1	288	219	147	31	5	1	403	691
Whites	301	264	183	20	768	309	294	275	246	196	1,320	2,088
Total	979	521	206	22	1,728	921	697	379	263	203	2,463	4,191

Note: The total number of participants on the table does not amount to 4,202 because 11 of the participants did not indicate either their race, their sex, or their level. Also, fourth refers to managers at the fourth level and above, and fifth refers to managers at the fifth level and above.
[a]First level are supervisors of nonmanagers.
[b]Second level are supervisors of first-line supervisors.
[c]Third level are middle-level managers.
[d]Fourth level are upper-middle-level managers.
[e]Fifth level and above are upper-level managers.

The first finding relates to the new-breed manager whose satisfaction requires not only a job and a paycheck but also a pleasant work atmosphere/environment, interesting and challenging work, a rewarding career, and fair treatment as a human being. These common needs and concerns occur in career-planning, performance-evaluation, potential-evaluation, job-satisfaction, work-design, and training and development areas. Similarities in responses are clearly evident even between black men, who are usually the most pessimistic and most critical, and white men, who are usually the most optimistic and least critical of current corporate practices in these areas. Table 1-2 illustrates the similarity in the responses of white and black men to questions relating to these matters.

While commonalities occur across groups, some considerable differences are evident by managerial level. For those cases in which managers at higher levels are more optimistic and less critical than those at lower levels about career-planning, performance-and-potential-evaluations, work-design, and training-and-development needs, several practical explanations are available. One is that greater amounts of information are routinely available to higher-level managers as a requirement for their decision-making responsibilities. Also, upper-level managers are more likely to feel they have been successful, and thus they no longer require career planning, performance and potential evaluations, and training and development. In addition, because of their successes they look more favorably upon the governing policies. Finally, they find their jobs more satisfying and better designed because they control the structure of the organization and the large work flow.

With regard to the second major finding, the evidence shows that substantial race/sex/level differences exist among managers' views regarding EEO/AAP and the present overall situation and treatment of minority and female managers in companies. Blacks and Hispanics perceive the effects of EEO/AAP on their employment opportunities most positively, but they are also the most critical about the present problems and obstacles confronting minorities in the companies.

The hierarchy of responses finds that blacks are by far the most critical, followed by Hispanics, Asians, native Americans, and whites.

With regard to women, black women are the most critical about their work situation, followed by white, Hispanic, native-American, and finally Asian women. As minorities have found allies in white women, primarily at higher levels, so have women managers found allies in many black men, who are unique in that they identify with the overall concerns of women managers. In general, all other groups of men express very little identification with most of the problems facing women in the corporate world.

Considerable evidence suggests that minority and female managers, especially black men and white women at higher levels of the corporate

Table 1-2
Managerial Concerns and Problems as Viewed by White and Black Men
(percent)

Concerns	Race	First	Second	Third	Fourth	Fifth+
Managers who say they need training on performance, potential, and career planning	Black	53	42	27	8	NA[a]
	White	43	36	23	18	18
Managers who say their jobs involve a whole and identifiable piece of work	Black	43	47	52	56	NA
	White	48	48	54	59	67
Managers who rate their company's career-planning system good or excellent	Black	Approximately 31 at all levels[b]				
	White	26	26	31	42	58
Managers who are not at all informed about career opportunities and requirements	Black	58	46	35	25	NA
	White	52	44	34	22	14
Managers who believe bosses are at least somewhat helpful in the area of career development	Black	Approximately 53 at all levels				
	White	Approximately 55 at all levels				
Managers who feel they are not performing their job as effectively as possible	Black	Approximately 50 at all levels				
	White	Approximately 43 at all levels				
Managers who believe their bosses' potential-evaluation procedures are not objective	Black	Approximately 31 at all levels				
	White	Approximately 25 at all levels				

[a] NA means not applicable.
[b] "Approximately ____ at all levels" means no significant differences appeared in the managers' responses by level.

ladder, are more, and not less, critical of their situation. Since this finding holds true even when age and length of employment with the company are controlled, the critical views held by higher-level minority and women managers apparently are the direct product of their own corporate experience.

White and native-American men see the fewest positive effects of EEO/AAP. Many of them believe that the "fair-merit system" they believe to have existed previously has been replaced by a system based largely on race and/or sex, rather than on merit. They feel that this system leaves them at at great disadvantage. They perceive minority and women managers' present situation to be basically nonproblematic and in accord with democratic ideals.

Table 1-3 illustrates the extreme difference between the views of black and white men on these issues.

Table 1-4 shows the sex-difference views by comparing white women's and men's responses on similar issues.

In sum, companies are faced with one set of managerial problems that is a function of the new value system and the managerial level. A second set of managerial problems, however, stems directly from differences in race and sex. This book suggests that many of the value-system problems and many of the race/sex concerns will disappear in direct proportion to the solution of managerial problems relating to work design, performance and potential evaluations, career planning, and training and development. Implementation of objective, systematic employment policies and practices will help alleviate some of the conflict and stress. Many current policies are idiosyncratic, subjective, and nonsystematic. This permits managers to blame their employment-related problems on others and on their race and/or sex, rather than on their own deficiencies and/or the deficiencies of the total employment system. The present system also provides a scapegoat for managers who have difficulty discussing subordinates' deficiencies with them. Such managers blame lack of advancement, poor ratings, and boring jobs on others higher up and/or on the imagined need to fill EEO objectives rather than on the real deficiencies of their subordinates and/or employment policies and practices.

While many of the overall value problems and race/sex concerns can be solved with systematic employment policies and practices, not all of these concerns are soluble within the corporate context. Since corporations are reflections of the society in which they exist, they will only be able to totally solve these problems successfully when society as a whole solves its race/sex problems and new value problems. At the same time, corporations are a major factor in society, and improvements in the corporate world are reflected in the society at large.

Table 1-3
Corporate Race and Sex Problems as Viewed by White and Black Men
(percent)

Problems	Race	First	Second	Third	Fourth	Fifth+
				Level		
Managers who agree affirmative action lowers hiring and promotion standards	Black	Approximately 14 at all levels[a]				
	White	Approximately 84 at all levels				
Managers who indicate women have problems and/or obstacles in at least three out of four work-related areas	Black	20	31	34	50	NA[b]
	White	Approximately 5 at all levels				
Managers who indicate minorities have problems in three out of three work-related social-interaction areas	Black	44	52	67	80	NA
	White	Approximately 7 at all levels				
Managers who are aware of numerous sexist tendencies in their company	Black	30	32	43	58	NA
	White	19	14	12	11	9
Managers who believe their career opportunities have improved since EEO	Black	45	49	56	58	NA
	White	Approximately 2 at all levels				
Managers who believe their career opportunities have been hindered since EEO	Black	Approximately 7 at all levels				
	White	59	66	50	22	6

[a] "Approximately _____ at all levels" means no significant differences appeared in the responses by level.
[b] NA means not applicable.

Table 1-4
Corporate Sex-Discrimination Problems as Viewed by White Men and Women
(percent)

Problems	Sex	Level				
		First	*Second*	*Third*	*Fourth*	*Fifth+*
Managers who believe their career oportunities have improved since EEO	Females	27	47	77	60	NA[a]
	Males	Approximately 2 at all levels[b]				
Managers who believe female managers are as qualified as male managers	Females	Approximately 95 at all levels				
	Males	63	66	72	76	79
Managers who believe women face three out of three social-interaction problems	Females	26	39	43	50	NA
	Males	Approximately 15 at all levels				
Managers who believe women have problems and/or obstacles in at least three out of four work-related areas	Females	25	26	44	45	NA
	Males	Approximately 5 at all levels				
Managers who believe minorities face at least four out of five racist tendencies	Females	7	12	20	40	NA
	Males	Approximately 6 at all levels				

[a]NA means not applicable.
[b]"Approximately _____ at all levels" means no significant differences appeared in the managers' responses by level.

History of the Study

During 1974-1975, increasing numbers of minority and female managers, behavioral scientists, and professionals in private industry and government questioned whether minorities and women needed special training to become effective managers in corporations. Many of these people claimed that the primary reason greater numbers of women and minorities are not placed, especially in middle- and upper-management positions, is due to the difference in cultural backgrounds and/or socialization patterns.

This study was initially designed to determine whether minorities and women needed such special training. During preliminary investigative interviews with managers from all race/sex/level groups in five companies, the study's original focus appeared to be too narrow. It had neglected to consider the possibility that similarities in training needs and concerns about corporate careers existed for *all* managers. More specifically, it had not considered that managers, regardless of race or sex, have certain similar training needs and career concerns because of poorly designed, poorly implemented company policies and practices. It also had not considered the question of who really needs special training—minorities and women or white men. The original question supposed that minorities and women needed the training. This, of course, assumed that women and minorities were the cause of problems, rather than white men. The results of the preliminary interviews suggested that the source of many problems and the real need for special training may lie primarily with white men.

In brief, the responses clearly indicated that the study should look at (1) the effect of overall employment policies and practices for managerial utilization and (2) the overall atmosphere in which managers perceive they currently work. The study was, therefore, expanded to:

> Identify problems associated with the development and utilization of managerial talent, with particular attention to minorities and women;
>
> Identify problems associated with the current work atmosphere;
>
> Provide a foundation from which to develop recommendations for changes in employment policies and practices, and related procedures to assure optimal utilization of the talent in corporations and a work atmosphere conducive to good employee morale and productivity.

Research Instrument and Study Steps

The data were collected through a self-administered questionnaire that had both open-ended questions, for which managers were able to give their own responses, and close-ended questions, for which participants chose from specific responses. Thus, both quantitative statistical data and qualitative individual comments are presented to assist the reader in a better understanding of the managers' feelings, beliefs, and attitudes. Trained professionals administered the questionnaires to groups of ten to fifteen managers. This procedure ensured that all participants' data would be collected. It also gave the participants an opportunity to ask questions of the professionals if they found any of the questionnaire material confusing. Note that only four managers refused to participate.

The content of the questionnaire was determined primarily from preliminary group interviews with over 350 managers, which were conducted in five of the companies with men and women of all races and managerial levels. The questionnaire included the following sections:

Biographical Data,

Career Planning,

Performance-Evaluation Procedures,

Potential-Evaluation Procedures,

Advancement,

Training and Development,

Special Training,

Work-Design Information,

Boss Relationships,

Work-Group Relationships—Peers and Subordinates,

Equal-Employment Opportunity/Affirmative-Action Program,

Women Managers,

Minority Managers,

Relocation,

Remaining with Their Company,

Job/Work History.

The specific questions came from previous studies, the comments of the 350 managers in the preliminary interviews, and suggestions from internal and external consultants. A pilot questionnaire was tested on 350 other managers in two companies who did not participate in the final sample. The final draft of the questionnaire was based on a careful item-by-item analysis of the pilot instrument.

Once the data had been collected for the years between 1976 and 1978 and a preliminary analysis had been made, feedback was given to a randomly selected 10 percent of the sample to gain their reactions and insights into the data. Some of the sessions were in homogeneous groups and others were in heterogeneous groups. This grouping greatly facilitated the final analysis, interpretation of the data, and development of recommendations.

If those who read this book approach it with an open critical mind, they will gain a great deal of insight and knowledge to assist them in understanding and/or prospering in the corporate world of the 1980s.

2 Different Minority Groups

Economic issues are probably the chief factors in determining the level of racist attitudes within this society. (For a detailed discussion of racism and sexism see the appendix.) Although political and social competition are important, the competition for desirable land, money, and good jobs determines, in large part, the intensity and depth of the threat felt by white society. Once a minority is perceived as taking something to which the dominant group feels exclusively entitled, it is subjected to all the harassment, exploitation, manipulation, and oppression a dominant group can muster. The acutal size of the minority group and its skin color also determine the white attitudes and behaviors directed toward its members. In return, the minority group's response to society, and of course to the corporation, is greatly influenced by the attitudes and behaviors directed toward them, attitudes and behaviors initially caused by the white response to perceived threats.

The discrimination encountered by each minority group in this study differs in kind and degree. Each group has been the target of racism in many similar and some different ways. Each group has differing positive and negative stereotypes placed upon it, not only by the white majority but also by other minorities. The degree of hostility with which each group views its treatment by American society differs.

The greatest burden of racism appears to have fallen upon the black race for a number of reasons: the bitter legacy of slavery, its darker color, its larger numbers, and its location throughout the country. The results of this greater burden, as shown throughout the data collected in this study, is that black managers are the most sensitive and empathetic to the plight of minority managers and the most outraged at the racist treatment they observe in the environs of American corporations today.

The Hispanic group, the next-largest minority in the United States, is second only to blacks in its negative views about the treatment and situation of minorities in corporations. However, within this large, umbrella term, *Hispanic*, are five distinct groups. When their responses are analyzed, we find that Puerto Ricans, many of whom have black origins, respond more similarly to blacks than do the other Hispanic groups. People who classify themselves as having "other Spanish" origins (Spain) are usually white in color and respond similarly to whites. This information strongly implies that the skin color of the Hispanic managers greatly influences their responses in this study.

The Asian-Americans are more acceptable than blacks and Hispanics to the white majority, probably in part because they are very small in numbers compared to blacks and Hispanics and lighter in skin color. As a result of this greater acceptability, they have tried to assimilate into white society more than the other minority groups, and their responses reflect this assimilated attitude.

Finally, it is important to note that of all major race groups, the responses of the native Americans are most similar to those of the whites. The main reason is that 39 percent of the native Americans have little, if any, native-American blood. In addition, the extensive assimilation policies the U.S. government has pursued at times with regard to the native Americans have had an impact on their value systems, attitudes, and opinions. This impact is especially strong on those native Americans who have left the reservation and joined American corporations.

Power and Stereotypes

A common factor in the history of each of the minority groups presented in this study is the power struggle with the dominant white population. Many whites view minority groups as a threat to the status quo. They fear the loss of power, control, and social position. This power struggle has caused competition over access to scarce resources such as jobs, land, housing, and education.

Every minority group has faced severe discrimination and racial oppression. The long-hallowed myth of a melting-pot society has been debunked by a number of social scientists, including Melvin Steinfield, who summed up the racial oppressions different minorities have suffered in this manner:

> While Anglos and other immigrants from northern and western Europe were "melting"; blacks were enslaved, sold, denied voting rights, and lynched; Indians were shoved off the paths of westward expansion and massacred; Chinese and Japanese were excluded or interred; Mexicans were conquered and oppressed. . . .[1]

Nonwhites have often been defined according to their function with American society rather than by their race or minority grouping. Blacks were considered draft animals; native Americans, wild animals; Asians, domestic animals; and Mexicans, humorous or lazy animals.[2] If a whole race is labeled as being little different from animals, no guilt is experienced from exploiting and discriminating against them in the most-severe, blatant manner.

While whites have developed negative stereotypes to justify the exploitation of and discrimination against minorities, negative stereotypes are most common and resilient about blacks and blackness. Positive concepts of blacks have not prevailed in any period of white history. However, other minorities have been viewed negatively and positively at different times. For example, the following passage illustrates such fluctuations:

> In 1935 most Americans thought of Japanese as "progressive," "intelligent," and "industrious"; by 1942 they were "cunning" and "treacherous"; and by 1950 the image had changed again. When there was a need for Chinese laborers in California, they were portrayed as "frugal," "sober," and "law abiding"; when labor was plentiful and they competed with white workers, they became "dirty," "repulsive," "unassimilable," and "dangerous."[3]

Prior to the Los Angeles "zoot-suit riots" during World War II, newspapers stressed Mexican-Americans' positive traits including the romantic qualities of their heritage, their brave temperament, their culture—dance, arts, music—and their devout religious values. However, during the riots, the imagery changed to a clearly negative portrayal of the Mexican-Americans as law violators, violent, lazy, cowardly, superstitious, backward, and immoral.[4]

White society has never wanted to be black. In America the old saying is, "An ounce of black blood makes one black." This adage applies to no other minority group. White and Asian is Eurasian. Hispanics were classified as whites until 1970. At various times in the history of this country, whites have taken "pride" in finding a little native-American blood in their family.

In sum, white Americans' views toward the various ethnic/race groups, except blacks, have varied greatly. Their views toward blacks have been consistently negative.

Several studies support the proposition that blacks are the least-accepted minority group represented in this study. Emery S. Bogardus, in his classic studies on social distance, noted that white Americans see certain minority groups as being more desirable than others. The more-desirable groups are, in order, Chinese, native Americans, Japanese, Mexicans, and blacks.[5]

A point of interest is that estimates show that now more than 36 million white Americans have some degree of black blood and that the vast majority of black Americans have white ancestors. Therefore, notions of biological or racial purity and superiority are as invalid as saying that only English-speaking people are Americans.[6]

The Four Minorities of This Study

The following sections of this chapter offer a brief historical review of the minority groups that participated in this study. The historical review concentrates on the groups' entry into the work-force competition for resources and the resultant reactions of white society. This review will assist the reader in analyzing why the minority groups respond differently to the present situation and treatment of minority managers in corporations.

Native Americans

The history of the treatment of native Americans is probably the worst story of murder, stealing, cheating, and lying perpetrated upon any group of people for their land and resources in the history of the world. It is a credit to native Americans that despite enormous efforts to devastate their cultures, they have survived to the extent that they have.

Competition for native-American land brought out racial stereotypes that supposedly justified stealing it. Philip L. Berg noted that as the Puritan population increased and its economic interests grew, it began to develop distinct negative changes in its conception of the native American. The white man's greed for land and resources had made the native American a victim of racism.[7]

After hundreds of treaties had been broken and most of their land had been stolen, the native Americans were totally convinced that these treaties were not for their protection and best interest but designed to separate them from their lands. Native Americans and whites first skirmished and then fought openly. The fighting was ferocious and barbaric on both sides. This was especially true of the whites, as they were the intruders.

> Group by group, the native Americans rose in rebellion only to be crushed—the Southern Plains tribes in 1874, the Sioux in 1876, the Nez Perce in 1877, and the Ute in 1879. The Apache tribe fought throughout much of the 1880s and 1890s until Geronimo finally surrendered with his remnant band of 36 survivors. The massacre of more than 300 Sioux, mostly women, children, and old people, at Wounded Knee, South Dakota in 1890 marked the end of massive native-American resistance to white authority.[8]

All told, throughout the history of the whites and native Americans, periods of peaceful coexistence were brief. From 1607 to the Wounded Knee Massacre in 1890, the native-American population decreased from an estimated 2 million to 200,000. This was an attrition unmatched by the Black Plague, the Thirty-Years War, or any modern war.[9]

Beyond demographic destruction, the native-American population also, at times, was forced from its land and home. In addition, whites developed programs to systematically destroy native Americans' traditional values and religion, economic systems, political systems, and language. In short, whites tried to forge an artificial amalgamation of hundreds of diverse and distinct native-American cultures. That these cultures could be regarded as one was the white man's idea, and because he possessed the power to do it he succeeded in making the concept a partial reality in his community.

An example of this forced adaptation is when, from the late 1890s to the 1930s:

> Tens of thousands of native-American children were 'legally' kidnapped and forced to attend schools hundreds of miles from home. Often their parents could not pay for their transportation home during vacations, so the youngsters had to remain at school all year. The school curriculum made no concessions to the cultural history or needs of native-American children. Rather, it was designed and applied with the idea of eradicating all signs of native-American culture.[10]

The strength of the native-American people to resist the white-imposed value and cultural systems has led the government to vacillate in its views about what should be done with native Americans. These changing views have been expressed in policies ranging in purpose from total integration into our cities to total isolation on reservations for the native-American population. Today they are still one of the most-manipulated people on earth, as well as our nation's poorest and sickest. Native-American unemployment is ten times the national average, and as much as 90 percent of all housing is below minimum standards for health and safety. They also have the highest rate of alcoholism and tuberculosis of any group in this country.

The whites' desire for native-American land and resources has never ceased, but the native Americans are now fighting back. As they fight back, not with guns but through the courts, the white backlash is beginning. The motive for the backlash is more economic than racial. Native Americans, 1 million in a population of 236 million, control 2 percent of the U.S. land mass. This percentage includes much mineral-rich land whose importance has increased because of the energy crisis. Native-American tribes own one-third of the country's easily accessible low-sulfur coal, one-half of its uranium, and substantial oil and natural gas deposits.

As noted in a recent *The New York Times* article, native Americans have experienced victories in a rapidly snowballing list of decisions and settlements. These victories have dealt with matters as diverse as the right of a family to raise children on the reservation, rights to fish and hunt, and rights to control water vital to the population and economic growth of the Southwest.[11]

Similarity between Native Americans' and Whites' Responses. One of the most-perplexing findings in this study is that, despite their terrible history of oppression at the hands of the U.S. government and people, the native Americans' responses to the questions about EEO/AAP and minorities; and women's treatment in their companies are quite similar to whites'.

As was earlier pointed out, whites tried to assimilate native Americans and destroy their culture with some success. This factor may explain to some extent why most native-American managers respond similarly to whites in this study. These managers have adopted white society's values and have moved to, and remained in, urban areas. In addition, they may see themselves as an elite of their race group who had to work hard to attain their position. They have little sympathy for other minority people who have not made it.

These native-American managers may also respond so conservatively because they are not true native Americans. Thirty-nine percent of the sample of this group is actually only one-eighth or less native American. Fifty percent of the sample are one-quarter to one-half native American, and only 11 percent are three-quarters or more native American. According to a white third-level manager, "Any white person who wanted to claim he/she had any Indian blood could be classified as 'Indian.'" A more-accurate criterion for determining native-American heritage, one accepted by the federal government, is that only individuals who can demonstrate that they are minimally one-quarter native American and who are actively associated with a native-American tribe are recognized as native Americans.

Some of the "new Indians" are not necessarily enthusiastic about their racial switch and have demonstrated a need to distance themselves from any native-American origins. One second-level native-American manager indicated that everyone should forget the past massacre of native Americans. The other native Americans in the group responded enthusiastically, saying, "Forget about the massacres in the past and let's start anew." In another group session, a first-level native-American manager said "We should forget about the past and ask what the native Americans are doing for the native Americans."

As noted earlier, the data gathered in this study consistently reveal that these pseudo-native Americans have a response pattern very similar to that of white men and dissimilar to that of any other minority group. As a full-blooded native American at the second level says:

> Those Indians or Chicanos who have always identified themselves as minorities are much more supportive to minority problems and less inclined to talk about reverse discrimination than those who identify themselves as white.

Table 2-1 demonstrates the difference between the responses of native Americans who are one-quarter or more native American and those who are

Table 2-1
Native Americans' versus Whites' versus Blacks' Responses about
Discrimination and EEO/AAP

Managers Who Agree with Statements	Less than One-Quarter Native American	More than One-Quarter Native American	Whites	Blacks
A lack exists of qualified minorities for managerial positions.	76	59	70	27
AAP is lowering hiring and promotion standards.	88	74	78	18
AAP helps more people than it harms.	50	60	70	88
Minorities are penalized more for mistakes than whites are.	6	17	10	57

one-quarter or less native American. In addition, black responses and white responses are given for comparison. The results indicate that native Americans who are one-quarter or more native American are usually more critical than those who are not, but still their responses are more similar to whites' and other minorities' than to those of blacks.

In addition to assimilation, another explanation for why even those native Americans who are "real" native Americans are not as critical as other minority groups is found in their culture. Elizabeth Almquist noted:

> Indians typically avoid several types of behavior that in white society are thought to be essential for "making it" in managerial and professional jobs. These behaviors include verbal manipulation, criticizing others, . . . and finally, most are reluctant to describe their personal problems or to seek assistance in solving them.[12]

Asian-Americans

People of Japanese and Chinese descent comprise the largest percentage of Asian-Americans, although many other Asian cultures are represented in this country. Due to their numbers, only these two subgroups' experiences are discussed. Both Japanese- and Chinese-Americans have, on the whole, higher personal incomes, higher family incomes, and higher proportional representation among professional and technical occupations than do white Americans or any minority group. Asians are also statistically over-represented in the better-paying areas such as the natural sciences. In addition, they have a higher education level. The 1970 census data revealed that the average number of school years the Japanese-Americans completed was

12.5, while the Chinese-Americans completed 12.4 years, and whites completed 12.1 years.

In order to reach these high levels of achievement in America, both groups had to overcome very hostile, demeaning, and dangerous racist attitudes and behaviors.

Chinese-Americans. The California Gold Rush brought the first large influx of Chinese into California. As with other minorities, the Chinese came to America partly to find a life better than the depressed conditions they had left in China. Most of these Chinese, in the early stages of immigration, were recruited to work as miners and railroad laborers.

Initially, Chinese laborers shipped to California in the nineteenth century were locked into the holds of ships. Many suffocated or starved to death. Others stabbed themselves with pieces of wood or hung themselves. Yet, despite these tremendous losses, the Chinese population in America, almost exclusively in California, between 1850 and 1880 increased from approximately 1,000 to 100,000.[13]

While the Chinese population was increasing, economic conditions in California were worsening. The Chinese became targets of racism. These people, who had been regarded as a godsend and as desirable workers because they were a cheap and efficient labor force, were subjected to the most-outrageous expressions of bigotry.[14]

Not only were they stoned, robbed, assaulted, and murdered, but they were also the victims of discriminatory legislation. In 1882 the U.S. Congress passed the Exclusion Act. This was an anti-immigration law that was directed for ten years against the Chinese. It was renewed for another ten years in 1892 and extended indefinitely in 1902. The act was not repealed until 1943 when it was replaced by a new act allowing only 105 Chinese to enter the United States each year. This seems a less than magnanimous quota considering the important role the Chinese played in the Japanese defeat in World War II. Another example of blatant racism is found in the 1927 U.S. Supreme Court decision of *Gong Lum* v. *Rice*. The Court upheld the right of local school boards to force Chinese students to attend black schools miles from their neighborhoods instead of permitting them to attend white schools in their own neighborhoods.[15]

Other laws were passed banning interracial marriages between whites and blacks, Chinese, Mongolians, or Orientals. These laws were not overturned by the U.S. Supreme Court until 1967.

During World War II, China and the Chinese people's image changed to that of a valiant wartime ally holding their own against vastly superior Japanese forces.

After the war, while mainland China turned to communism and fought the United States in the Korean War, Nationalist China was still a respected ally and became a valuable U.S. trading partner. These two Chinese nations greatly influence American attitudes toward the Chinese, both negatively and positively. More recently, the normalization of relations between the United States and mainland China has eliminated most negative attitudes Americans have toward the Chinese. In fact, as our trade increases with China, the need for Chinese employees is crucial. A number of American companies have secured lucrative contracts from China because of the skills of their Chinese employees.[16]

Presently, the Chinese in the United States are seen as a "model minority," an excellent example of an American "success story" despite their early hardships. However, in reality, many Chinese still suffer from racial discrimination, poverty, and the resultant problems. The model-minority myth is not true. The social problems of poverty, illiteracy, disease, broken families, and racist victimization have not disappeared entirely.

Japanese-Americans. In the late 1880s, as the demand for menial labor increased and the abundant source of Chinese labor was prevented from immigrating to the United States, American employers encouraged Japanese people to immigrate to fill this need. While these new Asians were not warmly welcomed because of the racism that had developed toward the Chinese, the need for labor and the specific characteristics of Japanese society and culture made the Japanese acceptable to Americans and allowed them to survive in an atmosphere already poisoned by anti-Chinese attitudes. Charles Marden and Gladys Meyer pointed out that certain aspects of Japanese culture gave these new immigrants a good reputation:

> The authoritarian character of Japanese social organization produced markedly obedient and self-effacing personality traits. The strong sense of subordination of the individual to the welfare of the group was reflected in the solidarity of Japanese subcommunities in this country. To conform punctiliously to elaborate social rituals was a major drive in the Japanese personality, accounting for the reputation for courtesy and good manners which the nineteenth-century Japanese acquired.[17]

In 1890 only several thousand Japanese were in the United States. However, by 1900 there were around 100,000, and this increase in the number of Japanese and the resulting competition with whites quickly kindled racist attitudes and behaviors on a large scale.

As early as 1890, white-male union members were participating in physically violent racism. For example:

> Japanese cobblers were attacked by members of the shoemakers' union. In 1892 a Japanese restaurant in San Francisco was attacked by members of the local cooks' and waiters' union. From then on, anti-Japanese activity

grew steadily in California, rising to a climax in the famous School Board Affair in 1906, when the San Francisco Board of Education passed a resolution requiring the segregation of all Oriental children in one school. At the time there were ninety-three Japanese attending twenty-three different public schools in San Francisco.[18]

Other significant and repressive incidences occurred. According to Steinfield, in 1905 the Hearst newspapers launched a major attack upon the Japanese. In 1907 President Theodore Roosevelt, by executive order, stopped Japanese immigration from Hawaii, Canada, and Mexico. He negotiated the famous Gentlemen's Agreement with the Japanese government that put an end to immigration. However, these measures did little to halt the tide of anti-Japanese prejudice.[19]

With the antagonism toward them increasing in the cities, the Japanese turned more and more to farming. However, their success in this endeavor posed an economic threat to whites. The California legislature responded by passing severe, restrictive legislation regarding alien landholding. The first act, in 1913, said aliens who could not become citizens could lease land for no longer than three years and could not own it. Marden noted that when it was discovered that the Japanese were buying stock in land-owning corporations and acquiring land in the name of their native-born children, a new act was passed. This act in substance prohibited the leasing of land by any method to foreign-born Japanese. Similar laws were passed by other Western states. Their constitutionality was upheld by the U.S. Supreme Court in a test case in 1923.[20]

The wave of racism against the Japanese culminated in the Johnson Immigration Act of 1924 that banned the immigration of persons "ineligible for citizenship." This act was directly aimed at the Japanese and was not repealed until 1952. Throughout this period, Japanese-Americans discovered that college degrees, a good work ethic, and middle-class values did not guarantee them first-class American citizenship.[21]

The next significant event in the history of Japanese-Americans occurred at the beginning of World War II. Anti-Japanese attitudes and feelings broke loose after Japan attacked Pearl Harbor. The hatred toward the Japanese culminated in 1942 with the decision to place the Japanese "menace in relocation centers." These centers in reality were concentration camps. This action violated all the Constitutional rights of these Japanese-Americans, many of whom were second and third generation Americans. Since Germans and Italians, many of whom were new emigrants, were not placed in such camps one might conclude that white-skinned German-Americans and Italian-Americans could be trusted and yellow-skinned Japanese could not. This was an example of racist behavior at its blindest.[22]

Some second-generation Japanese-Americans were able to leave the camps because of a labor shortage, not because of America's trust in them.

They were sent to the mid-West and to the East Coast. Others joined the U.S. military to fight for "their" country in Europe. Many Japanese who did not volunteer were drafted. In the exploitative tradition of racism, the same individuals who were locked up and denied constitutional rights were also subject to the military draft as citizens. The drafted Japanese were placed in a segregated unit in Europe where they distinguished themselves as one of the most-decorated units in any branch of service. Others taught at U.S. Army language schools or worked for U.S. intelligence.[23]

Despite this shameful treatment, the Japanese remained undefeated and more determined than ever to prove themselves. Attempts to hamper their progress resulted only in enhancing their determination to succeed. This determination generated one of the most-remarkable processes of upward mobility in American history. The economic, educational, and professional achievements of the Japanese-Americans ranks as high or higher than any other ethnic group in this country.

Japan's rapid rise as an economic power, the importance of its relationship with Communist China, and the economic successes of its people have changed America's image of the Japanese. Today, like the Chinese, they are no longer considered the enemy but a model minority.

Asians' Responses Compared with Hispanics' and Blacks' Responses. The managers were asked to respond to three statements related to social interactions. They were asked the extent to which they agreed or disagreed with the following:

Minority managers are excluded from informal work networks by whites.

Minority managers are often excluded from social activities that are beneficial to advancement in corporations.

Many minority managers have a harder time finding someone who is particularly interested in their careers.

Figure 2-1 clearly shows that the Asian responses are more favorable than are those of Hispanics and much more favorable than blacks. For example, 16 percent of the black managers versus 48 percent of the Hispanic and 57 percent of the Asians believe minority managers face no problems in these areas.

These more-positive responses are a result of white society's more-positive views about Asian-Americans than about Hispanics and blacks. This positiveness occccurs mainly because this group is fewer in numbers than Hispanics and blacks; thus, they present a much-smaller threat to whites in economic, political, educational, social, and other areas.

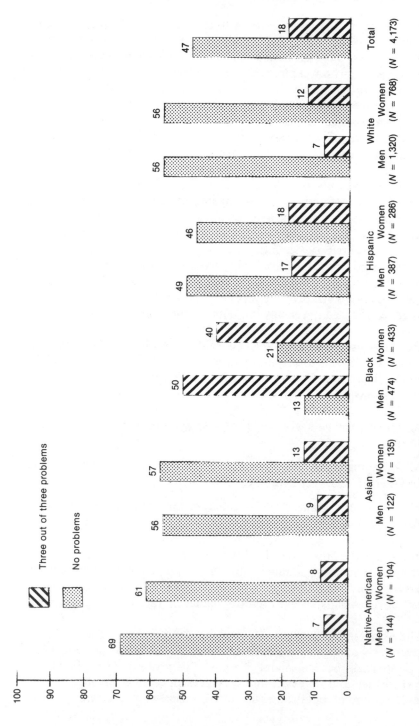

Figure 2-1. Percentage of Managers Who Believe Minorities Have Three out of Three Problems or No Problems in the Social-Interaction Area

Dr. Chalsa Loo, associate professor of psychology at San Francisco State, noted that cultural differences regarding expressed appreciation toward authority may also explain the different responses. She noted that traditionally Asians are trained to be more appreciative of and supplicant to authority. She also noted in evaluating these data that Asians may want to show themselves in a good light and want to be seen as responsible, diligent, and nonresistant. She believes they may be disguising their feelings or frustration and discontent because it is more socially acceptable to be positive toward company policies. Expanding on these points she wrote:

> . . . culturally and traditionally, Asian-Americans have tried to avoid confrontation with the Anglo society and Anglo authority, this being a means of survival in this country for them. . . . historically many feared that conspicuousness or resistance would result in harsher racist reactions from white Americans, thus their tendency to keep a low profile, accept whatever is handed to them, have few expectations of fairness and generosity from Anglos, be acquiescent toward authority, and work hard. . . . Through the product of one's work one gains acceptance into American society. Intelligence and hard work are means of reducing or ameliorating attitudes of racism towards Asian-Americans.[24]

In sum, the smaller number of Asians than Hispanics and blacks, combined with the Asians' desire to assimilate American culture and the economic power of their native countries, has led to their greater acceptance by white society. This has led to less discrimination against them, and thus they respond more positively to the treatment of minority managers in their companies.

Hispanic-Americans

Racism was directed against Asian-Americans primarily because of employment factors. Native Americans and Mexicans became targets of racism because of another factor—that is, they owned lands in the path of American expansion.

The first Hispanic-Americans were Mexicans whose land had been ceded to the United States in 1848. Not until the following century did other large numbers of Hispanic groups come to the United States. Large numbers of Puerto Ricans began emigrating to New York City during World War II and Cubans to Florida in the mid-1950s to escape Castro. However, the tone and stereotypes for all anti-Hispanic racism were set back in the nineteenth century in the Southwest.

Mexican-Americans. Mexicans lived in and controlled large sections of the western part of what is now this country for hundreds of years before Europeans and white Americans took most of it by conquest. In 1848 Mexico signed the Treaty of Guadalupe Hidalgo, ceding to the United States a vast territory that encompassed what is now California, Arizona, New Mexico, Nevada, Utah, and portions of several other states. Mexico had previously approved the annexation of Texas. The total area was greater than that of France and Germany combined. Under the terms of the Treaty of Guadalupe Hidalgo, Mexicans would become U.S. citizens if they remained in the ceded territory for more than one year. Most of them remained.[25]

The United States would have taken over more Mexican land if large numbers of Mexicans had not been occupying it. As Steinfield observed, the belief in the superiority of American institutions and the implied assumption of racial inferiority of Mexicans functioned as a restraint upon territorial acquisition. The fear existed that this alien race would cause much difficulty if it were part of American society. According to this view, sparsely populated regions could be annexed with a minimum of difficulty because Americans could populate them easily and become the dominant group. Mexicans were regarded with the same scorn as native Americans and were often not differentiated from them.[26]

Once landowners and leaders of a sophisticated ancient culture, Mexican-Americans soon found themselves powerless. They were labeled lazy, oversexed, dirty, and stupid. These are common stereotypes used to oppress any ethnic group seen as a threat. In this case the initial threat was possession of desirable property. Having been stripped of massive land-holdings, large numbers of Mexican-Americans were now available for exploitation on the labor market.

Before and during the Depression, Mexican-Americans who moved to the city experienced only limited success in improving their economic condition. They did find some relief in the various welfare programs, but jobs were extremely hard to find. Anti-Mexican feelings were widespread and overt throughout the Southwest in the 1930s as illustrated by the following:

> In the face of the hostility among minority groups and pressure from organized citizen groups, the federal and local governments tried to remove some of the surplus workers . . . one-third of a million Mexican-Americans were repatriated in Mexico between 1930 and 1933. Some people returned voluntarily. Others were politely coerced by welfare agencies which preferred to pay the costs of transportation rather than the costs of support, and many Mexican-Americans were ruthlessly rounded up and deported. The officials who carried out the deportation orders did not always check to determine whom they were sending to Mexico. Longtime citizens of the United States as well as illegal aliens were driven or flown to Mexico.[27]

If people never learn to speak English and are poorly educated, they can be excluded from the economic mainstream. Many American school systems managed to accomplish this exclusion for Mexican-Americans. James

Zanden reminds us that Mexican-American children were often segregated for purposes of instruction, in separate buildings altogether or in separate classrooms. On the basis of pedagogical considerations, some educators insisted that this separation of Mexican and white students was sound practice. Throughout most of the Southwest this segregation was considered desirable, but there was no overall pattern of separation. Segregation of the Mexican-Americans was more a matter of custom than of explicit law— quite different from the southern whites' treatment of blacks. Nevertheless, in some communities, Mexican-American segregation was strict and total.[28]

World War II provided opportunities for Mexican-Americans that their government had not provided. The labor shortages of the war allowed Mexican-Americans to enter into previously forbidden higher-paying jobs. As with other minorities, Mexican-Americans eagerly seized the opportunities.

Racial discrimination did not completely disappear, and it continued to plague them during the war. Neither the educational system nor the double-branded justice dispensed by Southwestern courts was affected. According to Stan Steiner, Mexican-Americans were denied unbiased trials. In Los Angeles, after a young Mexican-American youth was killed during a gang fight, twenty-four Mexican-American youths were arrested and nine were convicted of murder. The judge, the prosecutor, and the jury were all white. Two years later, all were freed because of lack of evidence.[29]

When the war ended, racial discrimination continued. Matt Meier and Feliciano Riviera noted that Mexican-American veterans found, to their dismay, that little had changed in the way the majority society viewed them. Even in death, they were not accepted by Anglo society.[30]

The problems do not go away. Job discrimination keeps Mexican-Americans' median income among the poorest in America. Health conditions and services in their communities are still poor. The housing situation is poor and inadequate. In the schools, Mexican-Americans are still treated as second-class citizens in too many areas. Educational facilities for Mexican-American children in the Southwest are poorer than for whites. Their teachers are in need of more practical training for dealing with minority children. A pressing need also exists for bilingual classes. Finally, a recent lack of rigorous prosecution by the federal government of civil rights violations against Hispanics has made the Hispanic community extremely angry.[31]

For Hispanic-Americans, the balance of power is changing. The American Latino community is increasing naturally, without immigration, at a rate of 20 percent a year as compared with white Americans' growth rate of 4 percent and black Americans' rate of 7 percent. These data were based on the national census, which traditionally undercounts Hispanics and misses the thousands of illegal or undocumented aliens. Census estimates of 12 million Hispanics in the United States are disputed. Other experts estimate the number at closer to 19 million, which means that the percentage of Hispanics in the U.S. population is somewhere between 5 and 9 percent.

As the Mexican government attains power through the newly found "petrodollars," it may demand legal recognition of the illegal aliens in the United States and an open-border policy. The Mexican government could also use this power to further push for social progress for Mexican-Americans. If this occurs, in unison with the increased population of the Hispanic citizens, social progress may become more rapid.

Cubans. The Cubans represent the second-largest Hispanic group in this study. The vast majority of Cubans live and work in the Miami area where over 600,000 of them live. Many immigrated around the time of Castro's revolution. They were mostly white, middle and upper class, and had been associated with Batista and/or opposed to Castro's Marxist orientation. Although wealthy in Cuba, their real and personal property was confiscated by the new communist state. This well-educated, urban high-status, primarily white-looking Hispanic group received a much-warmer reception than did Mexicans and Puerto Ricans. Because of their relative acceptance and high-status backgrounds, the Cuban population is the next-most-successful immigrant group to Asian-Americans. Almquist wrote:

> U.S. citizens were especially receptive to the majority because their anticommunist views made them dislike the Castro regime. They felt a deep sympathy for those who were displaced, and they recognized that the Cuban refugee held values which were very similar to their own. In addition, the Cubans who migrated brought qualities and skills which were usable in their economy: high educational levels, sophisticated occupational training, and a middle-class ethic and style of life. The middle-class ethic brought by Cubans included capitalistic values emphasizing "individualism, self-concern, personal right, and improvement of one's position in the stratification system as one's main worldly goal."[32]

The history of the Cuban community in the United States is brief, and while some discrimination exists, especially against those who are dark skinned, their concentration in the Miami area has allowed them to become both a political and an economic factor. These factors have made their transition into American society much faster than that of the Mexican-American.

Puerto Ricans. The third-largest Hispanic group participating in this study is Puerto Rican. Puerto Ricans, as many other immigrant groups before and after, came to America looking for better lives and opportunities. Large numbers of them immigrated to the United States to fill the unskilled-

and semiskilled-labor vacuums during and after World War II. Since that war, well over a million have come to the United States seeking their "pot of gold." Sixty percent ended up in New York City where many New Yorkers regarded them as another undesirable immigrant group.[33] This opinion exists primarily because most of them are uneducated, poor, speak little or no English, and many of them have obvious black origins. Thus, in comparison to the Cubans, the Puerto Ricans who come to America are on opposite ends of the educational, economic, and color spectrum, and this leads to more discrimination and less acceptance by white society.

Almquist summarized the present situation of Puerto Ricans in this manner:

> Despite their U.S. citizenship, Puerto Ricans are culturally different from Anglo majority. Spanish is their native language, few have completed a high school education, and many are from rural areas. The emphasis on family value and on the Catholic church serve to set Puerto Ricans apart from the dominant group. More important, Puerto Ricans are economically distinct . . . . Seventy-seven percent of all Puerto Rican families and a staggering 58 percent of female-headed families have incomes below the poverty level.[34]

Hispanics' Responses Differ among Ethnic Groups. The Hispanic minority of this study contains five major groups: Mexicans (375), Cubans (98), Puerto Ricans (75), South or Central Americans (21), and other Spanish (112), the latter primarily white Hispanics from Spain.

Since they come from different racial backgrounds, the Hispanics' responses understandably differ from ethnic group to ethnic group. While 88 percent of the entire Hispanic group agrees with its ethnic group's classification, South Americans and Puerto Ricans are most likely (100 percent and 91 percent), and Cubans least likely (84 percent) to do so. Eighty-seven percent of Mexicans and 85 percent of other-Spanish managers agree with their classifications. These figures are important because they demonstrate an unusual phenomenon. In this study, a much-higher proportion of Hispanics classified themselves as "other Spanish" than one would expect considering the small numbers of pure Spaniards in the United States. This high percentage of other Spanish might mean that some Mexicans, Puerto Ricans, and Cubans are attempting to disassociate themselves from people of color and instead associate themselves with white Western-Europe Spaniards. The fact that 15 percent of the Hispanics disagree with their racial classification and that 99 percent of these want to be classified as white supports this position.

Part of the conflict in racial identity is that, except for participants from Spain or of Spanish lineage, most of the other Hispanic groups are of mixed racial ancestry—native American, black, and white. Clara Garcia noted some of the identity conflicts Hispanic managers have in corporatons. She wrote that the inner conflicts experienced by Hispanic managers may be a result of their overlapping memberships and conflicting loyalties. They have a Latino surname and are a product of the Latino culture. Yet they are supposedly a member of the white society.[35] In resolving these issues she posited that assimilation is a solution only when the whites accept the idea, and for whatever reason, the Hispanics concur. That many Hispanics want to assimilate was evident in her study in which the majority of the Hispanic managers identified themselves as "white" or "white Hispanic." However, she correctly noted that the white corporate structure allows them to assimilate only to the extent that they do not threaten the longevity of the dominant white-male group.[36]

When the responses of the various Hispanic groups are analyzed, we find that Puerto Ricans' responses are closest to blacks' responses. The Cubans', South and Central Americans', and Mexican-Americans' responses are similar to each other, and other Spanish responses are similar to the whites' responses. Table 2-2 demonstrates these differences in responses.

The Puerto Ricans, who have the greatest mixture of black blood, and the other Spanish, who have none, are on opposite ends of the spectrum, like the blacks and whites. Thus, the Puerto Ricans' negative views may be a reflection of the prevalent discrimination they face because many of them have visible African origins.

Almquist, in addressing the same issue, points to the lack of prejudice based on color in Puerto Rico and the problems the immigrants have when they come to the United States:

> Racial prejudice on the mainland makes occupational and cultural assimilation difficult, in both direct and indirect ways. Many Puerto Ricans are black or of mixed black and white ancestry. Mainlanders tend to discriminate against people who are not white, and Puerto Ricans suffer from this color prejudice. The severity of racial prejudice is somewhat surprising to Puerto Ricans, who are accustomed to making class distinctions but not race distinctions. In Puerto Rico, people who are of the same social class mingle at dances and parties regardless of color. On the mainland, however, they are ostracized for racial intermingling, and the tension surrounding black/white relations spills over into the Puerto Rican community. Puerto Ricans do not always understand the severity of racial discrimination. They are reluctant to link up with blacks in the civil rights movement, and white Puerto Ricans are fearful of being labeled as black.[37]

In sum, the extreme differences in responses among the various Hispanic groups can be directly related to their race origins and skin color. Hispanics who are darker face more discrimination than do those who are lighter. As a result of this increased discrimination, dark-skinned Hispanics respond more similarly to blacks than do light-skinned Hispanics.

Table 2-2
Hispanics' Views about Discrimination and EEO/AAP as They Compare to Blacks' and Whites' Views

Managers Who Agree with Responses	Blacks	Puerto Ricans	South and Central Americans	Cubans	Mexican-Americans	Other Spanish	Whites
Minorities are excluded from informal work groups by whites.	65	40	29	34	29	24	29
Whites bypass minority managers and go to their superiors because they feel uncomfortable dealing with minorities.	43	37	19	21	18	10	10
Minorities must be better than whites to get ahead.	83	65	57	45	47	28	17
Minorities are penalized more for mistakes than whites are.	53	34	24	18	25	12	9
Minorities are made to feel that they got their jobs because of EEO targets and not because of their abilities.	74	63	57	67	56	50	29
A lack exists of qualified minorities to fill jobs.	27	41	48	33	48	52	68
AAP helps more than it hurts.	88	82	76	73	78	59	70
AAP forces companies to lower their hiring and promotion standards.	18	38	38	52	44	67	78

Black Americans

While many similarities exist in the social history of blacks and that of other minorities in the United States, there are some crucial differences. Because of their background in slavery and because their appearance is the most different from whites, blacks started from further behind than any other race group in this country. The dual liabilities of the stigma of slavery and color have made the way up steeper and the climb more arduous. To emphasize the violence and oppression visited upon black people is not to ignore the discrimination other minority groups have suffered, but it is to argue that the black experience has been different in kind, not just in degree, from that of any other American group. Joel Kovel remarked on the differences in degree of experiences. He noted that of all the various exclusions practiced in America—including those based on religion, sex, age, national origins, and economic status—none approaches in strength that of blacks by whites, the distinction of superior self and inferior other according to race, particularly as is revealed by the mark of skin color.[38]

A number of scholars have written that all the problems that blacks associate with racism are simply manifestations of the difficulty every rural and/or urban immigrant has had adjusting to city life. Such an argument reasons: since blacks are among the newest of groups, their difficulties have not had sufficient time to be worked out. Once they are worked out, blacks will become part of mainstream America just as the Europeans have done in the past.[39]

Charles Silberman and Robert Blauner disagree with this point of view and pointed out that blacks carry two burdens that other rural migrants never bore—their color and their heritage of slavery. Silberman stated unequivocally that racism against blacks is more virulent and intractable than is racism against other racial, ethnic, and religious groups.[40] As de Tocqueville observed in the nineteenth century, while slavery receded, the hatred and prejudice which supported it did not.

As with the other minority groups discussed, job competition was a major reason that whites developed racist attitudes toward blacks. The fear that blacks would compete for whites' jobs dates back even to the slavery days. This fear has ebbed and flowed with the existing economic situation. William Wilson described the situation as follows:

> In the antebellum North, where a more-industrial system of production enabled white workers to become more concentrated and better organized, laws of racial oppression, especially in the nineteenth century, increasingly reflected the interests of the white working class. The demise of northern slavery was quickly followed by laws to eliminate black competition, particularly economic competition. However, as the economy of the South gradually drifted toward industrial capitalism in the last quarter of the

nineteenth century, the white working classes were finally able to exert some influence on the form and content of racial stratification. White working-class efforts to eliminate black competition generated an elaborate system of Jim Crow segregation that was reinforced by an ideology of biological racism.[41]

During World Wars I and II, the lack of sufficient labor opened up opportunities previously closed to blacks, as well as to Mexican-Americans and Asians. However, like the Asians and Mexican-Americans, the blacks still faced racial discrimination. Earning a living became easier during World War II, but racist constraints on how and where one lived remained as strong as ever.

While blacks made progress through the 1950s and into the 1960s, the rate slowed considerably in the 1970s. During the mid-1960s, black people in this country had a strong feeling of change in conventional racial patterns. This feeling was expressed in both their perception of increased contact with white people and their sense of "real change" in their situation. As the 1960s ended, black perceptions appeared to have reached a plateau from which they did not change during the 1970s. This sense of change "for the better," which seemed strong during the 1960s, appears to have diminished during the 1970s. Today, after three-and-a-half centuries of racial oppression, overt and covert racist acts still occur daily. The expectation of continuing progress toward equality was not fulfilled in the recent decade, as evidenced by a variety of publicized events and statistics.

For example, housing remains a major problem for blacks. Newspapers, magazines, and television frequently report the harassment and damages that confronts blacks as they move into predominantly white areas. For example, after a high-level black IBM executive's family moved into their home in a white neighborhood in August 1979, an explosion and fire destroyed it. The fire officials believed it was arson and racially motivated. Five members of the family were injured.

It is not surprising, then, that an *Ebony* survey, twenty-five years after the *Brown* v. *Board of Education* 1954 decision, found that 68 percent of blacks do not believe that America has moved with all deliberate speed in ending discrimination in elementary and secondary schools. Fifty-nine percent think the same of colleges, 26 percent of transportation, and 25 percent of public accommodations. Sixty-six percent of blacks believe also that white racism is still a major factor hampering black progress.[42]

U.S. Supreme Court Justice Thurgood Marshall said in a speech at Howard University that people tell him the same troubles they did twenty and thirty years ago when he first sounded the positive note that "things are going to get better." "Only, guess what I'm getting now," he said. "You not only told me that but you told my father, too, and he's no better off. Are you going to tell my children that, too?"[43]

One would expect increased concern from blacks who know their struggle for equality is far from over and who see the focus of governmental concern and action shifting to other groups. Indeed, throughout the results of this study, greater levels of dissatisfaction, criticism, and anger occur among blacks, both male and female, than in any other group.

Black Managers' Responses Are Most Critical. Black managers, as is seen in table 2-3 and figure 2-1 are by far the most-critical minority group regarding the corporate treatment of minorities. For example, as table 2-3 shows, more than half of all black managers (males, 55 percent; females, 49 percent) believe minorities are penalized more for mistakes than are whites. Slightly less than one-quarter of Hispanic managers agree with this statement. Only one out of every six (16 percent) Asian male managers and white female managers agree. Least likely of all to agree are white men (5 percent) and native-American men (4 percent). In other words, given an identical work situation, one out of every two black managers sees evidence of racism that would be perceived by only one out of twenty white-male managers.

A number of important findings also are demonstrated by figure 2-1. First, black managers once again are most critical of the minority status in corporations, followed by Hispanics, Asians, whites, and native Americans. Second, in every race/sex group, except for black men and women, managers are more likely to say that minorities have no problems than they are to say that minorities have three out of three problems listed in the area of social interaction. Furthermore, larger percentages of black men and women than other race/sex groups assert that minorities have three out of three problems in the area of social interactions. Finally, black managers are least likely to state that minorities face no social-interaction problems. These two sets of data clearly demonstrate a hierarchy of alienation, isolation, and criticism that various minority groups experience concerning the treatment of minorities within white corporations.

The hierarchy of alienation is based in large part on whites' nonambivalent feelings toward blacks. They feel more threatened by blacks because blacks are the largest minority in this country and compete with them more intensely, in all areas, than any other minority. For example, blacks have been competing in the labor market on a much broader scale and over a longer period of time than any other minority group. Most native Americans are geographically limited to the reservation. Hispanics are found mostly in particular areas of the United States and are limited to certain jobs. Asian-Americans have been more-narrowly restricted both in the American labor market and geographic location.

Briefly, nonambivalent attitudes and the size of the black population have made blacks the biggest threat to the whites' dominant position in this society. As a result, blacks face more types of discrimination and more-

Table 2-3
Minority Managers Are Penalized More for Mistakes than White Managers
(percent)

To What Extent Do You Agree or Disagree that Minority Managers Are Penalized More for Mistakes than White Managers?	Native-American		Asian		Black		Hispanic		White		Total
	Men (N = 143)	*Women (N = 101)*	*Men (N = 121)*	*Women (N = 135)*	*Men (N = 474)*	*Women (N = 425)*	*Men (N = 384)*	*Women (N = 285)*	*Men (N = 1,306)*	*Women (N = 754)*	*(N = 4,132)*
Strongly agree	0.7	3	3.3	3	19	14.7	3.4	4.9	0.3	3.3	5.3
Agree	2.8	8.9	12.4	21.5	35.9	34.7	19	18.6	4.7	12.2	15.8
Disagree	74.8	82.2	74.4	73.3	43.7	49	68.5	69.8	76.3	72.4	67.8
Strongly disagree	21.7	5.9	9.9	2.2	1.5	1.6	9.1	6.7	18.8	12.1	11

severe discrimination. This leads to more-critical views of minorities' positions in corporations. The extreme differences in minority responses become clearer in the next chapter.

Conclusion

Regardless of what has been said about the different experiences of minorities, the important point to remember is that the responses of white Americans to the competition of minorities typically has been to blame the victims of racism—the minorities—and not the perpetrators of racism—the whites themselves. Thus, racism became an ever-expanding vortex fueled by greed and fears on the part of whites and anger and paranoia on the part of minorities.

3 The Present Situation and Treatment of Minority Managers

I, as a black male, have a problem in just one area: to be able to do the job without incurring great stress because of a feeling that I must perform 150 percent in order to be successful and to obtain a promotion.

I am a Hispanic woman who has never been a complete member or even a "token" member of the informal work group.

As an Asian male, I have a very technical job. I made a minor mistake six months ago and my Anglo boss has not let me forget it. This never happens to my white peers—even big mistakes are overlooked.

I am a native-American woman who has been made to feel as if I got my job because of quotas and not because of my ability—this is in spite of the fact that I have a college degree and only one of my seven male peers has one.

Economic Return on Personal Achievement

Facts or fiction? Do these minority managers really have such problems? One measure of the truth of these statements is provided by what has been learned about minorities' economic return on personal achievement. Numerous studies show that characteristics such as age, education, occupational status, job duration, and job experience affect whites' salaries more positively than those of minorities. This is especially true for blacks and Mexican-Americans.

Robert K. Jobu found that Japanese-Americans have achieved socioeconomic equality with whites, while Chinese-Americans are nearly equal. However, Mexican-Americans, followed by blacks, are far from economic equality with whites. He found that a one-unit change in education meant a salary increase of $522 for whites, $438 for Japanese, $350 for Chinese, $340 for Mexican-Americans, and $284 for blacks. When he analyzed the effect of age on salary, he found that a one-unit change in age meant $174 more for Chinese, $84 for Japanese, $79 for whites, $76 for Mexican-Americans, and only $33 for blacks. Occupational status and prestige converted into the following dollar-value increases for each step up the occupational status hierarchy: Chinese, $1,501; Japanese, $1,088; whites, $969; Mexican-Americans, $752; and blacks, $471.[1]

Findings in a survey of eight large corporations in 1975 showed that a college degree alone meant an increase of close to $1,000 more for a white manager than for a black manager. Further calculations in the same study showed that a one-unit change in job duration meant an increase per year of $360 for a black but $520 for a white. For each additional year of outside work experience, the white earned $220 more per year than the black.[2]

Racial discrimination clearly has had a negative impact on the income capacity of minorities. Although information about native Americans' salaries related to specific assets is not available, of all ethnic groups native Americans have the lowest median income in the United States. Data gathered in 1976 showed that native-American men had a $3,509 median income; women, $1,697. In the same year, the median income was $4,735 for Mexican-American men and $1,892 for women. Japanese men made $7,574 and women made $3,236.[3]

Obviously, wide differences exist in median salaries among the different ethnic and sex groups. While childhood poverty and poor schooling are contributing factors to the low earning power of some minorities, the data presented above show that differences in salary between groups with similar assets leads unquestionably to the conclusion that continuing discrimination against minorities is a controlling force.

Stereotypes about Minority Corporate Managers

As noted in chapter 2, white society has developed many stereotypes about minorities. Condescending acknowledgements are carried, of course, into the corporate world. Middle- and upper-level managers who are willing to do so can recall that almost every discussion pertaining to the upward mobility of a minority-group member has included statements implying some type of presumed social characteristics. The slightest behavior, real or perceived, that supports these assumptions is used against the minority-group member. Whole sets of such characteristics, in the minds of traditional white managers, render minorities, especially blacks, less than well suited for influential positions. A major study of several large corporations found that the most-frequently expressed negative racial attitude characterized blacks as lazy, dumb, or slow. It pointed out that often whites were curt toward blacks and would not give them the courtesy of an explanation because they assumed the blacks were too dumb to learn.[4]

In the same study of corporate managers' views, only 10 percent of black managers and 27 percent of white managers believed they worked in a situation in which whites did not seem to have any negative racial attitudes. In addition, only 9 percent of the white managers did not agree with racist statements and did not make any racist statements themselves about blacks.[5]

To ascertain the degree of negative racial attitudes held by managers who participated in the present study, they were asked the extent to which they agreed with the following statements that managers in the preliminary interviews mentioned most frequently:

Most minority managers use race as an alibi for many difficulties they have on the job.

Many minority managers come from different cultural backgrounds that are not conducive to their success in management.

Most minority managers are not as qualified as most white managers.

Overall, 49 percent of the managers surveyed do not agree with any of these stereotyped characterizations of minority managers. Thirty-five percent of the native-American men and 40 percent of the white men agree to none of the stereotypes as compared to 51-62 percent of the other ethnic groups. Figure 3-1 shows the managers' responses by race and sex.

Many whites and a surprising number of minority managers agree with these statements. Acceptance of these kinds of generalizations frequently prevents many whites from treating minorities fairly and causes minorities to adopt feelings of self-doubt that can affect their job performance.

Significant differences by management level occur in the responses of white women and white and Hispanic men. White men and women at lower levels are less likely than white men and women at upper levels to express stereotyped views of minorities. The increase in the percentage agreeing with the stereotyped statements is demonstrated by the response of white men:

First level	54%
Second level	62%
Third level	62%
Fourth level	63%
Fifth level	68%
Sixth level	69%

This finding is very disturbing because the achievement of equal opportunity requires the full support of upper management. If many upper-level managers believe in the stereotypes about minorities, their support for steps toward the achievement of equal opportunity will be limited at best. These executives will be easily convinced that minor concessions contribute substantial good-faith efforts. This lack of support will permeate the entire organizational structure. In addition, they will not easily accept minority peers whom they cannot view as equals. Thus few, if any, minorities will be promoted to upper levels of management.

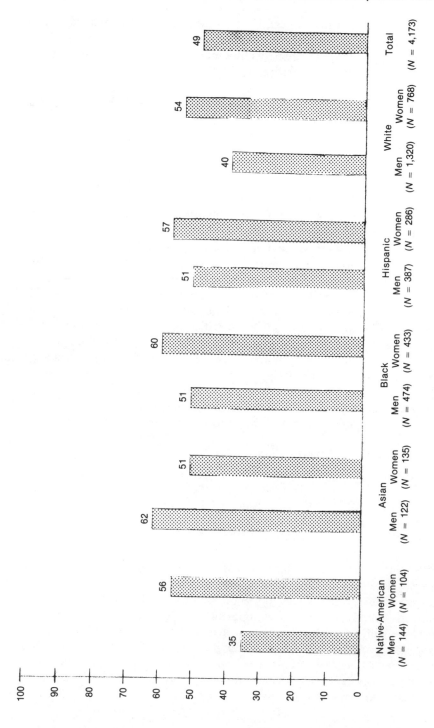

Figure 3-1. Percentage of Managers Who Express No Stereotyped Opinions about Minorities

The educational level of the managers surveyed does not have a consistent correlation with the extent to which they express racial stereotypes. For example, of the white women in the 30 + through 40 age group who express no agreement with stereotyped statements about minorities, 57 percent had no college, 50 percent had some college, and 62 percent had college degrees. Of white men in the 40-and-over age group, the figures are 41 percent, 42 percent, and 36 percent respectively. This finding supports the view that racial bias is not exclusive to less-educated people. Judith Caditz found that the racial attitudes of many well-educated white liberals are as affected, as are those of working-class and lower-class people, by threats to job security, prestige, lifestyle, and their children's class destination.[6]

Also, when controlling for age, no consistent pattern appears in the responses. For example, 45 percent of the white men aged 30 and under with some college express no agreement with the stereotypes. This is true for 26 percent of the 30 + through 40 age group and 42 percent of the over-40 age group. These data mean that corporations cannot depend on a young, educated work force to increase the acceptance of minorities. This is because managers are products of the overall society, a society in which the growing-up experiences of blacks and whites are still largely segregated and influenced by racist institutions.

Do Minorities Use Race as an Alibi?

"To what extent do you agree or disagree that most minorities use race as an alibi for many difficulties they have to face on the job?" is obviously a racist question. Managers would not be expected to respond affirmatively. Only 13 percent of the managers agree. However, the affirmative responses range from 22 percent of the native-American men and 15 percent of the white men and women to 7 percent of the Hispanic men. Managers who believe minorities use race as an alibi will have severe difficulty in accurately assessing legitimate problems that confront minorities because of their race. An Asian woman complains:

> Many whites in my organization dismiss legitimate minority complaints simply because they come from minorities. They try to make you feel guilty, but I do have many difficulties because of my race and also sex.

Because of paranoia some minority members will inaccurately attribute some of their difficulties to their race when they should not. However, many times minorities face problems on the job that are in fact related to their race. Both the paranoia of minority managers and their legitimate complaints about racial discrimination must be dealt with if corporations are really concerned about effectively developing and utilizing the large pool of minority managerial talent available.

Do Minority Managers Have Cultural Backgrounds Not Conducive to Managerial Success?

Thirty-seven percent of managers agree that the different cultural backgrounds of minority managers are not conducive to success in management. As table 3-1 shows, responses by the various race/sex groups who agree range from 43 percent of the black men to 31 percent of the white women. A black man at the second level comments:

> I come from a black ghetto background. The experience my white peer gained through school activities and through working in his father's store, I didn't receive. Therefore, being behind in this necessitates a more-extensive and -intensive training and development program.

A white man at the third level makes similar comments:

> Background, family, education, etc., have not given them [blacks] a good basis. They need training to build their confidence and also technical, professional knowledge to adequately do the job.

The previous two comments contain some truth for some deprived and uneducated minority people. However, these comments belie a major problem. Many whites and minorities make distinctions about poor, uneducated whites versus educated, middle-class whites, but they do not make these same distinctions about minorities. This conflicting approach may be embodied in the fact that 97 percent of the blacks surveyed and 60-90 percent of the other minority groups believe that most minorities are as qualified as whites, while at the same time 32-43 percent of them believe that most minorities come from different cultural backgrounds that will interfere with their managerial success. Is this a measure of self-doubt? Have some of these minorities internalized racist views about minority cultural deprivation? Are different minority groups referring to other minority groups but not their own? For example, are blacks saying, "we are qualified," but Hispanics, Asians, and native Americans are not qualified because of cultural differences? In all probability the answer is yes to all of these questions.

The persistence of such racial stereotypes is more likely to be caused by a lack of understanding and interaction than by vital cultural differences. Minorities, especially blacks as the "most-different" minority group, are not given a chance to disprove the white attribution of undesirable char-

Table 3-1
Minority Managers Have Different Cultural Backgrounds
(percent)

To What Extent Do You Agree or Disagree that Many Minority Managers Come from Different Cultural Backgrounds that Are Not Conducive to Their Success in the Corporation?	Native-American		Asian		Black		Hispanic		White		Total
	Men (N = 142)	Women (N = 101)	Men (N = 122)	Women (N = 135)	Men (N = 471)	Women (N = 431)	Men (N = 384)	Women (N = 283)	Men (N = 1,294)	Women (N = 747)	(N = 4,110)
Strongly agree	2.8	2	6.6	3	7	3.9	6	2.8	1.5	1.3	3.1
Agree	36.6	33.7	25.4	33.3	35.5	28.5	30.7	30.7	39.2	30	33.8
Disagree	54.2	60.4	60.7	56.3	41.2	52.2	53.6	59	55.5	59.7	54.6
Strongly disagree	6.3	4	7.4	7.4	16.3	15.3	9.6	7.4	3.9	9	8.5

acteristics. Many minority managers interact effectively with whites every day, but many white managers are unable or unwilling to acknowledge effective interaction. The white managers are not comfortable in these interactions, but they do not identify their own uncertainties as the cause. A white, middle-level manager admits:

> The white community considers blacks to be different without really knowing them. Their lack of social and business contact with blacks has tended to segregate them [blacks] in their own minds. Therefore, they categorize blacks into one group.

The fact that white managers have great difficulty acknowledging this scrutiny or the attitudinal bias behind it may relate to the social unacceptability of such attitudes in all but reactionary circles today. It has been effectively argued that cultural differences among American blacks, Asians, Hispanics, native Americans, and whites are not significant in terms of objectives or means of reaching objectives. The cultural differences that do exist between whites and minorities are not observable in organizational results, and for a very specific reason—that is, biculturalism.

In order to survive, minorities must develop bicultural competency at a very early age. This ability is developed both consciously and unconsciously through all of our society's organizations. Charles Valentine explained the survival strength demonstrated by the development of bicultural competency:

> Most minority people are prevented from activating or actualizing their lifelong socialization into white patterns, the same patterns which so many Euro-Americans easily use to achieve affluence and ease. Most minorities are reduced to peripheral manipulations around the edges of a system which might have crushed them entirely long ago if they had not acquired and developed such multiple competencies as they could.[7]

Put another way, the cultural argument against equality is not justifiable because it is used in a racial and a class manner, rather than in an individual manner. Although many minorities come from lower-class backgrounds, many variations exist in life-style and attitude within a given class, much less an entire race. Further, more and more minorities are coming from middle-class backgrounds. Nevertheless, a minority person who grew up in deprivation should have no more difficulty than a white person who has overcome an underprivileged status to be effective managers.

In sum, the vast majority of the minority managers are bicultural and can operate effectively in the corporate structure if given the opportunity. Since they have a choice, and because many minorities choose not to adopt an exclusively white culture, they are labeled as culturally handicapped. Many whites assume that the white culture is the only functional one for the business world and that other cultures are incompatible with white culture. They cannot understand that other cultures have as much meaning and value as theirs. This results in their trying to ignore and/or suppress the minorities' culture. Thus, U.S. corporations find themselves confronted with serious problems related to low productivity and low employee morale. They might well benefit from adopting some of the cultural and value differences that minorities bring into corporations.

Perceptions of Racist Tendencies in Corporations

Many white managers claim that, while they submit to negative stereotypes about minorities, these attitudes do not affect their behavior in the corporate world. A fifth-level white manager says, "Certainly I have stereotypes about minorities, but I also have them about white ethnics. They never affect how I treat people in my department. I treat them all equal." We will see that blacks, and to varying extents, other minorities, are definitely affected by racist stereotypes. To analyze such racist tendencies in the participating corporations, an index was developed based on the managers' agreement or disagreement with the following statements:

Minorities are excluded from informal work networks by whites.

Minorities are often excluded by whites from social activities that are beneficial to advancement in corporations.

Minority managers have a much-harder time finding someone particularly interested in their careers.

Most white managers have made minority managers feel they got their jobs because of EEO targets and not because of their abilities.

Whites are generally unable to work comfortably with minority managers; they bypass these managers and go to their superiors.

As figure 3-2 indicates, the responses on awareness of racist tendencies range from 19 percent of the managers who indicate an awareness of four to five situations, to 34 percent of the managers who state that none of the conditions indicating racist tendencies is present in their companies. When one examines race and sex responses, the figures show that 52 percent of black men and 44 percent of black women report the presence of at least four or five racist tendencies in the companies. The other groups' responses show a high of 20 percent for males and 19 percent for females.

Level differences exist for white women in this index. As the managerial level increases, higher percentages of white women report the existence of between four and five of the conditions:

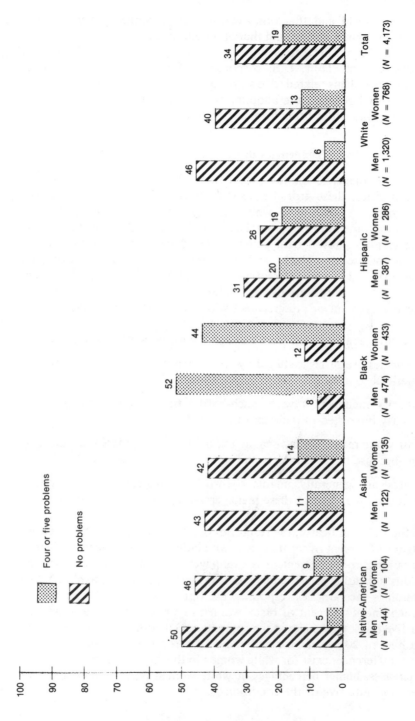

Figure 3-2. Percentage of Managers Who Are Aware of at Least Four out of Five or No Racist Tendencies in Their Companies

First level	7%
Second level	12%
Third level	20%
Fourth level +	40%

This finding can be partly explained by the fact that as women move up the corporate ladder, they operate less in an interracial and/or predominantly female environment and more in a white-male environment, where they are more exposed to racist tendencies toward minorities. They also are exposed to more-sexist tendencies than are lower-level white women because they are now operating in a male-dominated environment. Their additional oppression makes them sympathize with the minority situation.

Minorities Are Excluded from Informal Work Groups

In analyzing a number of the previous statements from the index in more detail, some important points become clearer. Thirty-six percent of the managers surveyed observed that whites exclude minority managers from informal work groups.

Between 21 percent and 31 percent of the native-American, Asian, Hispanic, and white managers of both sexes believe that minority managers are excluded from informal work groups. By contrast, 71 percent of black men and 59 percent of black women believe this is true. Table 3-2 illustrates the manager's responses by race and sex. Among whites and blacks of both sexes, upper-level managers are more likely than those at lower levels to believe minority managers are excluded from informal work networks by whites. For example, the figures by level for black men and white men are:

Black men		White men	
First level	64%	First level	19%
Second level	76%	Second level	26%
Third level	78%	Third level	29%
Fourth level +	100%	Fourth level	33%
		Fifth level	38%
		Sixth level	35%

These data offer substantial support for the belief that racist attitudes are affecting minority managers' equal and full participation in their work environment.

A black woman at the first level notes, "My peers never invite me to informal discussions, meetings, and luncheons, and many times they discuss

Table 3-2
Minority Managers Are Excluded from Informal Work Groups by White Managers
(percent)

To What Extent Do You Agree or Disagree that Minority Managers Are Excluded from Informal Work Groups by White Managers?	Native-American		Asian		Black		Hispanic		White		Total
	Men (N = 143)	*Women (N = 102)*	*Men (N = 122)*	*Women (N = 134)*	*Men (N = 473)*	*Women (N = 430)*	*Men (N = 385)*	*Women (N = 284)*	*Men (N = 1,303)*	*Women (N = 755)*	*(N = 4,131)*
Strongly agree	0	2	4.9	4.5	18.2	13	3.9	6	1.2	4.5	5.8
Agree	23.1	18.6	18.9	21.6	52.4	45.8	25.5	25.4	27.6	24.4	30.5
Disagree	73.4	74.5	66.4	70.9	27.5	39.1	65.7	62.3	67.3	65.6	59.5
Strongly disagree	3.5	4.9	9.8	3	1.9	2.1	4.9	6.3	3.9	5.6	4.2

issues related to my job." A second-level Hispanic woman made these comments: "I am never included. If I were included, it would not be to discuss work-related things—probably sex."

As noted by a group of first- and second-level black women, middle- and upper-level white-male managers have a fraternal sort of organization, "the club." When a white man is promoted to the middle and upper levels of management, he may not immediately belong to the club, but he is known, he is a brother, and before long he will fit in and become part of that group because other white men pave the way for him. When a woman or minority person is promoted, few women or minority members are available to sponsor their admission to the club. They have to make their own way or hope for a white-male sponsor. Researchers have pointed out that the system can be expected to react to threats to its members (white men) by functioning in such a way as to make it even more difficult for women or minorities to become a part of it.[8]

This finding is cause for great concern to anyone aware that the informal system is at the heart of the middle-management function and grows still more critical with every step up the corporate ladder.

Important interactions in the corporations, especally in their top echelons, are characterized by a high degree of informality, much of it in an exclusive, clublike context—luncheons, coffee breaks, social activities, and athletic events. These informal settings are used to test ideas, gain important, at times secret, information ahead of time, and obtain support or the right contact to move ahead successfully.

The basic question remains: Do these findings reflect reality? *Are* blacks much-more likely to be excluded than are other minorities, or is their response indicative of paranoia? Due to the support this issue receives from the white-male responses, especially at higher levels, paranoia is not the answer in most cases. Data in chapters 1 and 2 indicate that nonblack minorities and whites see blacks as the least-desirable minority with whom to interact. These data suggest that substantial validity exists to the black managers' responses.

A point not to be dismissed is that achievement of a higher status within the company does not insulate a minority manager from feelings, or the reality, of being excluded. If anything, reaching the upper levels makes exclusion more apparent and more painful, since fewer same-race individuals are in those levels who can be used as sounding boards and support systems. Another possibility is that minorities, especially blacks at higher levels, feel excluded because they naively believe when first entering the system that they will be judged on the basis of ability and work performance and thereby included in the informal networks. After a few years or after they reach the higher levels, the reality of racism becomes clear. Ability and performance begin to take a seat farther back in the bus, and total conformity comes forward as the prerequisite for admission to the club. Since race and sex are unalterable, it is impossible for minorities and women to become fully accepted members of the club until the club changes its admission criteria.

Whites Are Uncomfortable with Minorities and Bypass Them

Since better than one out of three managers believe minorities are excluded from informal work groups by whites, one would expect that some whites would feel uncomfortable about working with minority managers and would bypass them to go to their superiors. Almost one out of five managers agrees this is done. Forty-three percent of black managers agree, while 23 percent of Hispanic women and between 8 and 15 percent of the other race and sex groups agree. Managerial level does not significantly apply to this question, which means that these managers, regardless of level, see this bypassing happening to the same degree throughout the corporate hierarchy.

The consequences of exclusion and bypassing of any manager in most cases can be very detrimental to organizational effectiveness and efficiency. However, forcing too strict a chain of command is also detrimental to an organization because of distortion caused by filtering information through corporate ranks. Another reason that a strict chain of command can be detrimental is that the new-breed manager is not as inclined to follow and look favorably on a strict chain of command. They look more at the corporate structure as a team effort in which rank plays second fiddle to respect for corporate team members. Therefore, new-breed managers are more likely than older traditional managers to bypass the chain of command in order to accomplish their objectives, whether corporate or personal. If too much bypassing occurs in the chain of command, it clearly indicates a malaise in the respect and trust employees have in the organization. In addition, bypassing a person only because he or she is a minority or a woman not only undermines his or her authority and position but also smacks of racism and sexism. An Asian man at the second level notes:

> While I am the technical expert, many people, not my subordinates, go to my boss, and he must come to me for the answers. Some of my people lose respect for me when this happens.

A third-level black man puts it this way:

> How can I do my job when my boss encourages people to come to him? While I am certain some would still do it without his encouragement,

others would not. He just doesn't believe I have the ability to do the job.
He is very uncomfortable with me.

In short, for minorities and women to function effectively as managers,
bosses must understand that white men might be approaching the boss
about an issue when they should be approaching the minority or female
manager. Boss acceptance of deliberate disruption of the chain of command
because of race and sex not only affects organizational efficiency, but it also
perpetuates stereotyped attitudes about minorities and women.

Minorities Are Made to Feel They Got Their
Jobs Not on Ability but Quotas

One of this study's most-important findings is that almost half of the
managers (46 percent) believe that most white managers make minority
managers feel they got their jobs because of EEO targets, rather than
because of their ability. Once again, as table 3-3 clearly shows, extremely
large differences exist in the response between blacks and other groups. A
53 percent difference in responses exists between black and white men.
White men at lower levels of management who have the most contact with
minority managers are more likely to believe white managers make minority
managers feel they got their jobs because of EEO targets. This belief is
almost three times the percentage of first-level managers versus sixth-level
managers—34 percent versus 13 percent.

The postinterview-feedback discussion groups referred frequently to
this problem and to the disastrous consequences it has for minority
managers. The self-confidence of minority managers is influenced by the
way they are perceived and the cooperation their work groups give them.
When a manager hears "you got your job because of your race/sex rather
than your ability," his or her self concept and, ultimately, job performance
can be affected. A work group will not assist and cooperate as much with
managers whom they consider incapable as they will with managers they
perceive as capable. These factors set up a self-fulfilling prophecy that can
eventually lead to the manager's isolation and failure.

A native-American woman at the second level comments, "My special
problem is feeling that I have been put in a position just because of my
status. This has interfered with my job performance."

A group of first- and second-level Hispanic women indicates that they
have questions about whether they got their jobs because of EEO statistics
or their ability. On one level, they know it is because of their ability.
However, they hear so frequently that they got it because they met a target
that on another level some of them begin to believe it. This conflict in-

Table 3-3
Minority Managers Are Made to Feel They Got Jobs because of EEO Targets
(percent)

To What Extent Do You Agree or Disagree that Most White Managers Have Made Minority Managers Feel They Got Their Jobs Because of EEO Targets, Not Because of Their Abilities?	Native-American		Asian		Black		Hispanic		White		Total
	Men (N = 143)	Women (N = 102)	Men (N = 121)	Women (N = 135)	Men (N = 471)	Women (N = 431)	Men (N = 384)	Women (N = 284)	Men (N = 1,301)	Women (N = 751)	(N = 4,123)
Strongly agree	2.8	6.9	5.8	8.9	27.4	29	13.8	15.8	0.8	6.1	10.6
Agree	28.7	35.3	32.2	37.8	50.1	41.5	41.9	43.3	23.8	35.7	35
Disagree	65	54.9	57.9	51.1	21.9	27.6	42.7	39.8	70.7	53.5	51.2
Strongly disagree	3.5	2.9	4.1	2.2	0.6	1.9	1.6	1.1	4.7	4.7	3.2

troduces additional problems for minorities and women with which white men are not required to deal, even though many of these white men are promoted because of their personal associations and conformist attitudes, rather than their ability.

The information in this section has demonstrated that minority managers, especially blacks, believe they are confronted with racist reactions from whites. And, while some minorities might be a bit paranoid because of their victimization, their views receive considerable support even from white men. The overall impact of excluding, bypassing, and robbing them of self-esteem renders many of these minorities unable to function effectively in corporations. Clearly, racism has an incapacitating effect on many minority managers and is detrimental to corporate goals.

Managers' Awareness of More-Rigorous Demands and Obstacles Faced by Minorities

Racist stereotypes and tendencies complicate minorities' corporate work life even further when they are combined with more-rigorous demands and obstacles in the workplace. To determine how participating managers in this study view the demands and obstacles minorities face, they were asked to what extent they agree or disagree with the following statements:

Minority managers are penalized more for their mistakes than are whites.

Many minority managers are placed in dead-end jobs.

Most minority managers do not have the same power as do whites in similar positions.

Many minority managers' careers are held up because departments are reluctant to give them up due to their EEO goals.

Minority managers must be better performers than whites to get ahead. (As is the case with the vast majority of the statements in this study, these statements were suggested by managers who participated in the preliminary interviews and the pilot study.)

Figure 3-3 shows that more than twice as many managers believe minorities face four or five of these obstacles than those who believe minorities face none of the five. As would be expected, larger percentages of black men (45 percent) and black women (41 percent) than of any other race/sex group believe that minorities face four or five of the obstacles. Only 2-19 percent of other race/sex groups believe this is the case. White men are the only group more likely to say minorities face no obstacles than

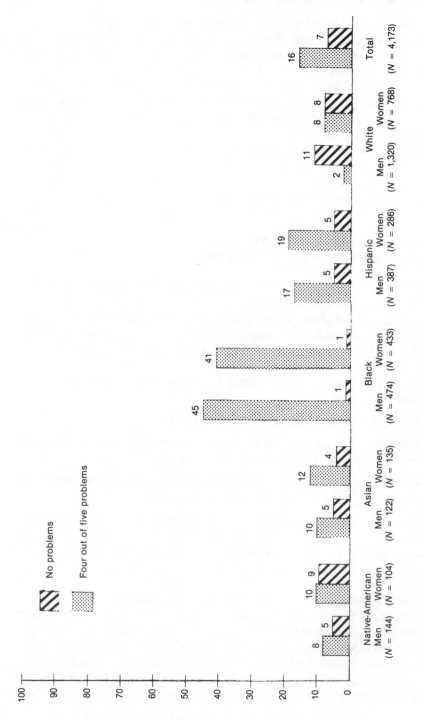

Figure 3-3. Percentage of Managers Who Agree Minorities Face at Least Four out of Five or No Obstacles in Their Companies

to say that they face many. This suggests that white men may have more difficulty than other groups in seeing problems in their system. However, 89
percent of the white men believe minorities face at least one of the five problems, suggesting they perceive some degree of unfairness in the system.

Consistent with other responses in this study, higher-level black men
are more likely than are lower-level black men to believe minorities face
four out of five of these problems:

First level	43%
Second level	45%
Third level	53%
Fourth level +	75%

These responses reflect the fact that black men moving up through the
hierarchy are very likely to observe these obstacles impeding their progress
and that of other minorities. Rather than encountering an atmosphere of
peer acceptance due to the commonality of the upper-level position, they
find themselves isolated from other blacks and not quite acceptable to their
white peers. Far from feeling secure in upper-echelon positions, blacks continue to face obstacles themselves and are privy to the decisions that place
similar obstacles before blacks at lower levels. They find themselves with
little power or support to change things. This, of course, has its effect on
their self-concepts and confidence in the system.

The ever-critical attitudes of black men, especially at upper levels,
reflect in part the fact that the white-male-dominated society has developed
stereotypes about black men that involve both hatred and admiration. Over
the centuries whites have basically developed an image of blacks that is, in
the final analysis, frightened. Not necessarily at a conscious level, they see
black men as the biggest threat to their dominant position, and therefore,
black men are most likely of any group in the corporate structure to face the
most-severe racist attitudes and behaviors.[9]

When age and education are analyzed, except for white men the
younger, more-educated groups of managers are more likely than the older,
less-educated groups of managers to believe that minorities face more
obstacles and demands than do whites. For example, in the combined group
of Hispanics, Asians, and native Americans, 20 percent of managers 30 or
younger with a college degree and 8 percent of those over 40 with no college
degrees believe minorities face four or five of these problems. This finding
supports those social scientists who predict that when educational levels exceed economic, political, and social rewards, those educated people will
become more militant and critical.[10]

Among blacks and white women, the college-educated 30+ through 40-
year-old group is the most critical. Fifty-nine percent of black men, 50 percent
of black women, and 19 percent of white women say minorities face four to

five of the obstacles. This feeling can be attributed to their association with, or involvement in, the struggle for minorities' and women's rights in the past two decades. Also, they probably face a more-hostile atmosphere because they are competing with white men for the few lucrative middle-and upper-level management positions. Finally, they have few, if any, minority or women peers and thus feel isolated and alienated.

Minorities Must Be Better Performers

The extreme differences among blacks, white men and other groups become more apparent when the obstacle statements are analyzed individually. An analysis of table 3-4 shows a 73 percent difference in responses between black managers (83 percent) and white men (10 percent) concerning the proposition that minorities have to be better performers than whites. A 1975 study of black and white managers found that 33 percent of white managers versus 88 percent of black managers agreed with this statement. Thus, while whites see minorities as being more-fairly treated today than in 1975, the views of blacks seem not to have changed.

This statement produces the largest difference in responses between black and white men in the entire study. A black man at the second level concludes:

> I cannot afford to be average or to meet the minimum requirements for a position. It's almost mandatory that I am from the right school with a little higher degree and be blessed with the favoritism of my boss.

The extreme differences in responses between black- and white-male managers can be attributed in part to the black managers' view of themselves as a very educated, ambitious, impatient group. They see white men, many with little or no college education, getting promoted, while minorities are frequently told they need more experience and training. One success story is usually sufficient to get white men promoted, but minorities and women usually need more. The fact that years of education and work experience benefit a white person more, in terms of dollars, than a black or Mexican-American clearly supports the argument that corporations require minorities to be better than whites for the same jobs. Evidently, the stereotypes override the facts of qualifications so that blacks and Mexican-Americans cannot afford to be mediocre.

A white middle-level manager from a large bank aptly sums up the present situation in the corporate world regarding qualifications: "Most minority executives are superminorities—mediocrity is the privilege of the white male."

Table 3-4
Minorities Must Perform Better than Whites to Get Ahead
(percent)

To What Extent Do You Agree or Disagree that Minorities Must be Better Performers than Whites to Get Ahead?	Native-American		Asian		Black		Hispanic		White		Total
	Men (N = 143)	*Women (N = 102)*	*Men (N = 122)*	*Women (N = 135)*	*Men (N = 474)*	*Women (N = 462)*	*Men (N = 385)*	*Women (N = 284)*	*Men (N = 1,308)*	*Women (N = 755)*	*(N = 4,140)*
Strongly agree	0.7	4.9	10.7	8.9	33.8	38	9.1	12.7	0.7	6.2	11.6
Agree	9.1	21.6	27.9	44.4	47	46.5	32.7	38.4	9.4	23.8	26.4
Disagree	71.3	69.6	54.9	45.2	18.6	14.8	51.7	44	72.1	58.4	52.2
Strongly disagree	18.9	3.9	6.6	1.5	0.6	0.7	6.5	4.9	17.8	11.5	9.8

Minorities Are Placed in Dead-End Jobs

Not only do some minorities and whites believe that minorities must be better performers, but also many believe minorities are in dead-end jobs. Twenty-one percent of the managers believe this is the case. The responses range from 51 percent of the black managers to 6 percent of the white males. The other groups fall in the 11-26 percent range. The managers surveyed define dead-end jobs as staff jobs in areas such as personnel or operations staff and some departments from which few people are promoted. A black third-level man comments, "Even though I have a technical degree I am in personnel and I see no getting out." A second-level Hispanic woman remarks, "My department is a dead-end department; people aren't promoted, they are just retired."

Managers who believe they must be better qualified, who believe their jobs are dead-end, are without the same power to act as their peers, and managers who believe they are more penalized for mistakes will not be optimally productive employees and may eventually become nonproductive, possibly counterproductive. This is especially true with the new-breed managers.

Conclusion

A pervasive tendency is to deny the very great impact of race on the corporate life and careers of minority managers. Americans in general, and white men in particular, do not like to think of themselves as unfair. Deep cultural and psychological conflicts occur among Americans because they have ideals of equality, freedom, God-given dignity of the individual, and inalienable rights on the one hand, yet they engage in practices of discrimination, humiliation, insult, and denial of opportunities to minorities on the other hand.

Many minorities are paranoid because of their treatment by the dominant society. Retreating into a self-imposed ghetto may be the minorities' only psychological defense against the unbearable pain perpetrated upon them by a racist society.[11]

Some black psychiatrists found that some healthy aspects exist to this paranoia. However, they note how difficult it is to keep the paranoia positive and not self-destructive. "To maintain a high degree of suspicion toward the motives of every white man, and at the same time never allow this suspicion to impair the grasp of reality, is walking a very thin tightrope."[12]

Certainly occasions occur in which minorities, because of their socialization and experiences, will interpret specific acts as racist when they really are not. While some paranoia truly exists, the new forms of racism also are difficult to detect and interpret and are often dismissed as the unfounded complaints of hostile or incompetent minorities. Thus, to conclude that minorities, especially blacks, are simply paranoid and unnecessarily critical would be shortsighted.

The support minorities receive from white women, especally those at higher levels, and from white men on some issues suggests that minorities' responses are valid in many cases. It is important to remember that 89 percent of white men believe minorities face some obstacles in these companies, 54 percent believe minorities face some racist tendencies, and 60 percent agree to some stereotyped remarks about minorities. Thus, the truth of the present treatment and situation of minorities in these corporations is somewhere between the extreme responses of black and white men. Regardless of what the exact truth is, the corporation's best interest cannot be to have managers working in an atmosphere in which racist stereotypes exist, in which minorities are excluded from informal work-related activities, or in which they are made to feel they did not get their jobs because of ability. The belief that one must be better than a white to get ahead, that one is penalized for more mistakes than whites, or that one is in a dead-end job is not conducive to good employee morale or productivity.

4

The Present Situation and Treatment of Female Managers

The basic function of sexism is similar to that of racism: It keeps power and privilege in the hands of white men. (For a detailed discussion of sexism, see the appendix.) The economic, political, and social institutions, as well as the legal system, culture, customs, and morals of this society in the United States are all determined by white men in order to sustain their privileged and dominant position. Domination may underlie women's subjugation to a greater extent than the profit system's exploitation.

In *Woman's Estate*, Juliet Mitchell calls the oppression of women the "primary oppression in all societies, whatever their mode of production. . . ." She points out that radical feminism is the "belief that women's oppression is first, foremost, and separable from any particular historical context."[1]

This chapter reviews the history of women in the work force and analyzes the effect of sexism on the present situation and treatment of women in the companies represented in this study. The influence of sexism on women's earning power is covered, and special emphasis is placed on the hierarchy of sensitivity to women's concerns and problems in the corporate world among the race/sex groups.

A Brief History of Women's Participation in the Work Force

The view of women as the weaker, inferior sex has little basis in fact. The vast majority of women have always worked. What has varied has been the location and conditions of their labor. Prior to the Industrial Revolution, both men and women performed most jobs, and all members of the family had to work. Little distinction was evident between men's work and women's work. This was especially true for the hard and strenuous labor jobs:

> No work was too hard, no labor too strenuous to exclude women. Among the masses of people still emerging from serfdom and existing in terrible poverty, the family was an economic unit in which men, women, and children worked in order to survive.[2]

The Industrial Revolution tolled the knell for the cottage industries that had been a preferred work location for women expected to bear and raise children while also producing marketable products.[3] The revolution, which was based on the exploitation of the working class, resulted in a labor situation not much different from serfdom. Women and children, as young as age six, were forced to work fourteen-hour days, seven days a week, in factories and sweatshops for less than subsistence wages. Heating, lighting, and ventilation were inadequate, if not totally lacking. Anyone who missed a day's work because of illness or any other reason was automatically fired.[4] In his 1906 revelation of the inhuman working conditions for women in Chicago's meat-packing industry, Upton Sinclair described how they stood all day long, ankle deep in briny water, freezing in winter and sweltering in summer.[5]

The emergence of the middle class accompanied the Industrial Revolution. This development allowed some men to provide for their families single-handedly. Women, increasingly freed from menial home labor by the new technology, were able to pursue other tasks. These other tasks were limited and clearly defined—that is, only certain types of work were acceptable for these women. Their primary social role was as a nurturing force, and the work they performed had to improve their power to fulfill this role with precision.[6]

While the Industrial Revolution created a multitude of jobs for women, in both factories and offices, it is crucial to point out that in general, and especially for middle-class women, few women doubted that any employment they had would be anything but temporary in order to assist or perform for some immediate need. Women were not to think about careers. Their full-time career was in their home.[7]

Women, encouraged to think of themselves as part-time workers, did not expect or press for advancement and equal pay. They were defined as temporary workers by their employers who were reluctant to advance them or raise their salaries.[8]

As previously noted, the temporary-work attitudes appear to have been held primarily by white middle-class women. For many minorities and lower-class immigrant women, working was not temporary. It was permanent and necessary.

Throughout history, men have determined when women could work and what work they could do. The usual practice that men have followed in defining women's work has been to hire women for positions that men, because of social class, education, or national needs such as war, were either unwilling or unable to fill.[9] This basic concept was demonstrated during the Depression and World War II. Female workers were the first, along with racial minorities, to be fired or laid off during the Great Depression. High rates of unemployment led to pervasive efforts to circumscribe the work of women who appeared to be depriving the male heads of households of their livelihoods. Women were still welcome to work in specified low-paying fields, but any woman presuming to compete for a "man's" job met with hostility and resentment. Government policy during the Depression was to "Get the Men Back to Work" and to spread the impact of the few available jobs. In 1932, a "married-persons" clause for federal civil-service workers specified that the first employees to be dismissed during personnel reduction were to be those who had spouses holding another federal position. Three-quarters of those dismissed under this act were women, even though the law did not specify that the husband was to retain his job. Under the New Deal, men received preference for Work Progress Administration (WPA) jobs, and single women, some lacking all other resources, were at the bottom of the list.[10]

World War II forced a complete reversal of this attitude, and "Rosie the Riveter" emerged as a patriotic folk heroine. Women poured into the labor force and proved to be competent laborers in many areas heretofore restricted to men. The nation had little choice. Women were needed to fill both "women's" jobs and "men's" jobs. In steel mills, women were found pounding typewriters in the offices and rolling steel next to the furnaces. These war jobs clearly were only temporary and an emergency measure, even though women were encouraged by the government to take them.

At the end of the war, women were urged to return home to make room in the labor force for the returning veterans. Employers were surprised to find that many women preferred to remain at work, even though they were often demoted from their wartime positions. Women were developing a new ethic, a new self-worth, and a new independence.[11]

Mary Ryan noted dramatic changes in educated women's attitudes about work and careers that were reflected in their goals. In 1943, 50 percent of the women at a prestigious eastern college wanted to retire permanently from the work force after becoming mothers, and 30 percent hoped to return to work after their children were grown. In 1971, only 18 percent of the women at the same college planned to retire after becoming mothers, and 62 percent planned to return to work later:

> These highly educated women of the 1970s were prepared to assume dual roles and an interrupted career pattern, apparently oblivious to or unconcerned about the likelihood that they would receive considerably lower salaries than their husbands who remained continuously in the work force."[12]

In 1940, almost half of the women in the labor force were unmarried and 30 percent were married. By 1970, 20 percent were unmarried and 60 percent were married. In 1972, over twice as many women with school-age children were working than in 1948—50 percent in 1972 compared to 20 percent in 1948 of working women from the total population. The most-dramatic rise was in working women with preschool children. In 1948, 10 percent of working women had preschool children, while in 1960, 19 percent had preschool children. In 1971, one-third of mothers with preschool children were at work.[13]

The number of women in the work force will increase further because women's changing attitudes about work will affect their children—especially their daughters:

> Whether or not the mother worked outside the home and what occupation she held, given that she was employed, affect daugher's location. In other words, mother's work matters for daughter's occupational location.[14]

While women's attitudes about work and careers have changed tremendously since World War II, most men's attitudes about women have not changed nearly as much. The men whose attitudes have changed the least are those whose wives and/or daughters do not work outside the home. These men have a very difficult time adjusting to female managers and especially high-level female managers in nontraditional jobs. They can accept and perceive women only in subservient roles. Doing otherwise creates tremendous conflicts. Their wives, their mothers, and their daughters are happy to play the subordinate role. Thus, these men do not understand the increasing number of women who will not play the subservient role and who want to move up the corporate ladder, especially in nontraditional jobs.

Sexism Translated into Dollars and Cents

As noted in the previous chapter, all other factors being equal, blacks and Mexican-Americans make less money than whites, due to racism. Comparing the salaries of women with those of men with similar characteristics, sexual discrimination clearly has a profound negative impact on women's salaries. Paul Burstein found, as expected, that white men earned a great deal more than minority men, and minority men earned somewhat more than white women, who made slightly more than minority women.[15]

Larry Suter and Henry Mitler found that men received $56 for each unit increment in occupational prestige while women received only $23. In addition, the net yearly return to men for each unit increase in education was $515 while women received less than half of that, $223. Women are unable to convert education and occupational status into earnings at the same high rate as men do.[16]

David Featherman and H. Robert Hauser also noted the severe effect of sexism on women's salaries. In fact, they determined that the ratio of female to male earnings declined even though the occupational and educational achievements of women have kept pace with and even exceeded men's. They stated, "Discrimination accounts for 86 percent of the earnings' gap in 1962 and 84 percent in 1973."[17]

In addition to the hard facts of lower pay and greater difficulty in securing jobs for which they are as qualified as men, women are subject to more-subtle pressures in the corporate world. Sexist attitudes have created problems for women in such areas as job placement, boss-subordinate-peer interactions, performance standards, and opportunities for promotion. The next sections reveal and explore the responses to specific questions about attitudes and behaviors toward women managers.

Hierarchy of Critical Responses on Sex Discrimination in Corporations

Sensitivity to sex discrimination in this study is revealed as a dual function of race and sex. In the responses to questions on sexism, the same pattern emerges repeatedly, revealing a clear-cut hierarchy of awareness on sexism in the participating companies. Black women are more critical of the treatment of women than is any other group. The next most-critical group comprised a cluster of native Americans, Hispanic and white women, then black men, closely followed by Asian women. Substantially behind Asian women are Hispanic and Asian men. White and native-American men are by far the least sensitive to the treatment of women. They rank by far below even the traditionally macho Hispanic men in this hierarchy. An overall combined index of questions on sexist tendencies, obstacles, and additional demands placed on women in the participating companies was formed and the results are shown in figure 4-1. The following questions make up the index:

Most male managers have made women feel that they got their jobs because of EEO targets and not because of their abilities.

Men are usually unable to work comfortably with women, so they bypass them and go to their superiors. Female managers are often excluded from informal work networks by men.

Female managers have a difficult time initiating informal work-related activities such as lunch dates and drinks after work because men misinterpret their behavior as a come-on.

Many women have a much-harder time than do men in finding someone who is particularly interested in their careers.

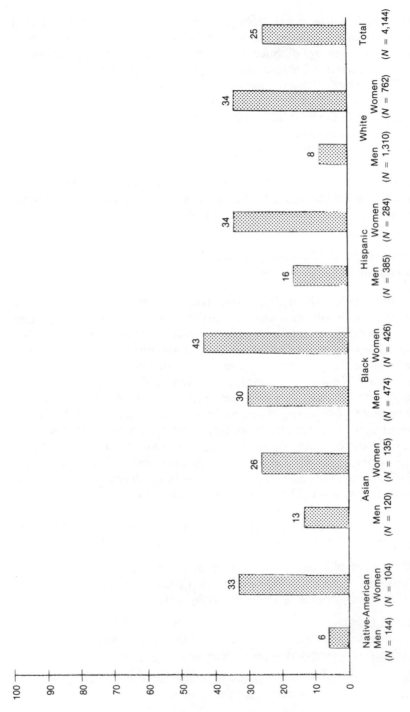

Figure 4-1. Percentage of Managers Who Are Aware of at Least Seven out of Nine Forms of Sexism in Their Companies

Female managers have to be better performers than men to get ahead.

Most female managers are placed in dead-end jobs.

Female managers are penalized more than men are for mistakes.

Most female managers do not have the same power as do men in similar positions.

Figure 4-1 illustrates that 43 percent of the black women believe that women have problems in seven of the nine areas. They are followed by 34 percent of the white and Hispanic women, 33 percent of the native-American women, 30 percent of the black men, and 26 percent of the Asian women. Following the Asian women are Hispanic men, 16 percent; Asian men, 13 percent; white men, 8 percent; and native-American men, 6 percent.

Why Are Black Women Most Critical about the Treatment of Female Managers?

What are some possible explanations of this hierarchy of criticism? One factor explaining minority women's more-critical responses is that they are stigmatized twice—once for race and once for sex. As perceived discrimination against race groups varies, so does the perception of sex discrimination. Black women are more sensitive to sexism because of the racial discrimination they suffer and more sensitive to racism because of the sexual discrimination to which they are subjected. Judging by their responses, black women suffer the same extreme racism that black men endure, presumably in accordance with Silberman's hypothesis that the darker one's skin color, the more hostile the prejudice to which one is subjected.

The history of the treatment of black women in the United States is one of deprivation and isolation, the dynamics of which evoked great inner strength in many black women. As the black man in slavery was degraded by being deprived of nearly every right of the white man, the black woman, in addition to being deprived of nearly every right of the white woman, was degraded by sexual abuse. This pattern continued into the postslavery period.

White society, because it considered the black women to be more docile and less threatening than the black men, allowed or forced the black women to serve the white family. Even though whites have looked more favorably upon black women than on black men, this has not prevented black men from gaining more than women by virtue of their gender. Despite having more education, black women consistently have a higher rate of unemployment and earn less money than do black men. In addition, they suffer many of the difficulties of white women due to the pervasiveness of sexism in our society. They are forced, in many cases, to bear the responsibility for family planning alone and are expected to cater to male desires and to assume a subordinate role.[18]

For a decade, black women were actively antifeminist because they felt that the feminists were competing with the black civil rights movement, or that feminism was just for the benefit of white middle-class women. Black women long believed that the major obstacles to success they faced in American society stemmed primarily from their race and not their sex. The negative reaction of many black-male politicians to Shirley Chrisholm's presidential candidacy in 1972 caused many black women to reevaluate their oppression as women.

Dr. Gloria Lindsy Alibarhou, once an antifeminist, has predicted that black women will become increasingly involved in the mainstream women's movement and that feminism as an ideology is beginning to take hold. However, she clearly states that this does not mean that racism will take a back seat to sexism.[19]

In short, black women are the most critical about the present situation and treatment of women in corporations, not only because they suffer sexist discrimination as all women do but also because they face the extreme form of racial discrimination that black men face.

Hispanic, Native-American, and White Women See Similar Discrimination

Hispanic, white, and native-American women are the next most-critical groups after black women. Several reasons put forth in the feedback sessions by white and native-American women for their critical views are:

They must deal with the white men's sexist attitudes both at work and in the home.

They believe white men see them as a bigger threat than minority women because the downfall of sexism will affect the entire white-male lifestyle, not just part of it.

They feel the women's movement has appealed more to them than to minority women because white middle-class women were the prime participants of the movement, and they can more-readily identify with it.

Thus, these women conclude that they are more sensitive to sexist attitudes and behaviors than are other women. However, because of their color—white or nearly white—they are not faced with the dual problems of race and sex and therefore are not as critical as black women.

Those native Americans who are "really native American" are less critical than black women because white society sees them as much-more acceptable, and many of them have adopted white values and attitudes. In addition, native Americans have cultural values that tend to make them less likely to be critical.

Hispanic women respond similarly to white and native-American women, not because Hispanic men have tremendous power in controlling society's institutions, but because of the Latino cultural concept of machismo. This concept basically labels women as second-class citizens, leading to Hispanic women's oppression and control.

Elizabeth Almquist wrote about Mexican-American women, and this passage can be applied to most Hispanic women:

> Because the first marriages were between Spanish patrons and Indian women they looked down upon, a partriarchal marital relationship was quickly established. Later, as a large group of Mexicans emerged, the values of the Catholic Church helped institutionalize a husband-dominant/wife-subordinate pattern.
>
> The Spaniards had already discovered that by socializing Indian women to the "Marianisma" concept, they were able to keep them controlled as servants. The Marianisma concept involves venerating the Virgin Mary and using her as the role model for Mexican women.
>
> The women should be submissive, altruistic, and self-denying. The veneration of the Mary image leads also to the downgrading of women who do not fulfill the ideal. Thus, there are only two types of women: the self-sacrificing mother who has an identity only as a mother and the whore who is the direct antithesis of the Virgin.[20]

Anna Nicto Gomez noted that while Hispanic women are anxious to achieve equality between Anglos and Mexican-Americans, they are caught in the belief that only men can be leaders and that the better jobs should go to men. Therefore, they have been slower to adopt the feminist movement than white women.[21]

Also, as was the case with native-American women, Mexican-American women do not respond as critically as black women because they are looked upon more favorably by white society. Therefore, while they face similar sexist oppression, their racial oppression in general is not as great as it is for black women.

Why Are Asian Women Least Critical of the Treatment of Female Managers?

Asian women are the least critical of the treatment of female managers, and this may be due to the influence of Asian concepts of women. Stanley Fong and H. Peskin explained the factors that influence Asian women's sensitivity to sexism—namely, that Chinese girls are still brought up with an emphasis on modesty, social niceties, patience, reserve, and submissiveness. They do not mind being protected and acknowledged as physically weaker than men.[22] Japanese women, according to Almquist, have family patterns and values similar to Chinese. "The traditional Japanese family was heavily patriarchal. Women's main functions were to serve their husbands and to produce male offspring."[23]

Dr. Chelsa Loo explained the Asian women's situation in this manner:

> Asian males traditionally have seen themselves as more competent and in higher-status professional positions than Asian women. As one Asian male candidly revealed, "Asian women should be less educated than Asian men. In a society where Asian men feel discriminated against and emasculated by racist attitudes, they need someone below them in order to feel some degree of superiority." Thus, for the Asian woman who wants the support and colleagueship of Asian men, conflicts over expressing her feelings about women's oppressions may be experienced. She may tend to downplay women's problems in order not to antagonize threatened males.[24]

That Asian women are the least critical of all minority women can also be explained, in part, by the fact that of all minority groups they are looked upon the most favorably by white society and thus face less racial discrimination. In short, their double stigma is much less severe than is that of other minority women.

Why Do Black Men Empathize with Female Managers?

The greater sensitivity of black men to the situation of women, when compared with the responses of other male groups, may possibly be explained by the fact that blacks have suffered greater oppression than other ethnic groups have over a longer period of time.

Diane Lewis made important observations and posited reasons why black men empathize more with women then do other men. Her basic argument is that African and Afro-American acculturation and socialization processes are much-less sexist than are the white Western European/American processes because they are not based on the dualistic nature of Euro-American culture.

As an example she noted that:

> . . . in black families, both males and females display similar styles of child care. They are nurturing and highly interactive physically with children. Both men and women value personal relationships and are expressive emotionally. Both are more adept at handling the world of interpersonal relationships than the world of objects and the physical environment.[25]

Dr. Alibarhou argued that not only cultural differences but also the low economic situation of most black males modified their sexist attitudes. Many more black women *have* had to contribute to the family support than white women.[26]

While a much-higher percentage of black men than other groups of men recognizes the oppression of women, all black men are not empathetic to women's situations. Some of them believe, consciously or unconsciously, as do many other men, that women's demands for equal rights are a threat to whatever masculinity they have been allowed by the larger society. Some resentment exists, particularly among middle-class black men, toward what is considered the preferential treatment in jobs for black women who are used as a double minority in affirmative-action hiring and promoting.

Why Do Hispanic Men Empathize Less than Black Men with Female Managers' Problems?

After black men, Hispanic men are the next group most empathetic to women's situation. However, they are far behind black men in level of identification. Part of the reason Hispanic men are less empathetic is the ambiguous nature of whites' attitudes toward Hispanics. Hispanic-Americans usually do not face as much discrimination and oppression as blacks do and are therefore less able to relate to discrimination and oppression against women.

Another factor that makes Hispanic men less likely to support women and women's positions is related to the concept of machismo in Hispanic cultures. A central concept of machismo is that women should always be subservient to men and that they are inferior to men. Pride in masculinity is the basis of machismo. Many Hispanic men believe that it is an insult to their manhood for their women to surpass them in the areas of work, career, or salary.[27]

A group of first- and second-level Hispanic-female managers made several comments about their relationships with their husbands. "My husband really doesn't want me to work. He feels it takes away from his manliness." Another commented, "I don't show my husband my pay stub because I make more money than he does. He sees my check, but I put enough in U.S. bonds and the savings plan that my check is less than his." Still another said, "My husband has no problem with my working or my position because he has a good job, but when I get to third level I fear his male ego will get hurt because I will have a greater position than he." These women all agree that Hispanic men prefer to see women stay home and be good wives, not only because of the reasons previously stated but also because they do not like "their" women dealing with men whom they do not know.

Explanations for Asian Men's Responses about
Female Managers' Treatment

The responses of Asian men are more conservative than are those of black men, but they are more liberal than those of native-American and white men. This can be explained, in part, by the extreme rigidity in the roles that traditional Asian society dictates for the sexes. Men, especially the fathers, are given the highest honor and almost total power over family members. Women are there to serve the man and take care of the home.[28]

It has been noted that Asian men who are actively involved in the movement toward racial equality consider competition from Asian women a threat to their masculinity. Moreover, while advocating freedom from racial oppression, many of the men in the movement are unable to see that, by relegating their Asian-American sisters to traditional low-level female roles, they are oppressing part of their own racial group.[29] Finally, Dr. Loo's comments about the passive, noncritical manner in which Asians approach authority helps explain the lack of empathy Asian men have for the present difficulties women face in corporations.

Explanations for Lack of Empathy Native-American
and White Men Have for Female Managers

Native-American and white men are the least likely, by a wide margin, to be sympathetic to women's positions. This fact is not surprising since they are the ones who will lose most in any equal treatment of women. Remember that white men represent only 37 percent of the population, yet they have controlled 95 percent of the lucrative positions in all society's institutions. Any movement toward equality necessarily means a threat to their dominant position. In addition, they will not only be threatened in the work environment but also in the home environment. Finally, since they control society's institutions, most are not likely to believe or admit that those institutions are sexist.

For most native-American men who are not white, their lack of support for the women's plight in corporations can be attributed in part to the native-American traditions and the manner in which the men have related to women in their own society. Dr. Hardy Frye wrote:

> The culture which most native Americans bring to the urban environment somewhat reflects the style of life practiced on the reservation. A strong dose of machismo appears to exist on the tribal reservation which makes a clear distinction between the *male* role and the *female* role, and this distinction is supported by both the isolation of the reservation from the rest of society and the strong traditions of the native-American people.[30]

Another very important finding involves a third variable: the effect of managerial level upon perceptions of sex discrimination. In many instances black men and white women at higher levels are much-more critical of the situation of women in their companies than are those at lower levels. Underlying these feelings is the fact that these managers at the upper levels are more isolated because of their fewer numbers. They are perceived as strong threats and as such are the targets of concentrated discrimination. Also, these managers, interacting with white men at higher levels, are more privy to the thoughts and behaviors of these men and are not optimisitc about what they see and hear.

Stereotypes about Female Managers

Numerous studies have shown that the negative stereotypes about women in society are carried into the corporate structure and that they grossly affect women's careers.[31] A case history of a white, third-level woman is illustrative. She has been with her company for seven years on their high-risk, high-reward management program for college hires. She is tall, very attractive, and everyone agrees, very intelligent. She does outstanding work. However, most of the men she deals with believe that she is too aggressive, too emotional, and not political enough. She has been accused of using her sex as an alibi for many of the problems she is confronted with on the job. She counters that most of her problems are related to sexist men who are intimidated by her height, brains, aggressiveness, and good looks. In addition, while she admits to making rapid progress, she believes she has had to be better than her male peers. She notes that on three occasions she was severely reprimanded because of small errors, while her male peers were and are not—even for their large errors. While two of her seven peers are friendly and invite her to informal meetings, the others attempt to keep her out of the informal work group, primarily through sexual harassment. Are the problems faced by this young woman atypical?

An index was constructed to measure the level of sexist stereotyping in the companies participating in this study. The questions from which the index was formed were suggested by the frequency of related comments by the managers during the preliminary interviews. The managers were asked to what extent they agree or disagree with the following statements:

Most female managers are not as qualified as most male managers.

Most women use sex as an alibi for many difficulties they have on the job.

Most female managers are too emotional to be competent managers.

Most female managers are not serious about professional careers

The rejection of such stereotyping by the female groups and black men is of statistical significance when compared with the responses of other male groups in the sample. Figure 4-2 shows that between 75 and 83 percent of the female managers, and 70 percent of the black men agree with *none* of the statements depicting stereotypes about women. In comparison, the other male groups' responses range from 58 percent of the Hispanic men to 41 percent of the native-American men.

The study found that the percentage of white men agreeing with any stereotyped comments about women decreases at the highest management levels. Quite the opposite was found with regard to their agreement with the stereotypes about minorities:

White men who agree with stereotypes about women		White men who agree with stereotypes about minorities
First level	54%	54%
Second level	52%	62%
Third level	39%	62%
Fourth level	44%	63%
Fifth level	36%	68%
Sixth level	35%	69%

The views of white men at upper levels of management possibly are more prejudiced against minorities than women because they believe that their power positions are less threatened by women than minorities.

The overall significance of the response to the questions about stereotyped views of women managers is that 34 percent of the participants agree with one or more of the sexist statements. A larger percentage likely harbors stereotypes but is unwilling to admit to them for various reasons. These managers are very likely to act out these beliefs consciously or subconsciously during interactions with, or decisions about, women in the corporate world.

When the variables of age and education are controlled, college graduates from all race/sex groups clearly are less likely to express sexist attitudes than are those who have some or no college education. For example, the real power brokers in these companies—white men over 40 years of age—agree with one or more of the sexist statements as follows: 55 percent with no college, 47 percent with some college, and 41 percent with college degrees express stereotypes about women. Noted that age does not have a

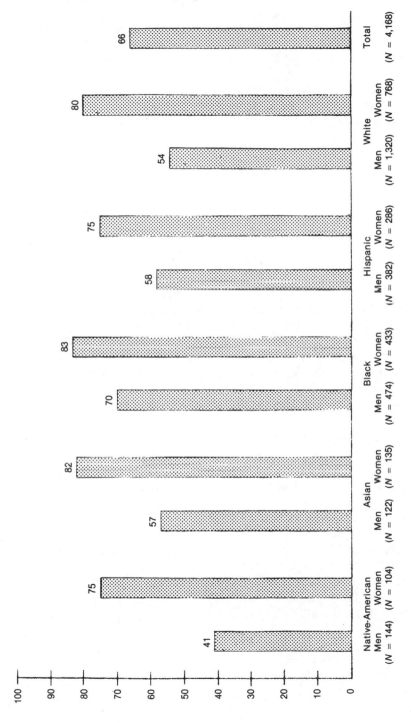

Figure 4-2. Percentage of Managers Who Express No Stereotypes about Women

great impact on whether or not managers express stereotyped attitudes. For example, almost half (47 percent) of minority men, excluding blacks, aged 30 and under, with college degrees agree with stereotypes about female managers compared with 43 percent between the ages 30+ to 40 with college degrees and 43 percent over age 40 with college degrees. Age also makes no statistically significant difference in white-male attitudes. Thus, we can conclude that while education seems to moderate sexist attitudes, age has no significant impact.

A detailed look at two of the sex-stereotype questions in this study defines more clearly the problems that stereotyping creates for female managers.

Women Are Too Emotional for Effective Management

The view of female managers as too emotional to be competent is held by 10 percent of the managers. Native-American men (20 percent) Hispanic and white men (13 percent) are most likely to agree with this stereotype. Table 4-1 presents the managers' responses by race and sex. The table also illustrates that a significantly higher percentage of female than male managers from each race group is likely to strongly disagree with this statement. This finding might suggest that many men who presently disagree, rather than strongly disagree, can easily be swayed to agree.

A white man at the third level responds, "Most women are not strong emotionally, and some do not have the background to lead a company or group of people."

While only one in ten managers agrees with this stereotype, it is important to note that among the dominant white-male group, three times the percentage at lower levels than at upper levels of management say that women are too emotional to be competent managers—that is, 18 percent versus 6 percent. In view of the fact that most women are at first and second levels, these attitudes can be very detrimental to their careers because no one wants a manager who they believe is too emotional to be competent.

The managerial competence of men can be challenged by the other side of the stereotype—that is, that men are trained not to be empathetic to human needs. David McClelland of Harvard was expressing the traditional view when he wrote that "men are interested in things and women in people."[32] Elizabeth Janeway responded:

> If so, men are in trouble, for command over things by physical skills has largely been made over to machines. Dealing with people, contrariwise, is becoming increasingly vital. Not only is it needed to manage the social strains apparent today but also, if we are to win a new sort of command over things by commanding and correcting our deteriorating environment,

Table 4-1
Women Are Too Emotional to Be Competent Managers
(percent)

How Strongly Do You Agree or Disagree that Most Women Are Too Emotional to Be Competent Managers?	Native-American		Asian		Black		Hispanic		White		Total
	Men (N = 143)	Women (N = 104)	Men (N = 121)	Women (N = 135)	Men (N = 472)	Women (N = 433)	Men (N = 381)	Women (N = 286)	Men (N = 1,306)	Women (N = 766)	(N = 4,147)
Strongly agree	1.4	4.8	3.3	3.8	1.9	4.8	3.1	6.6	2.1	5	3.4
Agree	18.1	7.7	6.6	1.5	5.7	1.6	10.2	3.1	10.9	2.9	7
Disagree	65.5	42.3	67.8	54.8	63	28.3	63.5	43.7	68.8	37.7	54.9
Strongly disagree	14.9	45.2	22.3	40	29.4	65.1	23.1	46.5	18.2	54.4	34.7

we have to begin by dealing with people, for we must persuade groups within our society to sacrifice their immediate needs to general, long-term goals.[33]

Management consultants Margaret Hennig and Anne Jardim stated that an element of truth exists in saying that some women are unable to manage their emotions or feelings. In our culture, women are socialized to express emotions freely and openly. It is entirely acceptable for women to cry. The cultural prohibition against the expression of feelings by men is so strong that to cry in front of other people is to be marked as someone who is uncontrolled, someone who cannot be trusted to make the right decisions. Secretary of State Edmund Muskie cried in the New Hampshire primary of 1972 and probably lost his party's support as a result. Without making value judgments, Hennig and Jardim pointed out that in organizations made up predominantly of men, women will find it expedient to manage their own emotions, particularly to avoid inappropriate responses such as tears in a business meeting.[34]

However, a word of caution is necessary about managing emotions—that is, anyone who has sought almost any type of therapeutic experience knows that emotion is not necessarily bad. Feelings are expressed one way or another. Holding in emotions can have a negative affect on both mental and physical health. When a manager is upset, it is better for the company and the person to express those feelings openly so that they can be dealt with in a constructive fashion. When feelings are not expressed, they can come out in indirect ways that negatively affect both corporate operations and the manager's mental and physical health.

Women Are Not Serious about Their Careers

The other stereotype to be considered is that women are not serious about their professional careers. More than one out of eight managers agree with this statement. Native-American men (22 percent) and white men (20 percent) are most likely to agree that women are not serious about professional careers. Between 11 percent and 18 percent of other minority men also agree; among female managers, only 4 to 9 percent agree. As with the previous stereotype, many more women are likely to strongly disagree than are men. Again, an element of truth does exist in this stereotype, particularly for some women who are married and/or have children at home. While from an early age men expect to work to support at least themselves and are encouraged to achieve, women, particularly white and/or middle-class women, have been socialized to find someone to support them.

As a result of these cultural expectations, many men and women emerge from childhood socialization with quite different ideas about jobs and careers. One result of this aspect is that while a man sees his career as an integral part of his life, a woman actively strives to separate personal goals from career goals. The process becomes particularly difficult when more managers impute traditionally home values to women managers and make assumptions about them.

Work as a manager often proves to serve as a resocialization agent for women. This is demonstrated by the fact that at upper levels, female managers are more enthusiastic than are female managers at lower levels about, or at least more willing to accept, transfers, put in unpaid overtime, make overnight business trips, or attend six-week training programs. Another very effective and instant resocializing experience is divorce. Some of the most-ambitious female managers are divorced. They represent a pool of women eager to accept transfers for developmental experience or promotion. This eagerness also holds true for single women who are heads of families and sometimes for women who are married and/or have children at home. Definite indications show up in the data that younger women take their careers far more seriously than did earlier cohorts of women and that they are selecting, in increasing numbers, traditionally male-dominated fields for their careers.

Changing work aspirations pose potential problems for the many two-career families in our society. Sometimes painful choices must be faced as to whose career takes precedence. This problem is now common enough to be recognized by corporations when contemplating the transfer of a valued employee. The *Wall Street Journal* recently reported that some companies are offering help in locating a job for the spouse of a transferee.[35]

Lee Gershuny made some cogent observations on the negative effects of stereotypes. Her remarks serve as a fitting summary for this section:

> The trouble with stereotypes is that they restrict behavior and understanding by constructing a static image of both sexes. Furthermore, assigning verbal qualities to each sex creates an illusion of biologically determined traits instead of suggesting their sociocultural origins or even an interplay of biology and environment. It is as though emotionality and passivity, usually assigned to the female stereotype, are qualities inherently absent in men. The passive man and the assertive woman are "unnatural" anomalies and are urged into psychotherapy to remedy behavior unbecoming the stereotype.[36]

Managers' Awareness of Sexist Tendencies in Corporations

While managers do not agree with stereotypes about women to the extent expected, 26 pecent believe women face four or five sexist tendencies, and only 15 percent believe women do not face any. Thus, 85 percent of all the managers surveyed believe women are facing at least one of the following sexist tendencies:

Most male managers have made women feel that they got their jobs because of EEO targets and not because of their abilities.

Men are usually unable to work comfortably with women, so they bypass them and go to their superiors.

Female managers are often excluded from informal work networks by men.

Female managers have a difficult time initiating informal work-related activities such as lunch dates and drinks after work because men misinterpret their behavior as a come-on.

Many women have a much harder time than men do in finding someone who is particularly interested in their careers.

Figure 4-3 illustrates that 43 percent of black women indicate an awareness of sexist tendencies within their company in responses to four or five of these questions, followed by between 33 and 35 percent of black men and native-American, white, and Hispanic women. These figures compare with 12 to 25 percent of Asian women and native-American, Asian, Hispanic, and white men.

Significant differences occur by level for black and white men. As level increases, the percentage of white men who are aware of no sexist tendencies also increases:

First level	18%
Second level	21%
Third level	22%
Fourth level	25%
Fifth level	25%
Sixth level	31%

This limited awareness of sexist tendencies in the corporate structure on the part of white men at upper levels may be the result of their inability to be critical of a system in which they have done well. Furthermore, they have had very little experience interacting with female managers and substantial experience interacting with nurturing wives and mothers.

In comparison, black men at higher levels of the corporate ladder are more aware of sexist tendencies. The percentages of black men who respond positively to four or five of the questions are as follows:

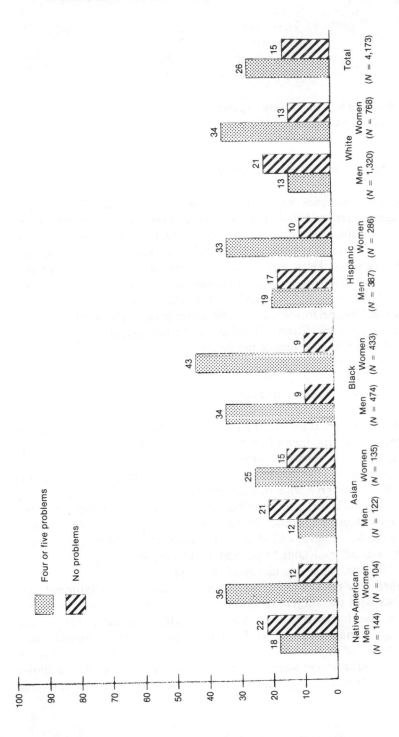

Figure 4-3. Percentage of Managers Who Are Aware of at Least Four out of Five or No Sexist Tendencies in Their Companies

First level	30%
Second level	35%
Third level	44%
Fourth level +	58%

Higher-level black men, having experienced oppression and competed successfully, are more empathetic to the woman's situation.

Women Do Not Obtain Jobs on Ability

Looking at the awareness of sexist tendencies in more detail, 54 percent of
all managers agree that most male managers make female managers feel
they got their jobs because of EEO targets and not because of ability.
Among women, blacks (74 percent) were most likely to agree and Asians (56
percent) were least likely. Among the male managers, blacks (71 percent)
were most likely and whites (34 percent) least likely to agree. These findings
are significant because any woman who is made to feel this way will suffer
in self-esteem. Her performance also will suffer because the work group will
not be very supportive. Chapter 3 discussed the consequences of this lack of
support on minority and female managers.

Social-Interaction Problems of Female Managers

Still another problem is that of the social interaction. Sixty-one percent of
all managers agree that men often exclude female managers from informal
networks, and black men (68 percent) and white women (67 percent) are
most likely to agree. Hispanic men (50 percent) and Asian men (49 percent)
are least likely to agree with this statement. Note that 57 percent of the
white men agree and that white and black managers at upper levels are more
likely to agree than are those at lower levels—that is, 85 percent of the white
women at the fourth level and above, 75 percent at the third level, 69 percent at the second level, and 57 percent at the first level agree. The consequence of this exclusion was discussed in chapter 3.
    Another area related to the exclusion of women from informal net-
works deals with the subjective interpretation of their motives. How are
women's actions interpreted when they try to include themselves in informal
gatherings or initiate informal work-related activities such as lunches, din-
ners, or drinks after work? Do many men create a problem for women
because they misinterpret women's actions as a come-on? Table 4-2 shows
the usual race/sex differences and that almost half of all managers agree
this is the case.

Table 4-2
Women Have Problems Initiating Informal Work-Related Contacts (percent)

Female Managers Have a Difficult Time Initiating Informal Work-Related Activities Such as Lunch Dates and Drinks after Work Because Men Misinterpret Their Behavior As a Come On.	Native-American		Asian		Black		Hispanic		White		Total
	Men (N = 143)	Women (N = 104)	Men (N = 122)	Women (N = 135)	Men (N = 474)	Women (N = 432)	Men (N = 383)	Women (N = 285)	Men (N = 1,312)	Women (N = 765)	(N = 4,155)
Strongly agree	0.7	13.6	4.9	11.9	9.3	12.1	5.8	9.2	4.3	14.3	8.5
Agree	39.2	32	27.7	31.3	42.4	34.8	46.1	32.6	39.2	35	37.2
Disagree	55.9	49.5	61.5	51.5	42.6	47.2	45.2	53	53.1	45.2	49.6
Strongly disagree	4.2	4.7	5.7	5.2	5.7	5.8	3	5	3.5	5.1	4.7

The managers' responses illuminate a very serious problem women are confronted with in corporations. Since many important decisions take place in informal settings, if women cannot initiate such contact, then they are at a tremendous disadvantage in being effective managers. While this question does not directly probe managers' views on sexual harassment, it indirectly indicates that many women might be confronted by such harassment if men misinterpret their initiatives of informal contacts.

The heightened consciousness of working women and the evolution of EEO case law have resulted in recent court decisions establishing legal precedents for bringing sexual harassment out of the realm of social rights and into the realm of sex discrimination. Recent articles and books indicate that sexual harassment has been the rule rather than the exception for all women who work.[37]

Women respond differently to the availability of sexual liaisons at work. Some women influence their careers by the manner in which they refuse sexual advances. The men who treat women with the expectation of a sexual type of response tend to become enraged if rejected abruptly. Some women manage to handle the problem delicately.[38] Of course, the question remains as to why they should have to handle this type of mistreatment at all.

Male chauvinism is reinforced by the behavior of some women who have strong negative attitudes toward the feminist movement. They are known by a variety of names such as the "fascinating womanhood." The modus operandi of these women is to appear helpless while artfully manipulating others. These women see life as being full of rewards for which their sexuality can be traded. Feminist condemn this approach as similar to, but more dishonest than, prostitution.[39]

Another group of women, particularly the young and inexperienced ones, are genuinely flattered by attention and flirtation. These women are usually, consciously or subconsciously, experiencing a need for male attention but are often not prepared for or interested in the more-serious needs for sexual attention on the parts of some men in positions of power.[40]

Consultants to women interested in careers as managers warn in no uncertain terms against mixing personal emotional involvements with working associates. Betty Harragan stated:

> What the unwritten and unverbalized canon of male ethics adds up to for women is clear: Any corporate woman employee who engages in intercourse with a fellow employee has jeopardized her chances of significant advancement within that particular corporate structure. She is irrevocably labeled "inferior" and must go elsewhere to move upward with a clear path.[41]

Unfortunately because of the prevailing double standard, men, especially white men, do not receive such counsel. In the poststudy-feedback sessions, black-male managers reported a related phenomenon: They are always accused of pursuing white women, even if they are not. They indicate that it is very difficult to form even a close working relationship with white women because white men quickly perceive a sexual connotation in the relationship. A number said that even a casual conversation with a white woman is sometimes looked upon in sexual terms by whites. Finally, several indicated that a few black men, but not white men, have lost their jobs because of affairs with white-female coworkers.

The potential for office affairs is ever present, and traditionally they have occurred between male power figures—managers and professionals—and powerless women—secretaries and clerks. The reality is that intimate relations will be on the upswing as more and more women fill the managerial ranks at various levels. Psychiatrist Robert Seidenberg noted:

> As people who have interesting careers have always noted, work is very sexy, and the people with whom one is working are the people who excite. A day spent launching a project or writing a paper or running a seminar is more likely to stimulate—intellectually and sexually—than an evening spent sharing TV or discussing the lawn problems or going over the kids' report cards.[42]

Corporate policies cannot stop sexual relationships at work nor should they interfere as long as such relationships are based on free choice and do not affect productivity. Unfortunately, unless both individuals have equal power and status, free choice is hard to determine. What must be changed in the corporate structure is the dual standard that permits only men, especially white men, to pursue whomever they want regardless of the woman's wishes. Considering the fact that many men still believe that women should be viewed predominantly in sexual terms, it is not surprising that 38 percent of the managers in this study believe that many wives do not like their husbands to work as equals with women or as subordinates to them. It is noteworthy that the higher the white woman is in the corporation, the more likely she is to agree:

First level	36%
Second level	46%
Third level	55%
Fourth level +	83%

The corporate women evidently are faced with a variety of sexist attitudes and behaviors that can hinder their performance, negatively affect their self-concepts, and create problems that frustrate their careers and interfere with the smooth functioning of the corporate structure.

Female Managers Face More-Rigorous Demands
and Obstacles than Male Managers

The previous series of questions dealt primarily with the social-interaction problems of women and the sexist attitudes that, indirectly or directly, affect women's perceptions of themselves and their ability to do their jobs. This section explores the more-rigorous demands or obstacles placed on women in terms of their work and careers. The managers were asked to what extent they agreed with the following statements:

Female managers have to be better performers than men to get ahead.

Most female managers are placed in dead-end jobs.

Female managers are penalized more than men are for mistakes.

Most female managers do not have the same power as do men in similar positions.

As in other questions pertaining to women in corporations, the responses to these statements vary by the race and sex of the respondents. From the percentages displayed in figure 4-4 one can extrapolate that 68 percent of the managers believe women face at least one of the problems characterized by the statements in the index. The figure shows also that 21 percent believe they face at least three of them.

The percentage of white women and black men agreeing with at least three out of four of the statements is highest at the fourth level and above:

White women		Black men	
First level	25%	First level	20%
Second level	36%	Second level	30%
Third level	44%	Third level	35%
Fourth level +	45%	Fourth level +	50%

There are a number of reasons why white women and black men at higher levels are more critical than are those at lower levels. They have probably had to fight harder and have faced more obstacles and demands in the early stages of their careers to get where they are. They are well aware that competent minority members and women below them are struggling to overcome similar obstacles despite EEO/AAP. Moreover, at these upper levels of management, they are in a position to see how the dominant white men operate to protect their status quo.

When viewing the responses by age and education, older white women, regardless of education, clearly are the most critical. Of white women with some college education, 51 percent aged thirty and under, 59 percent aged

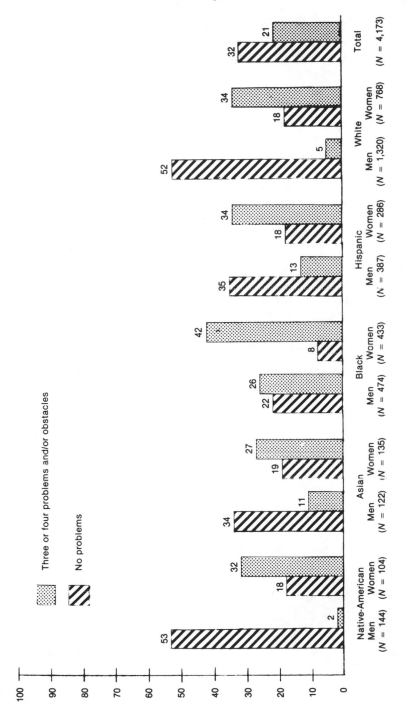

Figure 4-4. Percentage of Managers Who Believe Women Have at Least Three out of Four or No Problems and/or Obstacles in Their Companies

30+ to 40, and 69 percent over age forty believe women face at least three or four of these problems. Of those with college degrees, 49 percent aged 30 and younger, 54 percent aged 30+ to 40, and 75 percent over age 40 agree that women face three or four of the problems. Older women, especially college graduates, may be more critical because the discrimination they have faced previously was more overt and blatant than it is today and because the effects of such treatment have accumulated with time. White women over 40 years of age, with college degrees, are at higher corporate levels where there are few women. The isolation and alienation they face is often greater than for white women over 40 with no college degrees. These nondegreed women are, in many cases, concentrated in female-ghetto departments at lower levels of management because few women without college degrees move very far up the corporate ladder. In two out of three age groups of the other race/sex groups, except for white men, the findings are similar. White men's awareness that women face more-rigorous demands or obstacles than men do does not increase with age or education. As a group they tend to be less aware of or less willing to acknowledge differential treatment of women.

Women Must Be Better Performers

Looking at several of the questions that comprise this index, some interesting and disturbing facts emerge. Table 4-3 shows that two-thirds or more of all the women, regardless of their race, believe that women have to be better performers in order to advance. One-half of the black men agree. In comparison, approximately one-third or less of the remaining groups of men concur.

As white women move up the corporate ladder, the percentages of them who agree with this statement increase. For example, 60 percent of the white women at the first level, 72 percent at the second level, 82 percent at the third level, and 75 percent at the fourth level and above, reply that women must be better performers to get ahead.

A white woman at the fifth level comments:

Women, even in today's business world, must necessarily be overachievers just to become managers.

A Hispanic woman at the second level puts it this way:

I had to prove my ability as a manager more than a white female to show that I was promoted because of my ability and not my race.

A white woman at the second level concurs:

Table 4-3
Female Managers Must Be Better Performers than Male Managers to Get Ahead
(percent)

How Strongly Do You Agree or Disagree that Female Managers have to Be Better Performers to Get Ahead?	*Native-American*		*Asian*		*Black*		*Hispanic*		*White*		*Total*
	Men (N = 143)	*Women (N = 104)*	*Men (N = 122)*	*Women (N = 135)*	*Men (N = 474)*	*Women (N = 432)*	*Men (N = 383)*	*Women (N = 285)*	*Men (N = 1,312)*	*Women (N = 765)*	*(N = 4,155)*
Strongly agree	0	22.1	6.6	23	8.9	29.2	5.7	23.5	1.3	25.4	12.8
Agree	12.6	44.2	29.5	46.7	41.4	52.3	26.1	43.5	16.7	44.4	32.9
Disagree	76.2	33.7	55.7	28.1	46	17.6	61.9	31.9	69.5	28	48.1
Strongly disagree	11.2	0	8.2	2.2	3.7	0.9	6.3	1.1	12.5	2.2	6.2

> I feel I have to constantly prove that I am capable of doing a good job. Because I'm in a technical field, the men have trouble accepting the fact that I understand what they're talking about. I don't want "special" considerations—just the same as the men without the implication that I can't learn it because I'm a woman.

Finally, a Hispanic woman at the second level says:

> I feel the biggest problem I face is the reluctance still to trust women with anything of importance and to overcome the hostility of men who feel that except for AAP, they wouldn't have to deal with women at all. It's a paradox because I overcome this—I hate to confess this—by using whatever goes along with being young and attractive (not sex, just a little charm). Yet, that often seems to be the biggest obstacle to the next step. Mostly, our company promotes older, less-attractive women. They're less threatening.

This notion of proof of ability has been discussed extensively in the literature. In our society, men are expected, and themselves expect, to succeed in their chosen occupation, to receive financial rewards and satisfaction from their work, and to receive approval and support for their efforts from their families. When a talented man with demonstrated ability does not succeed, for whatever reason, it is unquestioningly apparent to him and to those who know him that he has been the undeserving victim of injustice or rotten luck.[43] This opinion is supported by the female managers in this study. For example, a white woman at the third level says:

> I personally feel women in the company have to continually prove their ability. This is not the case with the male manager. Many unqualified male managers are protected by their fellow male peers and bosses. To quote a former male boss, "It's difficult for one man to tell another man his faults, but easy to tell a woman."

Women "have to prove by their performance that they do belong . . . they have to prove success, and on a continuing basis. They have to prove that their careers will not be dual, discontinuous, and consequently marked by a lack of commitment—a burden of proof to which a man is never asked to submit."[44] When, to this sexist attitude, is added an atmosphere in which, as tokens, every action is performed under the critical scrutiny of the nontokens, it is not surprising or smacking of paranoia that many women feel pressured to perform as superwomen.

Are Women Penalized More for Mistakes?

Related to the fact that women believe they must be better than men at their jobs is the question, "Are women penalized more for mistakes than men?"

Almost one out of four of the managers believes this to be true. Only 5 percent of native-American and white men believe women are penalized more than men are for mistakes, compared with 44 percent of black women and 38 percent of Hispanic women. With regard to making mistakes, a white woman at the third level says:

> I believe a white female at a higher level of management is not permitted to make any mistakes. We are in a fish bowl and must perform at the highest level of proficiency at all times.

The implication of this attitude toward mistakes is that female managers can be programmed for failure if they are forced into a defensive posture that leaves no room for the risk taking inherent to managerial rsponsibility. Managers learn to manage. They learn best in an organizational climate supportive enough to allow an occasional mistake to be part of the learning process. However, if the climate is such that the organization overreacts to errors or failure, it stifles the growth process of its managers and threatens their self-confidence. An organizational climate that expects a woman to fail inhibits her willingness to engage in activities with uncertain outcomes. The organization's lack of confidence in a female manager not only destroys her ability to assume responsibility but also erodes the confidence of her subordinates in her ability to manage their working environment. (While this discussion is about women, the comments are applicable to all managers regardless of race and sex.)

Female Managers Do Not Have the Same Power
as Male Managers

Thirty-four percent of the respondents do not believe that women have the same power as men do in similar positions. The responses range from 53 percent of the Hispanic women and 44 percent of the black women to 25 percent of the white and Asian men. Women in each race group are more likely than men are to believe this.

Part of the reason that women are perceived as not having the same power as men is that 27 percent of the managers believe that men are generally unable to work comfortably with women; men bypass them and go to their superiors. Black women (50 percent) are most likely and white men (17 percent) are least likely to believe that men are usually unable to work comfortably with women and thus bypass them to go to their superiors. More than six times the percentage of white men at the first level (25 percent) than at the sixth level (4 percent) believe this to be the case. A good example of bypassing was given to this author by a high-level female friend. She was in Washington, D.C., at a speech given by Juanita Kreps, the secretary of commerce. Ms. Kreps made it quite clear that it would be much easier for her to do her particular job if she were a man. Many businessmen with whom she deals try to sidestep her because of her sex.

Power is not simply a question of individual orientations, such as a need for power, or achievment motivation. In an organizational setting, power is the ability to effectively protect and promote the interests and well-being of subordinates and followers. Research has found that no matter how sensitive and skilled managers are at human relations and interactions, group morale is low and subordinates' evaluations of bosses are low if they cannot count on bosses to exercise influence and power outside and upward from the group.[45]

Women Are Placed in Dead-End Jobs

Still another possible explanation for women's frustration in these companies is the fact that 34 percent of the managers believe that women are placed in dead-end jobs. Black women (53 percent) and Hispanic women (45 percent) are most likely to believe this and native-American (15 percent) and white men (20 percent) are least likely to agree.

A white woman at the second level expresses these views on the subject that vividly represent the concerns of most women who agree:

> I have been in this department, which is 99 percent female, for twenty years. New technology is making my job and my subordinates' job obsolete. I really don't feel like I am an integral part of the company anymore.

As is seen in later chapters, managers who believe they are placed in dead-end, boring, unimportant jobs are not likely to be productive employees. They could at some stage become counterproductive.

Conclusion

What is the present situation and treatment of female managers in the participating companies? Sexist attitudes and behaviors obviously are a very serious problem in these companies. While more than one out of three managers in this study express no stereotypes about women, almost one out of two of the white men who control the institutions does. These sexist attitudes are translated into numerous sexist tendencies and obstacles toward women. This is demonstrated by the fact that 85 percent of the managers (79 percent white men) believe women face at least one of five forms of sexist tendencies, and 68 percent of the managers, (48 percent white men) believe women face at least one of four sexist obstacles. Thus, the findings of the study show considerable support for women's perception that they are stereotyped, excluded from important work-related social interactions, have greater demands put upon them, have greater obstacles to overcome, and are made to feel inferior.

Corporations must begin to recognize that it is not the fault of women that they have been limited in their corporate career—it is primarily the fault of sexism and its assumptions of women's inferiority. Thus, corporations must take concrete steps to provide women fair and equal treatment. Put another way, it is in the corporation's best interests to minimize resistance to change in their managerial makeup, since resistance can be counterproductive. Those people who facilitate the inevitable change process by including women as full, equal members of corporations should be rewarded.

Corporations also must begin to recognize that they need all the talent available to be competitive in the new industrial era. To fail to incorporate women as full, equal members of corporate management is suicidal. No society or corporation will meet its full potential if it discriminates against women—after all, they do represent 52 percent of the U.S. population!

Finally, corporations must begin to recognize that female managers are bringing into corporations not only a vast untapped resource but also a set of values, some of which are more conducive to managing the new-breed employee. Chapter 7 shows that female bosses are preferred to male bosses by both sexes.

5 Advancement Goals and Aspirations

In the present corporate atmosphere, especially with the ever-increasing number of new-breed managers, no company can have a successful, efficient management force if many of its managers believe that they will not be able to satisfy their career needs, goals, and aspirations. Therefore, information on managers' feelings of progress, carreer goals, and aspirations are important in maintaining an effective managerial work force. No less important is the variation in feelings about these subjects among the different race/sex groups, especially among the white men who stand to lose in future advancement decisions.

Promotions and Qualifications

Advancement is of great concern to employees for a number of reasons. It brings greater financial and material rewards and higher status in society. Promotions gratify the ego and build self-esteem, and they validate the individual's sense of personal worth. They may offer an escape from an undesirable job or an unpleasant work environment. Promotions also allow a greater opportunity for fulfillment for those who desire power or a greater sphere of influence.

Corporations also benefit from promotions. The power to advance their employees gives corporations opportunities to exert great influence on the employees who want to be promoted. More specifically, it gives corporations substantial control over the lives, actions, and thoughts of employees who are upwardly oriented, influenced perhaps in proportion to the extent of upward orientations.

George Ritzer pointed out that promotions, while having a number of positive functions, also have some negative consequences. Stress can have a deleterious effect on the health of ambitious managers:

> The fact is that occupational stress, in whatever occupational category, is associated with a number of personal problems. Upwardly mobile managers, who typically have extraordinary workloads and great pressure and responsibility, have far greater incidence of heart disease, ulcers, arthritis, stroke, and various forms of mental illness. Then too, job-related stress may manifest itself in a series of behaviors such as alcoholism, drug abuse, and even suicide. Even those who are successful in their efforts to move up in the organization are subjected to stress.[1]

The promotion process itself also can have disastrous effects on the larger organization as illustrated through the concept of the Peter Principle. It says that in a hierarchy, employees tend to rise to their level of incompetence. Since most promotions are based on present performance, conformity, and likability by key people rather than on the potential to perform the proposed job, many employees are promoted until they reach positions they can no longer handle in the most-competent manner. To the corporations' detriment, these employees are likely to stay in those positions.

Part of the reason for the prevalence of the Peter Principle is the extreme difficulty of defining and quantifying the needed qualifications for managerial jobs. Primarily for entry-level management positions, companies in many cases will specify a degree or certification of training instead of attempting to define and enumerate the qualifications they seek. The hope is that educational institutions are able to define and provide the skills needed to fill a specific job such as writer, marketing manager, or engineer. A second method used by companies to avoid specifying qualifications is assuming that the only qualification necessary is to have demonstrated success at a comparable job in the past. This is often true with positions in areas such as personnel in which the problem of defining qualifications is more difficult than with certain technical jobs. This lack of definition makes even more awesome the attempt to determine the truly most-qualified person of a number of personnel specialists or electrical engineers.

As difficult as technical and professional skills are to evaluate, even less-readily identified or quantified are the intangible skills needed for managerial positions. Some of these abilities are leadership, organizing and planning, reasoning power, and communication. These abilities become increasingly important and far more abstract as one moves up the corporate ladder. The difficulty allows the subjective side of human nature to play a greater role in who eventually will be promoted.

Theodore Caplow astutely argued that the ultimate decision of who is going to be promoted rests "on the judgment, and hence on the good will, of one's superiors. . . ."[2] As early as 1930, social scientists noted that in many cases conformity is one of the major qualifications for getting ahead. What matters is how one meets and adapts to group norms in terms of race, sex, age, religion, educational institutions attended, social and political attitude, and how well one operates according to corporate politics.[3]

Recently, many people have argued that since EEO/AAP conditions have changed. They claim corporations have become more accepting of minorities, women, and other people who do not fit the elite white-male, Protestant, conservative-attitude mold. Data in the previous chapters question these claims, and a recent study by Frederick Sturdivant and Roy Alder of 444 executives questions whether this assumption even applies to managers who are white men. Far from revealing diversification, their study found that top executives are becoming a more-homogeneous group than were their predecessors:

Indeed, a more-uniform profile is reflected than the one of the supposedly "conforming 1950s." In addition to being exclusively male and Caucasian, predominantly Protestant Republicans of eastern U.S. origin, from relatively affluent families, and educated at one of a handful of select universities, as had been the case of the past, the executives in our sample share some new characteristics. Most significantly, the executives are closer together in age, and more of them have little or no work experience outside their companies.

The overall picture that emerges is one of a business leadership group lacking diversity of background and, indeed, becoming increasingly alike. Is this a profile that reinforces the easy, stereotyped view of those who see a gray-flannel mentality dominating the executive suite? Or is it a profile that simply supports the notion that "success breeds success?"[4]

The information conveyed by Sturdevant and Alder's study and other surveys underscores the fact that even for white men the promotion system has never been strictly based on merit or ability. Those white men who fit very rigid and subjective attributes and characteristics have comprised the vast majority of those promoted to the upper levels of corporate management. In short, what basically has been happening for years in corporate promotions is that when social criteria serve as measurement surrogates, managers tend to reproduce themselves. Filling management slots with people similar to themselves reinforces the belief that such people deserve high-level positions. This "managerial cloning" apparently serves as a risk-reduction mechanism in the face of the nonquantitative nature of potential measurement and the subjective judgment of qualifications.

A fourth-level black now sums up what has usually happened in corporate promotions:

Having been a minority member of this company's management for thirty years, I have observed that a minority male or female requires someone at fourth level or higher to help him or her to advance. Let's face it: What are the chances that a white-male supervisor would select a nonwhite-male or -female candidate for a position when there are a dozen competent white-male candidates to select from? You know even from this group of competent white males they are going to select the white male who is most like them.

Managers' Views of Advancement Progress

What are the goals and aspirations of the managers in this study? What do they think of past and future progress?

In order to answer these questions, managers were asked how rapidly they have progressed in their companies in terms of job level. A surprising number responded positively, as shown in table 5-1. Almost one in five of the managers believes they have progressed more rapidly than they expected, one out of four as rapidly as they expected, and one out of ten feel they advanced slowly at first but faster recently. Thus, at least 54 percent of the managers appear to be reasonably satisfied with their progress to date.

Considering the negative attitudes of many female and minority managers, especially blacks, toward their present situation, one might expect the vast majority to be dissatisfied with their past progress. Moreover, considering the numerous cries of reverse discrimination and the negative effects of AAP/EEO on the careers of white-male managers, one might expect most of them to be critical about their career advancement to this point. Neither of these is the case.

A noteworthy difference exists among the managers—that is, within each race group, women are more likely than their male counterparts to respond that they advanced slowly at first and then more rapidly. This response is, in all probability, related to the impact of EEO/AAP requirements in recent years. It is further supported by the fact that, as managerial level increases, both white and black women respond that they have progressed more rapidly than they expected:

	Black women	White women
First level	14%	18%
Second level	25%	19%
Third level	37%	26%
Fourth level+	N.A.[a]	40%

[a]N.A. means not applicable.

This study reveals that the attitudes of minority and female managers about past advancement are in line with other studies.[5] However, white men have become less satisfied with their progress in the past six years. Only 52 percent of white men in the present study seem to be satisfied, compared to 75 percent in a 1975 study.[6] A partial explanation for their views in this study is the slightly reduced number who have received recent promotions because they are now competing with women and minorities on a more-equal basis.

Over 60 percent of the managers in this study had been promoted within the preceding six years. The managers' responses cover a large range—76 percent of black women and 75 percent of Hispanic women compared with 41 percent of white men and 53 percent of native-American men. This percentage spread is reasonable, not only because comparatively larger numbers of minorities and women are being promoted but also because minority managerial pools tend to be vastly smaller than white-male pools.

Will the white men become increasingy disenchanted? Will minorities and women maintain the same level of satisfaction? The next sections give some answers.

Table 5-1
Rate of Progression within the Company (percent)

How Rapidly Have You Progressed in This Company?	Native-American		Asian		Black		Hispanic		White		Total
	Men (N = 144)	Women (N = 104)	Men (N = 121)	Women (N = 135)	Men (N = 473)	Women (N = 633)	Men (N = 387)	Women (N = 286)	Men (N = 1,313)	Women (N = 766)	(N = 4,162)
More rapidly than expected	12.5	15.4	11.6	11.9	18.2	18.5	14.5	23.4	18.3	20.9	18.1
As rapidly as expected	35.4	23.1	33.1	28.1	24.1	16.5	25.3	22	27.1	26.5	25.5
Less rapidly than expected	29.2	28.8	23.8	28.1	33.2	26.4	35.4	24.8	25.6	17	26.3
Rapidly at first but then more slowly	17.4	21.2	9.1	11.9	12.1	18.5	11.6	16.8	21.2	15.1	16.8
Slowly at first but then more rapidly	4.9	10.6	9.9	12.6	7	15.5	5.2	11.2	6.7	18.7	10.3
Have not been with the company long enough to answer	0.7	1	6.6	7.4	5.5	4.2	8	1.7	1.1	1.8	3.1

**Hopes and Dreams—Managers' Expectations
and Aspirations**

Looking into the future, more than one-fourth (27 percent) of the managers
never expect to be promoted. The range for this answer extends from a high
of 42 percent of white men to a low of 10 percent of black men. It is crucial
to note that only 10 percent of white men do not want to be promoted.
These data could lead to the conclusion that the white men's dissatisfaction
about promotional opportunities in the future will increase tremendously.

Sixty-one percent of the managers want to be promoted within two
years, and only 26 percent believe they will be promoted in that time frame.
The time expectations clearly differ greatly from time aspirations. The influencing factors are very similar to those influencing the managerial levels
that managers expect and aspire to achieve. Therefore, a detailed analysis of
the latter will suffice to understand the manager's overall attitude about advancement and the factors influencing these attitudes.

One of the main arguments put forth by many managers throughout
this study, almost exclusively at the fourth level and above, is that they do
not want to implement career planning and potential evaluations because
unfulfilled expectations and aspirations damage employee morale.
However, the results of this study show that the expectations and aspirations of managers are already out of line with projected rates of company
growth and employment attrition. For example, 31 percent of the managers
would like to advance to the fifth level or above, and 14 percent expect to
reach these levels. In reality, much less than 1 percent actually will reach this
level.

Effect of Race and Sex on Advancement Desires

Figure 5-1 illustrates the differences between the levels of expectation and
aspiration. Black men represent the largest percentage of managers both ex-
pecting and aspiring to advance to the fifth level and above. They also represent the group with the largest percentage difference between desire to rise
to these levels and expectation of getting there. Fifty-two percent of black
men want to advance to the fifth level, while only 23 percent believe they
will get there.

The responses of the black men are quite surprising in light of their very
negative views about the overall treatment of minorities in corporations. In
the poststudy-feedback sessions they gave explanations for the contradiction. They argued that the responses are not contradictory because they are
talking not about the fairness of their companies' promotional system but
about their confidence in their own abilities. If their present company does

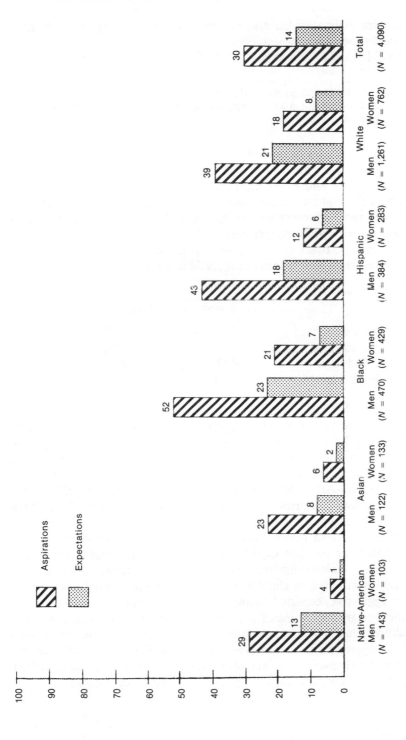

Figure 5-1. Percentage of Managers' Aspirations and Expectations to the Fifth and Sixth Levels

not recognize their abilities, another company will. Therefore, they have higher expectations and aspirations.

A third-level black man with an MBA from Wharton says:

> I have worked hard to get what white society says I must to "make it"; I'll be damned if I am going to let them hold me back. Of course, I have high expectations and aspirations.

The sexist attitudes of most men and the socialization of women being what they are, it is not at all surprising that women, regardless of race, have lower expectations and lower aspirations than do men. Black and white women have the highest aspirations among female groups to the fifth level or above (21 and 18 percent respectively) and also the highest expectations (7 and 8 percent respectively). It is crucial to point out that success breeds higher aspirations. Black and white women at higher levels of management are more likely than are those at lower levels to aspire to reach the fifth level or above:

	Black women	White women
First level	17%	5%
Second level	24%	10%
Third level	63%	43%
Fourth level +	N.A.[a]	79%

[a]N.A. means not applicable.

Asian and native-American women who are at the first or second level of management have much lower expectations and aspirations. They have not seen one member of their race promoted above the second level. Therefore, they have no success stories to emulate. As we will see, a reason that native-American women, many of whom are really white, have lower expectations and aspirations than white women is that fewer have college degrees compared to white women. Education does influence the advancement desire in many managers. While many more Asian women are educated, their very low expectations and aspirations can be attributed to the extreme male-dominated culture they come from. Also, as Dr. Chelsa Loo mentioned in chapter 2, Asian people as a whole are taught not to be aggressive, especially women. Hispanic women fall into the middle of the race groups. Some of these women are fairly well educated, and their culture, while based on machismo, does not possess values emphasizing lack of aggressiveness. However, the lack of Hispanic-female success stories and the Hispanic-male machismo partially would explain why their goals and aspirations are not as high as black and white women's are. .

Effect of Marital Status on Women's Advancement Aspirations

The traditional role of women, especially married women, still greatly affects aspirations. Female managers who have never married are more likely than are those who are married (25 percent more) to want to advance to the fifth level or above. They also are more likely than are married female managers to expect career advancement. Thus, one could conclude that many married women are still experiencing serious conflicts between their professional and family roles. Yet these data could also indicate that married women have lowered their aspirations because they feel corporations still look more favorably upon women who are not married.

The proposition that corporations look less favorably upon married women is supported by data from this study. White women at lower levels of management are more likely to be married than are those at upper levels. Fifty-eight percent of women at both the first and second levels are married as compared with 46 percent at the third level and 35 percent at the fourth level and above. These findings are in line with the corporate community as a whole. In another study involving female officers in over 1,000 major U.S. corporations, two-thirds were married or had been married in the past. One-third of those who had married were widowed, divorced, or separated. The proportion of divorcees was highest among the most-highly paid women.[7]

Regardless of women's present expectations and aspirations, as women are afforded opportunities, their expectations and aspirations will increase significantly.

Effects of Age and Education on Managers' Advancement Aspirations

Age and education also are factors in managers' aspirations and expectations. With few exceptions, larger percentages of younger managers, with educational backgrounds equivalent to those of older managers, indicate a desire to advance to the fifth level or above and expect that they will do so. In addition, as table 5-2 shows, college graduates are more likely than non-college graduates of the same race/sex/age group to say they would like to advance to the fifth or sixth levels.

The white-male responses are of interest because of the lower aspirations of white college-educated men aged 30 and under compared to those over 30 years of age. The lower aspirations of the 30-and-under age group

Table 5-2
Advancement Goals, by Race, Sex, Age, and Education: Managers Who Responded that They Want to Advance to the Fifth or Sixth Level

How High Would You Like to Advance in the Management of Your Company?	Other Minority		Black		White	
	Men	Women	Men	Women	Men	Women
30 years of age and under						
No college	36.8 (19)	10 (60)	33.4 (12)	7.1 (28)	16.7 (6)	0 (34)
Some college	48.7 (39)	6.8 (59)	41.2 (34)	29.4 (51)	30 (20)	15.4 (39)
College graduate	63.9 (122)	23.8 (67)	75.7 (111)	40.6 (64)	57.6 (33)	47 (66)
30+ through 40 years of age						
No college	11.1 (27)	4.5 (88)	33.4 (18)	16.2 (37)	11.3 (44)	13.2 (91)
Some college	21.7 (106)	10.3 (68)	33.8 (71)	15.4 (78)	30.6 (62)	15.2 (46)
College graduate	55.8 (122)	23.1 (26)	74.5 (110)	34.4 (32)	72 (157)	54.8 (84)
Over 40 years of age						
No college	6.5 (76)	0 (89)	12.5 (24)	8.6 (70)	8 (251)	1.2 (256)
Some college	15.2 (92)	2.2 (45)	15.7 (51)	14.8 (54)	16.3 (227)	8.3 (84)
College graduate	42.8 (49)	10 (10)	48.6 (37)	30 (10)	59.8 (448)	36.2 (58)

Note: Numbers in parentheses indicate number of managers responding by group.

might reflect the deterioration of the solid advantage of just being a white man in the present EEO/AAP atmosphere. Therefore, their expectations are lower, and consequently, they have lowered their aspirations. However, the fact that white college-educated men over 30 have very high aspirations reflects the view that they consciously or subconsciously know that the white man still has the major power to promote. They are not likely to easily allow their ranks to be filled with, nor their dreams threatened by, minorities and women. This tenacity is facilitated by three issues. First, many white men are already at the third level and above. Second, the EEO/AAP objective for middle management and above is one overall management-level objective and not separated specifically into levels three through six. Third, the paucity of minorities and women at the third and higher levels does not influence the white men to redefine their expectations and aspirations. Real competition at middle- and upper-management levels, in effect, does not exist.

College-educated white women, regardless of age, have higher aspirations than do black and other minority women. This is probably due to some extent to minority women's scaling down their aspirations because of the double stigma they face. In addition, as discussed earlier, the feminist movement has not had as great an impact on minority women, especially on the native Americans, Hispanics, and Asians as it has had on white women. These groups of minority women come from macho-oriented conservative cultures, a fact that might serve to contribute to their lower aspirations.

Importance of Advancement to Managers

According to the responses about the importance of advancement, 42 percent of the managers say that of utmost importance is advancement to the next level, and 43 percent say that such advancement is of moderate importance. Black (62 percent) and Hispanic (60 percent) men are most likely, and Asian women (32 percent) and white men (32 percent) are least likely, to say advancement is of *utmost* importance. The responses of the Hispanic and black men are predictable since they have the highest expectations and aspirations to advance.

In all race groups except white, women are less likely than men are to say advancement is of utmost importance. Women have frequently been told to look at their work as a job, rather than a career, so one would expect many women to believe advancement is not as important as performing well in their present assignment. However, regardless of race, at least 78 percent of the women and 80 percent of the men place at least moderate importance on the advancement of their careers. Of those managers who do not see advancement as important, little difference exists between men and women.

Words and Deeds—Formal Promotion Policies
versus Informal Practices

Regardless of the managers' own aspirations to advance, the amount of discontent and dissatisfaction promotions create among them will depend a great deal on how fair they perceive their companies' employment policies and practices to be.

When given the question, "Please make any additional comments about your company's promotional policies," 2,561 out of 4,209 managers responded. Table 5-3 shows the managers' detailed responses. Only 12 percent of these managers make statements indicating that they perceive the policies as fair. This figure is much lower than one from a 1975 study that indicated that approximately 25 percent of the managers viewed their companies' employment policies as fair.[8] The main cause of this decrease in perceived overall fairness can be traced to changes in the responses of white men. The effects, real or anticipated, of EEO/AAP upon their careers has made them more critical. White men evidently are, at present, more willing to express disapproval of a system that was discriminating against certain types of white men long before minorities and women were allowed to become managers. In short, many white men have joined minority and

Table 5-3
Managers' Perceptions of Promotion Policies of Their Companies
(percent)

Comments	Total (N = 2,561)
Promotional policies are not uniform or welldefined; therefore, they are subject to a high degree of subjectivity and politics	29.3
Promotional policies reflect, or are strongly influenced by, EEO/AAP. Preferential treatment is accorded minorities and women.	22.1
Policies are fair.	12.3
Current promotional policies frequently result in promotion of unqualified managers.	6.8
Respondent has insufficient knowledge about promotional policies.	5.5
Opportunities for promotion at present are limited.	4.8
Respondent needs better information to know promotional opportunities.	2.4
Age is a major factor in promotional policies—that is, discrimination toward older managers occurs.	2.3
Promotional policies are unfair to minorities.	2.1
Promotional policies are only fair because of external pressure.	2.1
Promotional policies are unfair to women.	1.3
Other.	9.1

female managers in criticizing the subjective, unfair promotion policies and practices that firms have used since their incorporation. The new-breed managers, regardless of race and sex, are perceiving the unfairness of many promotions more accurately and are more willing to express their dissatisfaction.

Data to support these statements are abundant in this study. In addition, according to many managers, the policies are becoming less fair. For example, managers are more likely to perceive ability factors such as accomplishments on the job, work experience, and technical, professional, or scientific knowledge as advantages contributing to their most-recent promotions. They are less likely to perceive ability factors as advantages contributing to the achievement of their desired positions. Seventy-six percent of the managers consider their professional, technical, or scientific knowledge advantageous in achieving their most-recent promotion, and by comparison, only 61 perent say these same factors would be advantageous to the achievement of future positions. When considering obstacles, managers are more likely to say that nonability factors such as race and/or sex would be obstacles to achieving their future promotion than they are to state that these factors were obstacles to their most-recent promotions.

To illustrate this point, 7 percent of the men say their sex is an obstacle to their most-recent promotion, contrasted with 32 percent who think it will be an obstacle to their future advancement. With regard to race, 40 percent of the black managers and 35 percent of the white managers are most likely to consider their race as an obstacle to achieving their desired position, while only 6 percent of blacks and 10 percent of whites believe race was an obstacle to getting their most-recent promotion.

Successful, upwardly mobile managers, as well as blocked and frustrated managers, usually state that promotions are based on luck or on being at the right place at the right time; on internal political connections such as friends and mentors belonging to the white-males club; or external political pressures such as EEO/AAP, the National Organization of Women, NAACP and other organizations; or on some combination of the three. Implicit in these opinions is an attitude of cynicism toward the company's goals and values and a questioning of whether the company really cares about its people. Following are some of the typical comments of managers. A third-level Hispanic woman says:

> Too often promotion depends on "being in the right place at the right time" or word of mouth through friends who recommend employees that they have run into. There is no formal way of opening promotions to all so that anyone could apply and be interviewed for possible promotion.

A second-level black woman says:

As long as the company continues to house white, aged males in fourth level and above, affirmative-action programs will continue to be a myth!

A fourth-level white man says:

> Some of the promotions which have been made have gone to the political maneuverers, the grandstanders, the apple-polishers who fool nobody except the man making the promotion. This greatly demotivates the knowledgeable segment of the employee group. I am not speaking in pique—I had my share of quick and early promotions (attaining third level in less than three years and fourth level in ten), but I was then working for men older than me who had nothing to lose. When I started working for men approximately my own age, I suddenly slowed down while they went on to greater glory.

A first-level white man says:

> Everything has stopped until the higher level has filled requirements of AAP. What has happened to higher-level "guts" to fight bureaucratic mandates? Are minority groups going to run this country through AAP. OSHA, ERA, etc.?

A second-level white man says:

> I think we have "reverse discrimination." Past company policy—i.e., discrimination against minorities—has come back to haunt us. However, I don't think it's right to make amends for past injustices. Promotions should be made on the basis of most deserving and best qualified, irrespective of race, sex, etc. I don't think it's right to grant promotions just to reach some numbers objective. It seems to me nobody would have a just complaint if *all* promotions were based on "most qualified." Why should some employees and the company suffer because of past mistakes?

Finally, a third-level black man says:

> The company's promotional policies will continue to be influenced somewhat by external pressures from the Justice Department. Promotions of protected group members will more than likely be made to offset possible deficiencies. If such a deficiency in the numbers does not exist, a promotion of a qualified protected group member would be seen as wasting a "resource" and probably would not be made. Rather, the promotion of a nonprotected candidate will be made to offset the "forced" promotions of protected individuals.

Factors Influencing Promotions

In order to get a more-detailed look at what factors the managers believe will be helpful, harmful, or irrelevant to their promotion, a series of non-ability- and ability-related items was given to the managers to rate. As table

5-4 shows, the managers' responses indicate that some important observations can be gleaned from their answers. More managers see ability-related criteria as advantageous to their promotion prospects than nonability-related criteria are. However, one factor that intrudes itself among the ability-related criteria is "help from someone particularly interested in your career." A sponsor is seen as advantageous by more managers than is their technical, professional, or scientific knowledge. This factor also is seen as more important than one's boss.

Even though a large percentage of the managers rate ability criteria as advantageous, more than a majority of the managers believe that race, sex, age, and politics are relevant to their career advancement in either a positive or negative way. In short, these data demonstrate and confirm the managers' statements that they do not believe their companies' promotional policies are fair and based solely on merit and ability.

Table 5-4
The Relationship of Certain Factors to Managers' Achievement of Their Desired Positions
(percent)

In Your Estimation, Is Each of the Following Factors an Advantage, Irrelevant, or an Obstacle to Your Achieving Your Desired Position? (N = 3,626)	Advantage	Irrelevant	Obstacle
Accomplishments and/or achievements on the job	89.4	9.4	1.2
Work experience	72.1	14.8	13.1
Help from someone particularly interested in your career	68.8	25.4	5.8
Technical, professional, or scientific knowledge	61	25.9	13.1
Boss	44.2	32.7	23.2
Educational level	41.8	31.5	26.7
Growth of business and economic conditions	33.9	26.5	39.6
Race of ethnic affiliation and/or identification	30	44	26
Political skill with the company	28.6	43.3	28.1
Sex	26.1	47.1	26.8
Age	24.2	48.1	27.7
Competition for the desired position	21	39.8	39.2
Seniority	12.9	66.7	20.5
Marital status	12.6	81.4	6

Effects of Race and/or Sex on Future Promotions

When comparing managers' perceptions of the effect of their race and/or sex on their careers, some interesting facts emerge. As table 5-5 demonstrates, white men believe their race and sex have an equal effect on their ability to achieve their desired position. A higher percentage of all the minority-group men see their race as more helpful than their sex is to their promotion prospects. In contrast, looking at the harmful effects of race and sex, a higher percentage of the minority men except for blacks regard their sex as more harmful than their race. Among black men, a much-higher percentage regards their race as more harmful to their prospects than their sex is (46 percent versus 10 percent).

Greater numbers of all groups of women see their sex and race to be advantageous rather than harmful factors. A very high percentage of white women (55 percent) see their sex as an advantage, but only 17 percent see their race as an advantage. Native-American women follow the same pattern, except more of them see their race as an advantage than do white women. Interestingly, white women are more positive than white men are about the helpfulness of race—17 percent of women versus 6 percent of men. Also, they are more frank about their sex being an advantage—55 percent versus 8 percent. Hispanic, black, and Asian women see their race and sex as almost equally beneficial (though percentages are different). However, while equal percentages of Asian women view race and sex as an obstacle, Hispanic women see sex as more of an obstacle than is race. The opposite is true of black women.

Table 5-5
Comparison of the Harmful and Helpful Effects of Race and Sex on Managers' Future Promotions
(percent)

Managers	Helpful		Harmful	
	Race	Sex	Race	Sex
Native-American men	23	5	15	45
Native-American women	37	49	6	22
Asian men	36	7	16	21
Asian women	49	49	12	13
Black men	31	15	46	10
Black women	40	43	32	25
Hispanic men	48	9	16	19
Hispanic women	58	58	8	13
White men	6	8	45	47
White women	17	55	11	17

These comparisons clearly point out that a manager's belief about the advantage or disadvantage of race and sex depends on the specific race/sex group of which the manager is a part. Also, those groups of men who have the most to lose in any movement toward equality, who have the most-sexist attitudes, and who are the least sympathetic to the plight of women in the corporate world are most likely to believe their sex is a disadvantage to their advancement goals. Minority responses about the effect of race reflect the fact that the native Americans, Asians, and Hispanics know that their race is more acceptable to whites than to blacks and thus less harmful to their promotional opportunities.

Who Is Benefiting Most from EEO/AAP?

This conflict about advantage or disadvantage of race/sex becomes more evident when analyzing responses about the effects of AAP/EEO on personal career opportunities. Two out of five managers feel their company's AAP has not affected their personal career opportunities. However, figure 5-2 shows that three out of ten managers say their opportunities have improved, and one out of five believes their opportunities have been reduced by AAP. Not shown in figure 5-2 is the fact that one out of five says he or she is unaware of the affect AAP has had on his or her career opportunities. For those managers who believe their chances have either not improved or grown worse, substantial differences exist in their responses as to who is really benefiting. Every race/sex group claims that one or more of the other groups are getting all of the advantages.

A black man at the first level says that women have become the number-one choice of affirmative action. A Hispanic man at the first level makes a similar comment, "I feel that the push on the women is stifling the minority males' opportunities." A Hispanic man at the second level comments, "I feel that I was well on my way to accomplishing my career goals before AAP became so popular. I don't feel that my most-recent promotion was accelerated. If anything, it might have been delayed because of promotions to white females." A black second-level woman says, "I face the same problem as white males: Promotional opportunities are available only after targets for white females are satisfied." However, a white woman at the first level believes her opportunities have become worse because, "In the area I work in they are putting more males in jobs that were before exclusively females." Still, a Hispanic woman at the second level says, "White females (meaning herself) are at a standstill while the company employs ethnic groups into management jobs." An Asian woman at the first level relates, "I feel my career is limited because most jobs are filled by males."

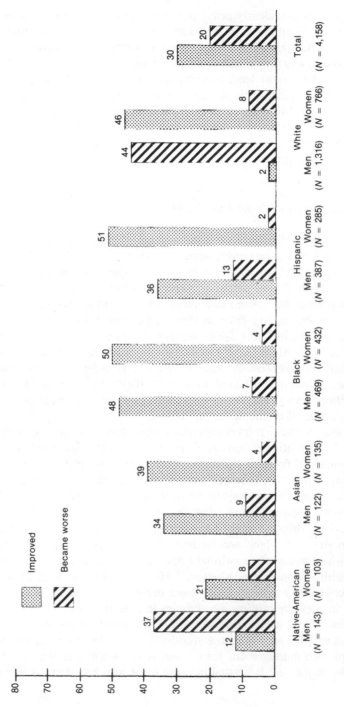

Figure 5-2. Percentage of Managers Who Believe AAP Has Had a Positive or Negative Effect on Their Personal Career Opportunities

Additionally, a native-American woman at the second level comments, "A traditional female job would be filled by a minority male before I would be given an opportunity to fill it."

What these responses suggest is that a number of minorities and women do not blame their lack of promotional progress on white men but instead on other protected groups. This is a serious conflict because it takes energy away from focusing on the real problem. In a society dominated by white men, the white men are still the favored group. They continue to receive most of the promotions, particularly at the higher management levels. This conflict allows white men to share only what they are forced to share, and that is very little. Put another way, while many minorities and women fight over only a small portion of the pie, white men sit back and continue to feast themselves on the largest piece. This is not to condemn white men, rather it is just to point out the psychological reality that people in power, regardless of race and/or sex, are not willing to share their power with others. Of course, as this study clearly shows, many white men would not agree with this statement. They believe they are the ones who are giving up everything to all the other race/sex groups. Two white men at the second level comment:

> I feel the scales have tipped the other way. What we have now is reverse discrimination, quotas, percentages, etc. Liberal treatment of law is ruining the esprit de corps not only in this company but in all companies.

> I have no career. My age group (30s and 40s) has been derailed and disenfranchised by the "just society." We have no upward mobility. We live well but we dare not aspire to a change in position. Until our generation finds full equality, the white male has had it.

These feelings are especially true of managers at lower levels, but a surprisingly significant number of white men in middle management and above believe they are at a disadvantage because of EEO/AAP. Forty-four percent of the white men believe AAP has had a negative effect on their personal career opportunities. By level the figures are:

First level	59%
Second level	66%
Third level	50%
Fourth level	22%
Fifth level	7%
Sixth level	2%

The view of first- and second-level white men has some connection to reality because of EEO/AAP-established goals and timetables for entry and low levels of management. Managers at the third level and above demonstrate some form of paranoia because women and minorities still pose little threat to them. White men continue to hold almost all of the power positions, and no goals and timetables exist for moving under-represented groups to the fourth level and above. Those white men are anticipating a new and unpredictable kind of competition with which they have never had to contend. A white man at the third level says:

> Emphasis on minorities and women will make promotion harder, even if I excel. Many assignments will be filled by a minority or a woman who can handle the job, rather than by one who can best handle the job.

A white man at the fourth level states:

> The opportunities and incentives for a white male in large U.S. corporations are becoming less and less, and this is more and more frustrating.

Another white man at the third level says:

> I don't believe AAP has had any effects upon my career opportunities to date. However, I know it will reduce my opportunities in the near future.

Finally, a white man at the fifth level says:

> As a white male, I believe career opportunities have diminished somewhat.

While some legitimate reasons exist for lower-level white men to feel that their opportunities have decreased, the issue is the starting point and the extent of the decrease. White men represent only 37 percent of the U.S. population and have totally dominated the managerial profession since its beginning. When laws were introduced forcing them to compete with the remaining 63 percent of the population, they began to recognize that their career opportunities would be greatly reduced if the laws were properly implemented. This increased competition does not apply to well-qualified, high-performing, high-potential white men but to the great masses of average and below-average white men who got their positions because of explicit or implicit preference for their race and sex. As a white man at the fourth level says:

> I believe that EEOC affects only the marginally qualified white male. Beyond that limitation, promotion becomes a matter of personal, social, and economic choice.

A realistic picture of the present situation for white-male promotions is painted by a black man at the fourth level who states:

Whites make the major decisions. Many decisions reflect racist/sexist attitudes. The myth of minorities and women making big gains at the expense
of white males is allowed to persist. Statistics do not bear this out.

His point is supported by the tremendous salary advantages white men are
awarded above those of women and minorities for similar educational and
work credentials.

Cries against preference were not voiced by many white men when the
quotas were 95 percent to 100 percent in their favor. In addition, people are
made to believe that the present numerical objectives are only established to
benefit minorities and women. However, numerical objectives often place
white men in nontraditional jobs. The purpose, of course, is to open choices
to all groups. Finally, the media and white men emit no outcries about the
quotas used by many fine universities such as Harvard. Quotas are used
there for the number of prep-school graduates, the number of affluent
students whose parents contribute large sums of money, and for the number
of students attending from each state, just to name a few of the nonmerit
selection criteria.

When the issue of opening up the job market to minorities and women
was first raised in the 1960s, before any numerical goals and timetables were
imposed, it easily could have been anticipated that those in power would not
relinquish any of that power voluntarily. Mass movements of groups create
turmoil as they move from an inequitable position to a more-equitable position, and concern grows among those people who must lose power in the
process. This is basically what is happening in this society and its corporations.

While 37 percent of native-American men and 44 percent of white men
believe their opportunities have become worse due primarily to their perception of corporate preference for minorities and women, only 2 percent to 13
percent of the other managers believe this is the case. Most of the reasons
that this other group of minorities and women believes their opportunities
have deteriorated center around the issue of other groups' receiving the advantages. They also see numerical objectives for minority promotion as
hindering, rather than helping, their careers. Exemplifying this position, a
black woman at the second level feels that "Numerical objectives decreased
my opportunity for promotions since now with a 'quota' system, once the
manager has his/her magic number, he/she does not actively seek black
women."

Do EEO/AAP Targets Hurt Minority Advancement?

Another basic reason some minority managers believe EEO/AAP is a detriment to their careers is that their departments are reluctant to promote them

because it will affect the department's own EEO targets. More than two out of five of all participating managers concur with this statement. More than three times the percentage of black than white men feel minorities' careers are often held up because of the departmental necessity to fill EEO targets—that is, 72 percent versus 22 percent. Table 5-6 displays the managers' responses. White men at lower levels who have more contact with minorities are much-more likely to agree than are those at upper levels:

First level	25%
Second level	27%
Third level	16%
Fourth level	20%
Fifth level	18%
Sixth level	13%

Several typical comments of the managers are illustrative. For example, a black women at the second level says:

> I feel my career might be held up because my department seems to be interested in keeping their EEO targets satisfied.

A Hispanic man at the second level says:

> I feel I have not had any major problems. The only negative feeling that creeps in is the one that tells me I may be "stuck" in an assignment because I "look good in the profile." In my last assignment, I did not move for five years, partially because I was performing well in an area that could stand a minority manager. I have broken away from that and am in a high-exposure job now. If I avoid the same "trap" as before, I'll be fine.

The irony is that the most-able minority managers might be the last ones departments are willing to release. Unless some central corporate procedure is developed by which managers are reviewed and made aware of opportunities in other departments, EEO could impede the upward progress of some minority managers, especially the high-potential ones.

Whom Does EEO/AAP Help the Most?

The conflicts among race/sex groups about the effects of AAP on their careers is less evident in the overall result that nearly one in two of the minorities and women believes his or her chances have improved since EEO/AAP. Few white men will admit that the 200-year exclusion of two-thirds of the population from competition with them has made a significant

Table 5-6

Reluctance of Departments to Give Up Minority Managers Is a Hindrance to their Careers (percent)

To What Extent Do You Agree or Disagree that Minority Managers' Careers Are Held up because Departments/ Establishment Areas Are Reluctant to Give Them up due to Their Own EEO Goals?	Native-American		Asian		Black		Hispanic		White		Total
	Men (N = 142)	Women (N = 100)	Men (N = 122)	Women (N = 379)	Men (N = 470)	Women (N = 426)	Men (N = 379)	Women (N = 281)	Men (N = 1,301)	Women (N = 753)	(N = 4,106)
Strongly agree	1.4	10	6.6	9.8	25.7	20.9	14	12.8	1.6	4.8	9.5
Agree	23.9	23	35.2	34.1	46.4	45.5	38.5	36.3	20	28	31.1
Disagree	64.8	65	54.1	53.8	27.2	31.2	44.3	48.4	66	58.6	52.6
Strongly disagree	9.9	2	4.1	2.3	0.6	2.3	3.2	2.5	12.4	8.6	6.9

contribution to their having achieved their position. The conviction of many minorities and women that they would not have had the opportunity to compete on remotely even footing with the dominant group is evident in numerous comments. For example, a white woman at the third level gives these reasons for saying AAP has had a positive effect on her career:

> As a woman, I would not have attained my present level or have potential for any future advancement if AAP had not been implemented. I would have deserved it because of my ability and performance, but I would not have been considered because of corporate sex bias.

A black man at the second level expresses it this way:

> My entry into the company and my promotions were directly affected by the company's Affirmative-Action Program. While I may have been qualified, it is doubtful whether there would have been any positive action without the program.

A Hispanic woman at the second level agrees:

> Five years ago, as AAP came into the picture there were no Hispanic females at second level in my division—I was the first. AAP influenced my promotion to second level. I have my doubts about the impact of targets on division level and where the policymakers are for minorities/women.

Why Do Managers Believe EEO/AAP Has Not Affected Their Careers?

Two out of five managers indicate that their career opportunities have remained the same. Qualitative data from the survey reveal a number of reasons why managers believe this is so. A Hispanic woman at the first level who has been in the company for five years expresses the conviction that AAP has not helped overcome sex bias:

> Even though I am a minority, I am a female. I have a college degree and have been rated outstanding in the assessment center. They have disregarded all these things.

Some women and minorities feel that they are competent and earn their promotions solely on ability and would earn them without AAP. For instance, a Hispanic woman at the first level states, "I believe I was promoted because I was qualified, and I was neither helped nor hindered by AAP." A white woman at the third level feels she achieved her present level on her own competence but that her career opportunities are now hurt because,

"We have many white females at my level, but also many of them are incompetent." The latter kind of response by minorities and women who were among the first to crash the barriers has been noted by researchers. As long as they are the only ones of their race and/or sex around, they enjoy a certain status because they are showpieces and like this special attention.[9]

Due to the fact that no affirmative-action goals and timetables exist at the upper levels of management and that very few minorities and women are there with whom to compete, it is not surprising that larger percentages of white men at the fourth, fifth, and sixth levels than at the first through third levels respond that their career opportunities have remained the same since the inception of AAP—27 percent at the first level compared to 85 percent at the fifth level and above.

In brief, most of the attitudinal data from this section confirm that white men are most likely to feel hostile to, skeptical of, and threatened by AAP/EEO, and minorities and women are most likely to feel positive about these developments. The fact that over 95 percent of the managers at the top of the corporate structure are likely to be white men is regarded by them as a reflection of fairness and merit, as "cream rising to the top." For them to seriously entertain the notion that sex and ethnic- or racial-group membership helps explain the position of white men undermines the legitimacy of the present structure of the organization.

Effects of EEO/AAP on Corporate Efficiency/Effectiveness

One of the racist and sexist ideologies put forth by the dominant white-male society in order to maintain its privileged position is that minority and female managers are forcing companies to lower their hiring and promotion standards. Judith Caditz noted that even liberals (not conservatives) with pro-integrationist attitudes had adopted negative attitudes about competition from blacks. She wrote:

> The major reason respondents report, when they express a clearly unfavorable attitude toward the entrance of blacks into their occupational fields, is the negative consequences that standards will be lowered. The presence of blacks in their occupations will be a "reflection that qualifications are not up to standards."[10]

In this study, a majority of the managers (57 percent) believes that affirmative action has forced the participating companies to lower their hiring and promotion standards. The question of the lowering of standards produces the second greatest difference in responses between black and white men in this entire study. Black men (14 percent) are least likely and white men (84 percent) are most likely to agree that AAP is forcing their companies to lower hiring and promotion standards. A white man at the second level says:

> My answers throughout this questionnaire make me look like a racist. I am not! I strongly feel that "excellence will be rewarded" and that we do not need artificial EEO programs to force an erosion of management. The price of our capitulation to political pressure will likely be great indeed but will not be fully felt for some years. Ultimately, the reverse discrimination implicit in EEO may destroy our company as we know it today.

The assumptions made by this white man and by many others neglect the reality that many of them who are average and below average got their jobs because 63 percent of the population was excluded from competing with them.

The responses of these black and white men are predictable. However, the responses of white women and other minorities also show high percentages who believe standards are being lowered, and this was not predicted (see figure 5-3). Based on findings reported earlier in this chapter and in chapter 3, these groups are probably talking about race/sex groups other than their own. Another possible reason for the agreement by surprising numbers of these groups is that they have basically adopted the inferior descriptions of themselves put forth by the dominant white-male society. A final possible reason is that, by sharing the views of the dominant culture, they may feel that white men will be more accepting of them. As noted in earlier chapters, this has been the case.

Not all groups of white women are as likely to agree that companies are lowering their hiring promotion standards. White women at upper levels are less likely to agree than are those at lower levels:

First level	68%
Second level	62%
Third level	54%
Fourth level +	48%

High-level white women probably have had to overcome the feelings of being inferior to rise to their present level.

A related question to lowering standards is about the effect of a racially mixed work force on productivity and service. The majority of the respondents indicates that the race/sex mix of the work force mandated by AAP does not, to their knowledge, interfere with their company's productivity or quality of service. Blacks of both sexes (each 90 percent) are most likely, and white men (61 percent) and native-American men (54 percent) are least likely to agree. Between 71 and 80 percent of the other race/sex

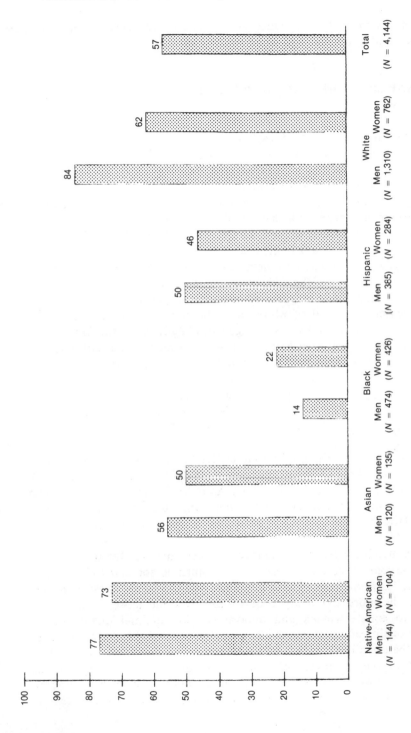

Figure 5-3. Percentage of Managers Who Believe Affirmative Action Lowers Hiring and Promotion Standards

group makes this response. Once again, except for blacks, rather large percentages of minorities and white women agree.

EEO/AAP and a Lack of Qualified Minorities and Women

The following findings are disturbing but not surprising in light of the responses to the previous two questions. Fifty-five percent of the managers say that a lack of qualified minorities exists, and 44 percent believe a lack of qualified women exists to fill available jobs. Figure 5-4 shows the comparative responses of the race/sex groups. For every group except black men, the managers believe a lack of qualified minorities is a greater problem than the lack of qualified women. Larger percentages of upper-level white men than of those at lower levels indicate a lack of both qualified women and qualified minorities as a problem. Sixty percent of white men at the first level versus 84 percent of the fifth-level and above managers feel, at least to some extent, that a lack of qualified minorities exists to fill available jobs. The percentages by level of white men who say that a lack of qualified women to fill available jobs exists range from 52 percent at the first level to 70 percent at the fifth level and above. A white man at the sixth level expresses the view of many men who do not view women as equals. He says:

> Most women aren't as qualified as males. Forcing people into jobs that they are not qualified for, nor will ever become qualified for, is impacting on selectivity for future requirements for advancement.

As noted earlier, this ubiquitous adjective "qualified" crops up in every book or article about affirmative action, as it did in many of the feedback sessions with respondents in this study. As Betty Lehan Harragan pointed out, "It is a word used constantly and indiscriminately by everyone whose life is affected by the changing attitudes of women (or minorities) in business."[11]

In discussion, a group of managers agreed that one factor hindering EEO is the contention that minorities and women do not have to be the best qualified. They have only to meet minimum qualifications. These managers feel that the more frequently people hear this, the more inclined they become to equate women and minorities with minimal qualifications. Defining qualifications is one thing, trying to determine exactly what constitutes "best qualified" is beyond the human subjective mind. What is best qualified to one manager will not be to another. In addition, many minorities and women believe that two qualifications systems exist: one for white men and one for their groups. A black-male manager who worked in

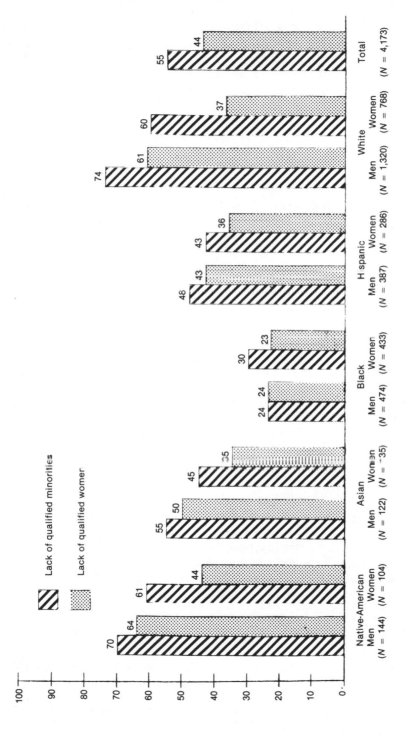

Figure 5-4. Percentage of Managers Who Believe a Lack of Qualified Protected Groups Exists for Available Jobs since AAP

EEO says that when women or minorities are being evaluated, a highly for-malized structure is used—that is, individuals have to meet every criterion or they do not get the job. White men have an informal structure and in-formal criteria. Individuals do not have to meet most of the criteria so long as they are likable white men and do an average job.

With regard to educational qualifications, as table 5-7 shows, all minority-male groups, except native Americans, obviously hold their own in terms of educational attainment compared to whites. When responses are analyzed by level, whites very clearly have had the advantage of being pro-moted without a college degree. For example, a comparison of black and white men having college degrees reveals a significantly higher percentage for blacks at every level:

Black men		White men	
First level	39%	First level	13%
Second level	68%	Second level	30%
Third level	74%	Third level	59%
Fourth level +	100%	Fourth level	59%
		Fifth level	84%
		Sixth level	90%

Looking at age in relation to education, table 5-8 shows that younger black, Asian, and Hispanic men, aged 20 to 30 years, are more educated than are their white counterparts. For example, 86 percent of Asian men, 70 percent of black men, 69 percent of Hispanic men, 56 percent of white men, and 32 percent of native-American men in this age group have college degrees.

These figures, along with the fact that white men receive higher finan-cial rewards for education and length of service, support a consistent claim made by the vast majority of the minority managers and supported by many of the white managers in this study—that is, minority managers must be much-more qualified than whites in order to attain equivalent positions. In addition, they support the proposition that despite fifteen years of EEO/AAP, many young white men are still being automatically awarded the privileged status of older white men.

Effects of Age on Promotions

Age discrimination is becoming a more-vital issue as American society becomes middle-aged rather than young. The 1964 Garda Bowman and 1975 Fernandez studies clearly showed that substantial majorities of managers believe that being under 45 should be a helpful factor for pro-

Table 5-7
Educational Achievement
(percent)

What Is the Highest Grade You Completed?	Native-American		Asian		Black		Hispanic		White	
	Men (N = 143)	Women (N = 96)	Men (N = 119)	Women (N = 133)	Men (N = 470)	Women (N = 426)	Men (N = 384)	Women (N = 284)	Men (N = 1,305)	Women (N = 762)
Eleventh grade or less	2.1	4.2	0	0.8	1.1	1.9	1.8	1.1	1.1	3.5
Twelfth grade	25.9	63.5	10.9	26.3	10.4	30	16.7	46.8	22.5	46.7
First year of college	12.6	13.5	11.8	21.1	8.7	17.6	9.9	12	7.5	11
Second year of college	28	10.4	10.9	11.3	13.6	17.1	15.4	14.4	10.7	7.6
Third year of college	10.5	5.2	10.1	6.8	11.3	8.7	5.7	6	5.7	3.5
College graduate	14.7	3.1	34.5	23.3	33.8	16.7	32	14.1	32	17.1
Graduate training	6.3	0	21.8	10.5	21.1	8	18.5	5.6	20.5	10.5

Table 5-8
Managers within Specific Age Groups Who Have Completed College
(percent)

Age	Native-American		Asian		Black		Hispanic		White		Total
	Men	Women	Men	Women	Men	Women	Men	Women	Men	Women	
20-30	31.6 (19)	14.3 (21)	86.1 (36)	54 (50)	70.3 (158)	44.8 (143)	68.8 (125)	32.7 (116)	55.9 (59)	47.8 (140)	53.7 (876)
30+ through 40	29.2 (48)	0 (34)	51 (51)	28.2 (46)	55.3 (199)	21.5 (149)	52.9 (153)	12.6 (103)	60 (265)	37.8 (222)	42 (1,270)
40+ through 50	17.7 (51)	0 (24)	34.6 (26)	13.3 (30)	30.8 (91)	7.4 (109)	23.8 (84)	8.5 (47)	56.8 (494)	14.2 (240)	33.3 (1,196)
Over 50	4.2 (24)	0 (17)	20 (5)	14.3 (7)	40.9 (22)	7.6 (26)	25 (20)	5.6 (18)	44.1 (488)	15.8 (159)	33.5 (786)

Note: Numbers in parentheses indicate number of managers included in each age group.

motions. For example, 76 percent of the managers in Bowman's study and 62 percent in Fernandez's said that being under 45 should be helpful for promotion. On the other hand, 54 percent of the managers in Bowman's study and 52 percent in Fernandez's believed that being over 45 was harmful to advancement.[12] From these studies, age clearly was believed to be, and actually was, a factor in promotions.

In this study, the managers' responses in table 5-9 show that not much has changed since 1964 or 1975. A majority of the managers believe their age plays a role in their advancement opportunities. The older the managers, the more likely they are to believe their age is an obstacle—13 percent of the managers 30 and under compared to 72 percent over 50 believe age is an obstacle to their advancement.

A sixth-level manager said that at the age of 50 he was considered too old to promote to his present level. It took his company nine months to make him permanent in his present position, even though everyone agreed that as an acting sixth-level manager he was doing a tremendous job.

To discriminate against a manager because of age is as nonproductive as discriminating against him or her is because of race and/or sex. People age at different rates mentally and physically—that is, some 65-year olds are younger in body and mind than some 40-year olds are. To use age as a promotion factor robs corporations of a vast supply of competent, energetic, creative managers—especially as our society becomes older.

Effects of Sponsorship on Advancement

At this point, it is quite evident that many managers believe their promotions are blocked or more difficult to achieve because of nonability factors such as race, sex, and age. However, the single most-important nonability

Table 5-9
Effect of Age on Achievement of Desired Position
(percent)

In Your Estimate, Is Age an Advantage, Irrelevant, or an Obstacle to Your Achieving Your Desired Position?	*30 and Under (N = 853)*	*30+ through 40 (N = 1,229)*	*40+ through 50 (N = 1,044)*	*Over 50 (N = 495)*	*Total (N = 3,621)*
Advantage	41.9	32.1	10.7	2.6	24.2
Irrelevant	45	58.7	49	25.3	48.1
Obstacle	13.1	9.3	40.2	72.1	27.7

factor that directly influences the role that race, sex, age, and ability play in managers' advancement opportunities is a sponsor or mentor. Eugene Jennings noted that many mobile managers at various times in their career patterns become protégés of some highly positioned superior.[13]

In a 1975 study, 82 percent of black managers and 62 percent of white managers believed pull with top management, or sponsorship, was a helpful factor in advancing in business.[14] A survey of over 1,050 companies' female officers in 1979 supported these findings. Fifty-three percent reported having had a mentor/protégé relationship. The higher the salary, the more likely that the female officer was to have had mentor relationships.[15] Gerard Roche noted in his study of top executives that not only did many see mentors as helpful but also that those who had had mentors along the way were happier about their careers. He wrote in 1977 that nearly two-thirds of the respondents had a mentor, that the number of these relationships is growing, and that those who have had them earned more money at a younger age and are happier with their career progress.[16]

In defining the concept of mentorship, Richard America and Bernard Anderson spoke of the nuances of these relationships:

> . . . sponsors should have confidence in the junior manager's discretion and judgment and be willing to reveal some of their own personal concerns, weaknesses, troubles, and doubts, as well as to hear those of others. A real sponsor will tell you things he wouldn't tell others in the firm. If such trust is absent, the relationship probably is not really a sponsoring one.

> Just what the sponsor gains should also be clear. Strictly altruistic sponsorship can be dangerously close to paternalism and cannot long be an attractive arrangement. A manager should recognize how sponsors receive tangible rewards from the relationship in professional, organizational, or technical support. If it is not reciprocal, then again, it is not really sponsorship.

> This fact often does not come through in conversation on sponsorship. Sponsors are frequently perceived as doing a favor, but it should be clear that sponsors also receive support and information, and the relationships, if sound, are reciprocal in their benefits. Some people make a point of this dimension and are alert for paternalistic dynamics that can creep into sponsoring relationships.[17]

Several important points America and Anderson did not make are that the mentors select their "mentees" and not vice versa. One can quickly become a political liability to the mentor and can find oneself out in the cold.

In this study, the significance of having a sponsor is demonstrated by the fact that respondents rank it third behind performance and work experience as being advantageous for obtaining desired positions. Sixty-nine percent of the managers consider help from someone particularly interested in their careers as an advantage, and only 6 percent considered it as an obstacle. Little variation is evident among the race/sex groups—between 67 and 76 percent believe a sponsor is an advantage. These figures demonstrate the universality of the concept of sponsorship in today's corporations.

That women and minorities have additional problems in finding sponsors is demonstrated by the fact that 40 percent of the managers in this study believe that many minorities, and 44 percent believe that many women, have a much-harder time than white men do in finding someone who is particularly interested in their careers.

Hennig and Jardim point out that the problem of sponsorship becomes more acute for people making the transition to middle management because "The learning system changes, the system of implementation changes, and in the nature of the relationships that white men traditionally establish with each other lies the key to both. White godfathers look after white godsons. Since women cannot be seen as substitute sons, nor can minorities because of color, their relationships with male (white) power figures are fraught with difficulties. The stereotyped labels placed on women come into play, burdening the female manager with either heavy sexual overtones or describing her as a hard, tough lady who is good at her job and nothing else.[18] The stereotypes burden the minorities with concepts about lack of intelligence and/or ability and lack of social and cultural similarity to the dominant whites.

Women and minorities have far greater risks attached to the development of relationships that would help them to learn and advance. This has been true because rarely have women or minorities been at higher levels who are available to serve as sponsors or mentors for lower-level women and minority managers. A group of native-American first-level women, in discussing their company's promotional policies, said that promotions are greatly influenced by sponsorship: "You need a sponsor and in the future you will still need a sponsor. Promotions will become fair once women get up into higher levels of management and can sponsor other women."

In concluding this section, some words of caution are appropriate. Many minorities and women, recognizing that they have a more-difficult time finding sponsors, attempt to become the "image of a promotable"—that is, they attempt to emulate the dominant race/sex group in thought and spirit in the hope that they will be more acceptable. This is a dysfunctional approach to the problem. The most-important factor minorities and women should bear in mind is that in most cases sponsors select their "sponsoree" not only because he/she has some common reference point but because the "sponsoree" has some unique quality that distinguishes him or her from the masses of managers.

Conclusion

This chapter has presented data that indicate that not only do managers have higher aspirations than expectations but also that they want to be promoted much sooner than they expect to be. Black and Hispanic men have the highest aspirations and the biggest gap between aspirations and expectations. In addition, considerable evidence shows that white men are scaling down their aspirations. Some encouraging information emerges on the increasing aspirations of women, especially younger college-educated women. Since career advancement is extremely important to most managers, and their aspirations already significantly exceed realistic possibilities of career advancement, corporations will become increasingly confronted with a dissatisfied group of managers. As these managers face an end to advancement opportunity, some may cope with it through disengagement from their jobs, which in turn will present problems for the companies. Previous studies have shown that depressed aspirations can take the form of disengagement from the work setting, low commitment, or nonresponsibility.[19] The response most damaging to the company occurs when the manager withdraws from responsibility. Kanter reported that Indsco Company culture had a name for people who had written off their careers. They were "mummies" or "zombies." They did only what they were told to do, took no initiative, and responded only to crisis, if then. One Indsco manager said of these people:

> Some people reach the state where the challenge they once had from their work no longer exists. They get into a job-oriented depressed state. They mope around. I think the company could change the atmosphere for people like that, help turn them on, if they could only be given a growth move.[20]

This study supports the alienation position, with almost two out of five managers saying they are not performing their jobs as effectively as possible, partly because of lack of motivation. People who see themselves in dead-end or boring jobs, people who doubt their abilities to improve their advancement situation, tend to talk more frequently about alternative possibilities. Close to one-half (46 percent) of the participating managers say they will leave their companies due to lack of advancement opportunities. Nineteen percent want more-interesting and -challenging jobs. (The issue of leaving one's company is discussed in detail in chapter 13.) Once again, as these managers face an end to advancement opportunity, some may cope with it through disengagement from their jobs, which in turn will present serious personal and productivity problems for the companies.

The dissatisfaction of managers will be greatly enhanced because of their negative view of their companies' promotion policies. Few of the managers interviewed believe that these policies are without politics, color, age, and sex blindness or are, therefore, fair. Many believe ability criteria play second fiddle to nonability criteria and that the influence of the latter is increasing. White men see themselves in the most-unfavorable positions for advancement despite their past advantages based upon traditional race and sex discrimination and by the fact that the power positions in their companies are still white-male dominated. Nonetheless, the white men will continue to have the advantage because they have the power. They will promote the individuals who fit their image of the most-promotable managers, which of course, are and will continue most frequently to be white men.

This chapter also points out that white men, particularly those at higher levels, are the most critical about the effect of EEO/AAP on the company. It is absolutely crucial to note that if they tend to believe that a serious lack of qualified minorities and women exists, if they feel that to promote or hire minorities or women lowers the company's standards, and if they believe the mixed work force interferes with productivity and service, then to expect them to have the genuine commitment necessary to maximally utilize women and minority managers is unrealistic.

A black woman at the second level aptly sums up what many minorities and women believe about upper management's commitment to equal promotion opportunities:

> Subjective data are still viewed as the tools for most promotions to second- and third-level positions unless pressure is applied through discrimination complaints filed by females and minorities. Even EEO targets are viewed as maximum efforts by higher management. There has been no overall commitment from higher management to fully develop *all* human resources. Only court orders or lack of compliance to consent decrees prod higher management into action. No formal disciplinary action has been taken against managers who constantly violate civil rights of many employees, even when the company is forced to litigate and pay cash to claimants whose allegations are found to have merit. This infringement costs companies money that could be more useful to the business if it were channeled into comprehensive developmental programs.

In short, the basic problem confronting corporations in advancement making and practice will be to sustain the interest and motivation levels of the work force. This will require the adjustment of aspirations and expectations to more-realistic and -manageable levels and the development of a fairer promotion policy. Solutions to these problems are discussed later.

6

Relocation: A Different Problem in the 1980s

Many large companies, because of dispersed facilities, require managers to relocate a number of times during their careers. Frequent relocation has caused managers from IBM ("I've Been Moved") or Proctor and Gamble ("Pack-and-Go") to be characterized as nomads. The Bell System has been similarly characterized because highly successful careers with Northwestern Bell Telephone Company, for instance, can encompass fifteen or more moves.[1] These moves are often considered as a sign of success for executives because company-originated moves are closely associated with promotions. Both promotions and lateral transfers for developmental experiences can add diversified experiences and test reactions to the new responsibilities, challenges, and surroundings expected of those who aspire to higher levels of management. Simple transfers to similar assignments with no developmental experience have less appeal to managers but are important to many large companies.

With the ever-increasing number of professional women in the work force and two-income-family working arrangements, relocation issues are becoming more complex and difficult for corporations to deal with in a satisfactory manner. Added to this difficulty is the new independence of some employees. Increasing numbers of employees are no longer complacently willing to move wherever and whenever their companies want them to. Many employees are placing their personal needs, concerns, and desires before those of their companies, which is in tune with the value system of the new breed of managers. Corporate success in addressing the emerging and changing attitudes of managers toward relocation is of paramount importance in the development and effective utilization of the managerial work force.

The willingness of managers to relocate is affected by two sets of variables. The first set relates to the overall issue of relocation. Variables in this set are sex, race, education, age, marital and parental status, level of management, previous relocation experience, and expectations of the effect of a refusal to relocate upon one's management career.

The second set of variables relates to the responses of individual managers to specific relocations. This set includes variables such as the nature of the new assignment, promotion, lateral with experience or lateral without experience, length of time since the last transfer, reputation of the location of the new job, and the personal/familial situation of the person at the time of the proposed relocation.

Frequency of Past Relocation

Over one-third (36 percent) of the managers in this study have relocated their homes at least once with their present companies, while 55 percent have never relocated. Table 6-1 shows that women in all of the ethnic groups are more likely to have never relocated than are their male counterparts. Among whites, 62 percent of the women and 36 percent of the men have never relocated. In the case of Hispanics, 69 percent of the women and 57 percent of the men have never been moved by their employers.

This difference for whites and Hispanics is partly due to the fact that many more of the men are at higher levels than the women; therefore, the men are more likely to have relocated. In general, upper-level managers are more likely than lower-level managers are to have taken an assignment requiring relocation. For example, the percent of white women who have never accepted assignments requiring relocation are:

First level	72%
Second level	64%
Third level	45%
Fourth level +	40%

Another possibility is that some groups of managers have been presented with more-frequent opportunities to relocate. During both the prestudy-interview sessions and poststudy-feedback sessions, women commented on the tendency of their bosses to assume that women will not consider relocating, particularly if they are married and/or have children. The comments of a white woman at the second level and one at the third level are both typical and revealing. The second-level woman says, "It seems that the company makes assumptions about my mobility without consulting me. I think they should ask for my preferences." The third-level woman comments, "Although I am married, opportunities for advancement by relocating should be discussed, because some husbands are also in a position to relocate if necessary."

Although some assumptions may be valid for some women, significant and increasing exceptions are indicated by the literature and confirmed by this study.[2] Single and divorced women, including those who are heads of single-parent households, provide a pool of career-oriented and highly ambitious managers. Although married women may be less likely to welcome transfers, many married women do welcome them. The assumption that

Table 6-1
Frequency of Relocation (percent)

How Frequently Have You Taken an Assignment that Required You to Relocate Your Residence?	Native-American		Asian		Black		Hispanic		White		Total
	Men (N = 144)	Women (N = 104)	Men (N = 122)	Women (N = 135)	Men (N = 473)	Women (N = 433)	Men (N = 386)	Women (N = 286)	Men (N = 1,315)	Women (N = 766)	(N = 4,164)
Once	18.1	12.5	8.2	5.9	16.1	7.4	19.9	11.5	13.7	12.1	13.2
Two or more times	24.3	14.4	6.6	3	9.7	1.6	10.1	3.8	18.3	9.5	11.5
Four or more times	20.1	3.8	0.8	0.7	1.1	0.5	4.9	0.7	28.4	4.2	11.3
Never	33.3	55.8	73	74.8	61.7	74.1	56.5	68.9	35.7	62.3	54.5
Not applicable (with company a short time)	4.2	13.5	11.5	15.6	11.4	16.4	8.5	15	3.8	11.9	9.5

any manager will refuse a transfer because of a characteristic such as sex, marital status, or age is not legitimate.

Another important point to be made is that not only are higher-level managers more likely than lower-level managers are to have relocated but that they are also likely to relocate more frequently. The responses of black women and white men illustrate this point:

Black women who have moved one to three times		White men who have moved four or more times	
First level	6%	First level	6%
Second level	11%	Second level	11%
Third level +	44%	Third level	32%
		Fourth level	46%
		Fifth level	60%
		Sixth level	72%

The conclusion appears to be that to move up the corporate ladder, one must be willing to relocate many times.

Variables Relating to Relocation

Sex and Race

Although, as table 6-2 shows, men are more willing than women are to relocate, regardless of race, it is inaccurate to predict managers' willingness to relocate on the basis of sex. Many of the women in this study are willing to relocate, and many men are unwilling.

A typical female position is put forth by a first-level Hispanic woman:

> This is one area in which men are different. Women do have to consider their husband's occupation, but if the same offer was given to a man, he would take the relocation without thinking about his wife's position (if any).

However, important exceptions exist, as indicated by the response of a Hispanic woman at the second level. She replies:

> Since I make twice my husband's salary, we have agreed we would relocate for my job, but not for his, since it obviously would not be to our advantage.

Men's and women's reasons for working may surprise some readers. Only 8 percent of the women and 1 percent of the men in this study are

Table 6-2
Willingness to Relocate for a Promotion (percent)

How Willing Are You to Relocate Your Residence Geographically for a Promotion?	Native-American		Asian		Black		Hispanic		White		Total
	Men (N = 143)	Women (N = 104)	Men (N = 122)	Women (N = 135)	Men (N = 472)	Women (N = 431)	Men (N = 385)	Women (N = 284)	Men (N = 1,306)	Women (N = 765)	(N = 4,148)
Eager	39.2	18.3	23	12.6	38.1	18.3	40.4	17.6	32.5	15.8	27.3
Willing	38.5	41.3	49.2	37.8	44.1	36.7	42.2	38.7	41.2	31.4	39.2
Reluctant	13.3	19.2	17.2	26.7	13.6	23	10.6	20.4	13.9	23.9	17.4
Unwilling	9.1	21.2	10.7	23	4.2	22	6.7	23.2	12.4	28.9	16.1

working to earn extra money. In addition, almost equal numbers of men and women are working because it fulfills their needs—34 percent versus 36 percent respectively. Finally, 62 percent of the men versus 49 percent of the women are working because of financial necessity. This seriousness about their careers affects women's views on relocation. Clark Kerr explained the fairly recent shift in reasons for many women:

> Let us acknowledge at once that most women work for money. Many women have no other source of economic support but their own work, and increasing numbers support their dependent children through paid work. Even when the burden of making a living falls mainly on the man, the money earned by the woman in most families has proven indispensable to maintaining a standard of living the family considers satisfactory.[3]

Education

Differences in the managers' responses to questions about relocation are also affected by their achieved educational level. Regardless of race, sex, and age, managers with no college education are less willing to relocate for a promotion than are those with college degrees. For example, of the black women 30 years or younger, 39 percent with no college, 65 percent with some college, and 75 percent with a college degree are willing to relocate for a promotion. A black woman at the third level with an MBA says, "I shall go wherever necessary if there are opportunities for advancement. . . ." These data on education indicate that as the work force becomes more educated, companies will find more and more women willing to relocate. This also applies to male managers. However, educated managers may also be more particular about why, where, and when they will relocate.

Age

When controlling for age, sex, and level of education, an interesting pattern emerges from the responses of those willing and/or eager to relocate for promotions. For male college graduates, the willingness to move as age increases declines steadily, such that mobility appears to decrease with age. A white man at the third level, age 50, put it this way:

> A number of years ago, numerous moves were customary and expected. With age, financial problems attendant with any move, disruption of the family and friends, relocation has become highly undesirable.

Women have a strikingly different pattern. White women of all ages are less mobile than are men of the same age group. However, significant differences exist between sexes in the youngest age group (30 years and under), and these differences lessen in the middle-age category (30+ through 40 years) and then greatly increase in the oldest-age category (over 40 years). While male mobility decreases from the youngest category to the middle category, the women in the middle-age category are most likely of the three age groups to be willing to relocate.

Obviously, something very interesting is going on in this 30+ to 40-year-old group of women. One possible influence is the impact of divorce upon women in this age range. Another possibility is that this group is the first cohort of a significant wave of career-oriented women. Since a greater difference in mobility rates occurs by sex in the youngest group than in the middle (30+ to 40 year old) group, this pattern is possibly a product of a combination of age and sex. Such a hypothesis would say that the youngest age group of women is more career oriented than the 40-year-old and older group was at the same age. Their inclination toward a career would be heightened by the impact of divorce when they are in the 30-to-40-year-old range. As these two younger groups of women reach the 40+ age group, the mobility rates may drop, but the rates of decreases will be smaller and the numbers of them willing to relocate will never be as small as the current 40+-year-old group of women.

Marital and Parental Status

Marital status is a factor found to significantly affect the willingness of female managers to relocate for promotions. Table 6-3 shows that male managers of almost any marital status are more likely than female managers are to be willing or eager to relocate for promotions. The biggest difference between married male and female managers of the same race group occurs among blacks—39 percent more married black men are willing to relocate than are married black women. The smallest difference occurs among whites—18 percent more married men than women are willing to relocate for promotions.

Several typical comments of married women who are unwilling to relocate are of interest. A white women at the first level comments:

> My husband is of such an age and his work such a nature that he cannot transfer nor can he obtain another job in a different area. Because of this, I cannot consider a change. This problem is not unique. If transfers were not set up to require moving the actual home, many women would be willing to take the new job.

A Hispanic woman at the first level notes:

> If I were single, my life would be my own, but now my husband's career comes first and mine second.

Table 6-3
Marital Status and Willingness to Relocate for a Promotion
(percentage of willing and eager responses)

How Willing Are You to Relocate Your Residence Geographically for a Promotion?	Native-American		Asian		Black		Hispanic		White		Total
	Men	Women	Men	Women	Men	Women	Men	Women	Men	Women	
Married	77.9 (127)	50.7 (67)	72 (93)	41.3 (87)	80.4 (369)	40.7 (243)	81.2 (320)	47.6 (172)	58.5 (1,220)	40.7 (417)	59.6 (3,115)
Never married	100 (1)	71.4 (7)	65 (20)	64.7 (34)	86.7 (53)	73.3 (90)	87 (31)	68.3 (60)	80.7 (26)	53.2 (214)	66.4 (536)
Divorced	100 (7)	76.9 (26)	85.7 (7)	75 (12)	92.8 (42)	64.5 (79)	90.9 (33)	73.9 (46)	76 (46)	57.7 (109)	72.2 (407)
Widowed	0	50 (2)	0	100 (1)	50 (2)	60 (15)	100 (1)	42.8 (7)	75 (12)	50 (24)	57.3 (64)

Note: Numbers in parentheses indicate number of managers in each group.

Even though some women appear to be tied to their husbands' careers, between 41 and 51 percent of all married female managers are still willing to relocate.

The comments of the two married women willing to relocate reveal another facet of the situation. One second-level white woman says:

> I would be willing to relocate depending on the job and location. However, as a married female, you are rarely asked. It is assumed you would not.

A third-level Hispanic woman gives a very valid reason why companies should not assume women will not relocate. She says:

> Relocation would be fairly easy for me as my husband works for a nationwide firm. As a wife, however, relocation would be contingent upon his ability and desire to move.

Married managers usually are less likely to be willing or eager to relocate for a promotion than are managers who have never married or who are divorced. For example, 48 percent of married Hispanic women—68 percent who have never married and 74 percent who are divorced—are willing to relocate for promotions.

A recent article in the *Wall Street Journal* reported that more and more female professionals, including married women, are accepting career relocation. The article detailed the successful efforts of their employers' personnel departments in aiding the women's husbands to find employment at the new locations.[4]

Managers with children appear to be as willing or more willing to relocate for promotions than are those who have no children. For example, of the married men, 66 percent with no children under the age of 18, 80 percent with one or two children under 18, and 79 percent with three or four children under 18 are at least willing to relocate for promotions. Among married women, 41 percent with no children under 18, 40 percent with one or two children under 18, and 58 percent with three or four children under 18 are willing or eager to relocate for promotion. Childless managers may be more-intensely involved in a social life-style and with groups of friends they do not want to leave behind. Managers with children take their primary social group with them on the move and are under additional financial pressure to make the extra money associated with promotions or transfers. The data indicate that the more children a manager has, the greater the need for money and security.

Level of Management

The gap between men and women who are eager or willing to relocate for promotions decreases at higher levels of management, irrespective of race.

For example, a difference of 25 percentage points separates the men and women at the first and second levels who are at least willing to relocate for promotions—that is, 75 percent of the men compared with 50 percent of the women. The difference that occurs between the sexes at the third level and above is 16 percentage points—that is, 80 percent of the men compared with 64 percent of the women. The taste of success tends to merge managers' views on relocation. In addition, women, at some levels, are as willing or more willing to relocate than are men at the same or different levels. By way of illustration, 81 percent of native-American women at the second level as compared to 75 percent of native-American men at both the first and second levels are willing to relocate for promotions. The prediction can be made that, as more women move up the corporate ladder, the gap in view-point between the sexes will decrease.

Previous Relocation Experience

Regardless of race, sex, or level, managers who have never taken an assign-ment requiring relocation are the managers who are least willing to relocate. Between 18 and 27 percent of the female managers who have relocated at least once, compared to 57 percent of those who have never relocated, are reluctant or unwilling to relocate. Evidently, for the majority of managers, the actual experience of relocating is more positive and less stressful than they anticipated and worth more in the long run.

Expectations of the Effect of Refusal

Though it may never have been written down in a company publication or personnel brochure, the implied or imagined threat is always present even though it may not be real: "If you want to get promoted, you must move." A variation of this ubiquitous bit of folklore is, "You can turn down one transfer, but if you turn down a second one, that's it. You'll never get another opportunity." A white man at the fifth level puts it this way:

> Relocation should be considered as part of the job when evaluating poten-tial. A "mobility" factor should be considered, and all employees should be aware of this.

Managers are more likely to believe that turning down promotions that re-quire relocating have more of a negative effect upon their careers than turn-ing down lateral moves that require relocation. Seventy-two percent of the managers feel that turning down promotions would have a very negative effect. Forty-nine percent believe refusing to relocate for a lateral position would have a similar effect.

Differences by race and sex exist in the degree to which managers feel their refusal to relocate would have affected their careers. Men within each racial group are more likely than their female counterparts are to state that refusing to relocate for a promotion would have a very negative effect. For example, 80 percent of the Hispanic men versus 66 percent of the Hispanic women make this statement. Table 6-4 gives managers' responses by race and sex. Managers who believe a refusal to relocate would have a very negative effect on their careers are more willing to relocate than are those who do not believe it would have any effect. An Asian man at the first level submits:

> I feel I have no control over my relocations if I want further opportunities.

A black woman at the first level sees it quite differently. She notes:

> I feel the company is more than fair in relocating. I feel they will do anything they can not to relocate when it could be avoided. Therefore, no effect would apply. They would not hold this against an employee if they were considered a valuable employee.

Variables Relating to Specific Relocation Directives

Nature of the New Assignment

It is not surprising that managers are most willing or eager to relocate their residences geographically for promotions (66 percent) and less willing or eager to relocate for a lateral transfer to a job that does not provide developmental experiences (8 percent). Thirty-eight percent of the managers are willing or eager to relocate for lateral transfers to jobs that provide developmental experiences.

Native-American men (50 percent), black men (50 percent), and Hispanic men (47 percent) are most likely to be eager or willing to take a developmental lateral transfer, and Asian women (26 percent) and white women (28 percent) are least likely to respond in this manner. In interpreting these response categories, questions arise regarding managers who respond "reluctant" or "unwilling." Individuals who give these responses might or might not accept transfers depending on many other variables.

Managers say that they want a better understanding of what a move means in terms of their careers. They are unsure of the gains or losses for their careers from a move or a refusal to move. A more-definitive statement of career plans and moving sequence from their companies would be helpful.

Table 6-4
Negative Effects of Refusal to Relocate for a Promotion *(percent)*

If You Were to Turn Down a Promotion that Would Require You to Relocate Your Residence or to Commute Farther, How Much of a Negative Effect, If Any, Do You Believe This Would Have on Your Career?	Native-American		Asian		Black		Hispanic		White		Total
	Men (N = 144)	*Women* (N = 104)	*Men* (N = 122)	*Women* (N = 135)	*Men* (N = 469)	*Women* (N = 430)	*Men* (N = 386)	*Women* (N = 283)	*Men* (N = 1,310)	*Women* (N = 760)	(N = 4,143)
Negative effect 1	53.5	43.3	43.4	34.1	47.8	38.8	55.7	42	51	43.4	46.9
2	26.4	20.2	22.1	23	28.8	21.6	24.4	24.4	25.6	22.9	24.6
3	11.1	11.5	15.6	21.5	12.2	19.8	9.1	17.3	10.4	15.4	13.4
4	4.9	10.6	9.8	8.1	6.4	10	5.2	9.9	5.3	7.9	7
No effect 5	4.2	14.4	9	13.3	4.9	9.8	5.7	6.4	7.6	10.4	8.1

Some comments from the managers help pinpoint these feelings. A white woman at the first level says, "If it involved a good promotion, I would definitely relocate." A Hispanic woman at the second level discusses both lateral moves and promotions. She says, "I will be willing to relocate on a rotational assignment as long as it is for a promotion and to further my career." A black woman at the first level answers, "I would never turn down a promotion. I would try to relocate if possible if it was a lateral for developmental purposes." Finally, a white man at the second level makes these representative comments. "My willingness to relocate would depend greatly on the area involved as well as the job responsibilities and expectations."

Time since Last Transfer

Company moving benefits and salary increases notwithstanding, managers are still concerned with the financial costs of moving. The various problems associated with moving and the demands upon the emotional reserves of the managers and their families are serious. While managers may accept the necessity of transfers, even when promotions are not involved, they resent being moved too frequently. A Hispanic man at the fourth level says:

> Make more of an effort to enable a management person to consider family hardships in choosing or not choosing to accept company moves with no penalty to career opportunities.

A black woman at the first level suggests a condition for which people might be more willing to relocate:

> Most employees are willing to relocate if the job offered was more permanent rather than on a one- or two-year basis.

Location of the New Job

Minority managers, particularly blacks, are often concerned about the section of the country and the size and makeup of the community to which they would be relocated. Areas or communities in which few members of the same race or ethnic group live or areas that have reputations for poor treatment of minorities may be expected to meet with high rates of refusal by minorities. Such concerns should not be dismissed as exaggerated or unfounded. Recent reports from a number of government agencies and commissions reveal that much racial discrimination remains in the United States, often taking more subtle forms than in the past.[5]

A recent survey by the Department of Housing and Urban Development found that a black family looking at homes or apartments stands a 75 percent chance of encountering discrimination. According to this study, blacks often are given incomplete or false data and are shown fewer homes than whites are, even when their background, income, and family size are similar.[6] Discrimination in education also continues. The U.S. Commission on Civil Rights reports that "equal educational opportunity for all children clearly has not yet been achieved" and that desegregation remains a distant goal in many localities.[7] Minority students are suspended and punished in disproportionate numbers, and bilingual programs are often soft-pedaled. In evaluating relocation, Hispanic-American and some Asian-American managers whose children are dependent on bilingual schools may be quite reluctant to accept transfers to areas where the school systems do not offer bilingual instruction.

Women also face prejudice when they try to arrange housing in a new area. This is particularly true if they have to rent rather than buy and if they are single-parent heads of households. Treatment by neighbors, particularly in suburban areas to which single women and minorities are moved, ranges from inconsiderate to cruel. All managers who relocate face the time-consuming task of finding reliable professionals such as orthodontists, internists, attorneys, service people, and so forth. Minority managers are not only concerned about the competence of such individuals, but they also must determine which professionals will treat them, their spouses, and their children without prejudice.

Many managers have concerns about the geographic locations of jobs regardless of race or sex, as the following comments suggest. A black man at the second level says:

> Relocation has many personal implications which have no relation to the job. Would you relocate to Alaska?

A white man at the third level comments:

> The "where" would be very important. Not interested in East Coast or Southern California (LA area), any place else would certainly be considered.

A Cuban (Hispanic) man at the second level likes his urban environment:

> I prefer not to relocate out of South Florida unless it is necessary or it will imply promotional opportunities.

Personal/Familial Situation

The complexity of any manager's personal/familial situation varies across time, and so does his or her attitude toward relocation. For many managers, sometimes relocation is minimally disruptive, and sometimes it can be greatly aggravating. There are countless reasons why managers at some point in their lives may feel that relocation would be very disruptive. For example, perhaps the manager needs another semester or two to finish night-school work on an MBA degree. Or, as studies have demonstrated, moving can be critically stressful for children when it comes at the time of other developmental crises such as striving for an identity or searching for models.[8] Transferring credentials at some stages and levels such as in the senior year of high school may be extremely difficult and can create stressful conflicts for the individual and the family. The following comments are representative of the overall concerns expressed. An Asian man at the first level says:

> I tried not to interrupt my children's educational process till high school.

A white man at the fourth level makes these strong comments:

> My wife and our family have relocated some fourteen times since we were married. It was easy and fun when we were younger. The social costs are now too high.

A black woman at the first level notes:

> Within the next ten years, my plans are to retire. Therefore, I will not consider relocating for any reason at this time.

One of the most-recent problems to surface is that of two-career families. As one career woman states, "I've moved with him for the last fifteen years. Now it's time for him to consider my career."[9] In the present study, when the managers are asked, "If your spouse had a new job that would require you to relocate your residence, would you?" more than one-quarter of the men (29 percent) indicate either they would go wherever necessary or move to most locations if their wives had to relocate. In contrast, 50 percent of all female managers would be similarly willing to move. Only small differences exist between the responses of men and women from the same race. The answers indicate that female managers are approximately twice as likely to encounter spouse resistance to accepting transfers. Although family economics may be increasingly dependent upon two incomes, apparently many men and women still accord higher priority to the man's career. This attitude is strongly reinforced by the fact that men still receive higher average salaries.

Of course, a manager's response to this one question can in no way be taken as predictive of future behavior. Dozens of other factors may jointly make the difference in whether a spouse flatly refuses, agrees to, or enthusiastically welcomes the proposed transfer. One illustration is that, if the spouse is a licensed professional, it is much-more complicated to move out of the state in which he or she is licensed than to move within the state. The impact of this factor runs the socioeconomic gamut from physicians and attorneys to real estate salespeople and beauticians.

Many women who were both married and employed in "good" jobs indicated to this writer that as their position improves they are spending more time trying to resolve work and marriage role conflicts. Whether the man or the woman in the two-career family is offered a transfer, both will have to deal with conflicts between the marriage role and the job role. Stress resulting from these conflicts could be anticipated and avoided or reduced if companies adopted more-flexible policies on matters ranging from relocation to scheduling vacation times.

Conclusion

Many factors affect managers' decisions to relocate. One cannot make any assumptions about relocation attitudes, whether they be about a specific group of people or about any individual. The only real way to determine whether a particular manager is willing to relocate is for the company to present all the facts and elicit the individual's responses. Companies should recognize that for the ever-increasing numbers of new-breed managers, relocation is becoming a more-complex issue. These managers are not going to just pick up and move because the company says to do so. The new-breed managers' attitudes are impacting on some of the older, traditional managers. A group of middle-level, middle-age white men told several interviewers:

> Before we moved because the company told us—no questions asked. But why should we do it now? We see women and minorities turning down relocation and it doesn't hurt their careers. In fact, we are glad they started doing it. Their actions give us some courage to look at our personal needs—not only the companies'.

Considering these views, the following suggestions are made. First, all managers should be given the opportunity to turn down or accept relocations—no assumptions should be made. Second, the company has to become more sensitive to the very complex relocation problems that are occurring because of the changing makeup of the work force. Third, in this age of two-career families, personnel services could be developed to aid spouses in locating suitable employment. Fourth, the companies must make certain that the hardships of relocation are adequately compensated.

Fifth, and most important, companies should think through the future managerial needs of the organization, identify the talents and experiences required to meet these needs, and present this information to individual managers in career-planning sessions. If companies were to give managers a more-comprehensive view of long-range possibilities, fewer refusals to proposed transfers would occur.

7

Boss, Subordinate, and Peer Relationships

For the past twenty-five years, psychologists and sociologists have stressed the importance of good working relationships characterized by high trust; supportiveness; and interest between and among subordinates, peers, and superiors in maintaining productive, efficient corporations. However, only in the past few years, with the emergence of the new-breed managers' demands to have an open, honest, sensitive, fair, human-oriented work environment, have corporations begun to focus on the "quality of work life." Corporate focus on improving the quality of work-group relations does not seem to stem in large part from a new-found humaneness but in the decreasing productivity and quality of products produced by their workers.

Good work-group relationships are enhanced by a getting-along-together attitude and by a lack of role ambiguity. Ambiguity occurs when a manager is prevented from having necessary information because the immediate work group of subordinates, peers, and/or superiors withholds understanding, trust, and support. If managers are already in an ambiguous position because of inadequate information about role responsibilities and/or access to information, they will have poor working relationships and conflicts. These conflicts could lead to the employees' having both physical and mental problems that will affect their job performance.

"Getting along" refers to the critical ability to influence others, particularly in terms of acquiring the necessary resources and information for successful job performance. Since more and more people demand to be treated as contributing human beings, the tangible and intangible resources are seldom accessible through formal position or authority alone, as was usually the case before the emergence of the new-breed managers.

In the introduction to Alfred J. Morrow's book, *The Failure of Success*, Chris Argyris expertly argued how work-group-relationship problems affect the effective functioning of the organization:

> Problems are equally severe at management levels where incompetent organizational structures create executive environments lacking in trust, openness, and risk taking. . . . The attitudes that flourish best in such environments are conformity and defensiveness, which often find expression in an organizational tendency to produce detailed information for unimportant problems and invalid information for important ones. This tendency ensures ineffective problem solving, poor decision making, and weak commitment to the decisions made.[1]

Because of the extreme importance of good work relationships to corporate productivity and efficiency and to employee mental and physical health, the following sections focus on boss, subordinate, and peer relationships in the participating companies.

Boss Relationships

As a member of an organization, many individuals can be beset by feelings of anxiety and alienation. As Erich Fromm noted in *The Sane Society*, many people do not see themselves as having control over their lives, but as powerless "things" dependent upon powerful others.[2]

Until recently, this idea has been descriptive of the status of subordinate and superior relationships in corporations. It is essential to understand that this description is becoming more and more outdated because of the new value systems of many corporate managers. However, bosses were, and always will be, one of the main reference points of a manager's official work group. They are in many cases the most-"significant other," the persons whom the managers are most anxious to understand and satisfy.

The relationships that subordinates form with their bosses can greatly affect the information, resources, and overall support the bosses give to them. In addition, certain social needs are often filled by the subordinate/superior relationship in a work situation. The most-satisfactory work environment for a subordinate is one in which he or she is treated fairly, appropriately praised, given consideration and understanding when mistakes are made, and told where he or she stands.

Many people believe that bosses feel prodded to assist their subordinates because of mutual dependency for success. This assumes that bosses are objective, rational beings and immune to occasional lapses into human irrationality. This assumption, of course, is incorrect. When bosses feel negative toward subordinates, they may deliberately withhold information or support in order to assert authority, increase dependency, or prove that the subordinate is not competent. Subordinates must, to the extent acceptable to their own personal values and needs, attempt to understand and deal with their bosses' idiosyncrasies, needs, and concerns in order to minimize the effect of these negative feelings on themselves. John B. Miner, commenting on the variety of traditional prenew-breed managers' boss/subordinate interactions, observed that:

> Subordinates are expected to behave in ways which do not provoke negative reactions from their superiors—ideally they will elicit positive responses. A subordinate must be in a position to obtain support for his/her actions at higher levels. This requires a good relationship with

superiors. It follows that a subordinate should have a generally positive attitude toward those holding positions of authority over him/her. Any tendency to generalized hatred, distaste, or anxiety in dealing with people in positions of authority will make it extremely difficult to meet job demands and personal goals. Interactions with superiors will either be minimal or filled with so much negative feeling that the necessary positive reactions and support cannot possibly be attained.[3]

For the new-breed manager, one must reword some parts of Miner's comments. While subordinates are expected to behave in ways that do not provoke negative reactions from superiors, many new-breed managers will take the wrath of their bosses if they strongly feel that the actions they are asked to take or actions taken against them by their bosses strongly offend their personal values. In addition, many of these managers do hold feelings of hate and distaste for their supervisors. However, in most cases they learn to control these feelings when they realize the higher levels in the corporate structure support their superiors' actions. In part, they control their negative feelings by making a conscious effort to avoid emulating their bosses' management style and philosophy with their own subordinates. Finally, we will see that the boss/subordinate relationships are not just the subordinates catering to the needs and dictates of their all-powerful bosses as Miner's comments imply. Subordinates also have power over their bosses, and they are beginning to recognize this more and more, especially among the new breed.

Demographics of Bosses in the Study

A staggering 95 percent of the bosses in this study are white. Although 13 percent of the American population is black, only 2 percent of the participating managers' bosses are black. The Hispanic proportion of the American population is estimated at 9 percent, but only 1 percent of the bosses are Hispanic. The remaining 1 percent of the bosses are native American, Asian, and others. Furthermore, while women comprise 52 percent of the national population, only 14 percent of the bosses are women. By age, 32 percent of the bosses are over 50 years of age, 38 percent are 40+ to 50 years of age, 24 percent are between the ages 30+ and 40, and 6 percent are 30 years old and under. Since managers' bosses must be at least second level, these statistics represent race/sex/age distributions for managers at lower-middle-level management and above.

Female managers are five times more likely than male managers are to have a female boss (26 percent versus 5 percent). Among women, whites are most likely to have male bosses and Asians are least likely at 36 percent. By levels, 66 percent of white women at the first level, 88 percent at the second level, and 96 percent at the third level and above have male bosses. Similar trends are found among the other female groups. Eighty-seven to 98 percent of the male participants have male bosses. Although other women are almost twice as likely overall to have female bosses than are white women, the causes of this sexual segregation are related to the organization of work, the departments to which women are assigned, and their level of management. The effects of this uneven distribution hold both positive and negative implications for the future.

The positive effects are indicated by the recent empirical testing of Kanter's hypothesis that the contextual environment—that is, the ratio of minority to majority persons in a group—is an important determinant for achievement by minority-group members.[4] Minority-group members are less likely to be high achievers by group standards as they become more isolated. In other words, minority-group members reach higher levels of achievement when they are with their own kind. Explanations of this phenomenon are discussed in the section on performance. Given the evident concentrations of women indicated in these findings, some women should be gaining personal strength from being in predominantly female departments.

The negative effects stem from the fact that women are being concentrated in particular "appropriate" departments and implicitly being kept out of others. This prevents them from gaining the experience necessary to equip them for higher levels of management. In addition, the departments in which they are concentrated are not considered important mainstream-power departments. This lack of coming up in integrated environments makes the eventual transition—for those able to maneuver one—more difficult. This is an additional adjustment, and one typically that men do not have to make. This separation seems to be even more the case for black and Asian women than for Hispanic and white women.

Managers' Perceptions of Their Bosses

In order to analyze the managers' perceptions about their bosses, they were asked a number of questions that attempted to focus on the relationships, communications, openness, efficiency, helpfulness, and honesty of their bosses. Put another way, the questions focus on whether or not the boss/subordinate relationships are healthy and mutually beneficial.

The data show that more than half of the managers (51 percent to 66 percent) say their bosses are doing a good or excellent job in each of the following:

Giving helpful suggestions on how to do your work (51 percent).
Keeping you informed about changes that affect your work (55 percent).

Having the information you need, when you need it (58 percent).
Taking prompt action on your questions, ideas, and complaints (61 percent).
Giving straight answers to questions (63 percent).
Explaining to you why things are to be done in a certain way (63 percent).
Asking for your ideas and suggestions about the job (66 percent).
Giving you support and help with a job when needed (67 percent).

An index constructed from these questions measures how many managers believe their bosses are doing a good to excellent job overall. While 50 percent rate their bosses as good to excellent on six out of eight questions, the other 50 percent do not rate their bosses so highly. On four out of five questions, 14 percent rate bosses high; on one out of three questions, 22 percent rate them high, and 14 percent of the managers do not rate their bosses good to excellent on any of the questions.

When managers' responses are divided into race/sex groupings, 45 to 55 percent of the managers rate their bosses good to excellent in at least six areas. Least likely to rate their bosses good to excellent on at least six of the areas are black men, 45 percent; Hispanic men, 45 percent; and black women, 46 percent. Most likely to rate their bosses high are native-American women, 55 percent, and Asian men, 54 percent.

It should be noted that the responses of white men at the first and second levels are similar to the most-critical groups. Following are the responses of white men by level who rate their bosses good to excellent on six to eight of the questions:

First level	45%
Second level	49%
Third level	53%
Fourth level	62%
Fifth level	71%

(Note that sixth-level managers in this study were not asked all the questions that were asked to fifth-level and below managers.) The responses show that black men and women, Hispanic men, and white men respond quite similarly at the first two levels of management. Since 14 percent of the white men at the first and second levels are 20-30 years of age compared to 36 percent of the black and Hispanic men, it does not seem that the white men's overall low responses are influenced by their youth. A more-plausible scenario is that these lower-level white men are not and probably will not become part of the high-level circles of management. Therefore, they are more likely to be critical of how their bosses operate than those at higher levels are.

White men at the higher levels begin to feel they own and control the organization so they are not going to be as critical about "their" corporations.

It is extremely important to note that most minorities and women at the third level and above remain consistent and quite critical about the treatment of minorities and women and about their relationships with bosses. Contrary to white men's responses, minorities and women do not develop a more-optimistic evaluation of their bosses' abilities as they move up the corporate ladder. One explanation for this discrepancy is that managers from the dominant group feel more a part of the group that helped them get there. For women and minority men, group identity diminishes as they progress up the management ladder because fewer same-sex or same-race superiors, peers, and subordinates are found in the higher levels. As their status becomes more-obviously "token," they feel more isolated and thus become more critical. A black man at the third level states:

> I feel that some of my bosses don't tell me everything or as much as some white males because they don't want me to achieve, and because if you're black, they exclude you from some duties or chairing group discussions where you're meeting many members of the opposite race. Many times I feel isolated and alienated.

A similar concern is expressed by a Hispanic woman at the third level who says:

> I believe the solid cultural differences existing in my relationship with my boss will adversely affect my career development in this company. I understand their culture, but they do not understand mine and they don't try. Their club is exclusive and really has no room for a Hispanic female.

Considering blacks' comments about the treatment of minorities and women, one would expect black managers to be more critical of bosses than their white-male peers are. This, however, is not the case for those at lower levels. Why? One likely explanation for this contradiction is that blacks might overestimate relationships with bosses as a form of self-protection. Their self-esteem would suffer if they admitted that their relationships with their bosses are not very good. It would be admitting that they are unable to overcome racism and deal with "the man." Another explanation could be that blacks, while sometimes paranoid about the treatment of minorities in their companies, respond quite similarly at the lower levels to whites when asked specifically about their own bosses. In other words, when an overall question about the treatment of minorities is asked, a higher percentage will indicate negative treatment. However, when a question is asked about the manager's own particular treatment, responses are more positive.

A rather disturbing finding is that one out of seven managers do not rate their bosses good to excellent in any of the areas. One-quarter of the respondents who are not performing their jobs as effectively as possible said that to some or a great extent, poor working relationships with their bosses are hindering their job performance. Here are some examples of why bosses are rated poorly. A white woman at the first level says:

> My boss expects things done his way whether right or wrong. I am in a job which does not give me much freedom and independence. He delegates an assignment but usually to more than one person. Not only to me but to all of the group. This just causes confusion and makes us look weak in the eyes of others.

A white man at the fourth level makes these cynical remarks:

> Keep a low profile. Don't irritate bosses. Don't ask for too much too often, regardless of the needs of the job. Good scouts and personal loyalty to a boss are more-often rewarded than performance. This would be easy to prove. Take a random sample of promotions to the first, second, third, fourth, and fifth levels. Then compare the promotees' [sic] performance figures with their competition.

A first-level native-American man comments:

> I have the feeling that higher management distrusts our judgments and abilities and that we must always protect ourselves.

A first-level Hispanic man says:

> I feel there is a personality conflict between my boss and myself. I can't be what he wants me to be. It is affecting my interest in the job.

Finally, a third-level black man sums up his relationship with his boss this way:

> I have been with this company ten years. I have progressed rapidly, but I am tired of being what my bosses think I should be. I have tried to accommodate most of their needs, but the higher I go the more they seem to want you to conform in all ways—looks, dress, attitudes, life-style—you name it. When are they going to recognize and accept me as a human being? The older I get, the more I want to be recognized for my own uniqueness.

Many of these comments epitomize the new-breed managers' concerns and problems with the style of management that is based solely on authority, power, and one-way communications. Some of them also bring out the attitude that they are not willing to be the passive recipients of their bosses' actions. As with most new-breed managers, they want to be active, respected partners in achieving corporate goals.

Communications a Major Issue

Many of the measures of bosses' effectiveness in the index deal directly or indirectly with effective communication. Effective, honest communications are one crucial sign of healthy boss subordinate relationships. In feedback sessions, two negative feelings came out repeatedly from the managers: (1) they do not have time to give sufficient attention to all of their subordinates, and (2) they are not trained to provide the kind of formal and informal feedback needed to relate to subordinates in a productively critical, yet unthreatening, manner. For example, a white man at the third level, reporting on his boss, says:

> No discussions. As a matter of fact very little personal discussion on any matter. He prefers to talk with his staff via a tape machine.

A Hispanic man at the first level shares his coping tactic:

> Only by exercising a tremendous amount of personal effort to keep myself informed of latest policies and information and by setting aside personality conflicts in performing my duties and responsibilities am I able to make it. My boss is of little help.

Many managers also believe that communication is poor because they cannot speak freely. Table 7-1 indicates that, overall, only a minority of the managers feels entirely free to express themselves on company matters without fear of reprisal from their bosses. White managers are least likely (46 percent) and black managers are most likely (62 percent) to report that they do *not* feel entirely free to express their own thoughts and feelings on company matters without fear of reprisal from their bosses. At least for minorities and women, this fear exists among almost equal percentages of them throughout the corporate hierarchy. For white men, more managers at upper levels than at lower levels feel entirely free to express their thoughts. Nonetheless, one out of three of the upper-middle-and-above-level white men do not feel entirely free to express themselves. Thus, this fear of expression seems to permeate the entire corporate structure.

This fear can be traced in part to the fact that most bosses are not comfortable communicating with subordinates, and therefore, they adjust in a number of ways. Some bosses avoid communicating with subordinates as much as possible. Some communicate in a dictatorial fashion that stifles any form of communication. Others communicate in a circumlocutory

Table 7-1
Freedom of Expression
(percent)

How Free Do You Feel to Express Your Own Thoughts and Feelings on Company Matters without Fear of Reprisal from Your Boss?	Native-American		Asian		Black		Hispanic		White		Total
	Men (N = 143)	Women (N = 104)	Men (N = 122)	Women (N = 135)	Men (N = 474)	Women (N = 432)	Men (N = 387)	Women (N = 285)	Men (N = 1,269)	Women (N = 765)	(N = 4,116)
Entirely Free	49.7	47.1	39.3	43.7	37.1	39.1	41.3	43.5	53.7	54.4	47.4
Fairly free	32.9	33.7	40.2	45.2	38.6	38.4	39.3	36.8	33	33.3	35.8
Not very free	14.7	14.4	17.2	8.1	17.3	16.9	16	13.3	10.2	9.4	12.7
Not at all free	2.8	4.8	3.3	3	7	5.6	3.4	6.3	3.2	2.9	4.1

manner so as not to offend anyone who is able to decipher what is being communicated. Finally, many bosses believe in the corporate position and consider any deviation as a form of disloyalty that should be punished.

Fear to communicate makes managers hide information and cover up important activities. It creates an atmosphere of oppression that eventually affects the functioning of the organization because in such an atmosphere creativity, new ideas, and the strength to take risks do not flourish.

Bosses' Supervisory Abilities

Managers perceive their bosses as having more difficulty supervising some race/sex groups of managers than others. Seventy-two percent of the managers feel their bosses are at least good in their ability to supervise white men, 66 percent feel they are at least good in supervising white women, and 57 percent say their bosses are at least good at supervising minority managers. The range of responses of those race/sex groups who rate their bosses good or excellent in supervising white men is 10 percent, from 67 to 77 percent. White women have a range of 12 percent, from 61 to 73 percent. The range for minority men is 15 percent, from 48 to 63 percent. With regard to supervision of minority women, the gap is even larger—a range of 21 percent, from 46 to 67 percent. More agreement clearly exists about managers' abilities to supervise white managers than minority managers.

The psychological defenses of denial and projection appear to be operating here. While between 34 and 44 percent of the managers believe their bosses have problems supervising various race/sex groups, only 13 to 16 percent of these managers indicate *they* need some training in supervising different race/sex groups of managers. It goes back to the old saying, "I have no problems. It is the other person who does."

Several additional points should be made. White-male managers are more likely to give their bosses better ratings on ability to supervise minority men, white women, and white men as the respondent's level of management increased. When comparing this trend to that of the white men's perception of their bosses' abilities to supervise white men, a 14-16 percent difference appears by level—that is, more white men see their bosses as good or better at managing white men than other race/sex groups. This may indicate that some of the managers recognize that race plays a role in managers' ability to supervise minority managers, which lends support to the black managers' views because they are the only managers to regard the race of their immediate bosses as a factor in the boss's ability to supervise minority managers. Black bosses are most likely (38 percent), and white bosses least likely (19 percent), to be rated as excellent by black managers. Furthermore, only 1 percent of the black bosses are rated poorly in supervising minority managers, and 19 percent of the white bosses are rated poorly. All other race/sex groups rate about equal percentages of the black and white bosses as excellent or poor in supervising minority managers.

A white man at the third level, who admits to having problems in supervising minorities, makes these essentially negative comments about minorities:

> I feel there is an undue emphasis on finding and promoting minority persons to middle management (third, fourth, fifth levels) without particular regard to previous job performance, achievements, interpersonal relations, or capacity to manage others. Their most-apparent deficiency is inability to supervise and relate to either peers or subordinates.

White managers, or any managers, with these views certainly will have difficulties supervising minority managers.

Are Female Managers Better Bosses than Male Managers?

Many negative myths about women as bosses have been adopted by society because of sexist attitudes imposed by the white-male-dominated institutions. These myths paint female bosses as picky, opinionated, emotional, and unpredictable. Several typical comments from white men are illustrative of these negative stereotypes. A white man at the first level makes these comments: "Women must be trained to handle men and in general learn what it takes to be a boss. They usually lack the experience because they are women." A white man at the third level says of female managers, "Decision making is weak. Empathy for subordinates often lacking."

The data in this study contradict the widely held myths. They show that female bosses are usually evaluated the same as male bosses but that they are rated better than male bosses in a number of critical areas. A higher percentage of female managers are rated good or excellent in their abilities to supervise various groups. For example, 82 percent of the male managers who have female bosses rate them good to excellent in ability to supervise white men. This compares to 69 percent who rate their male bosses as good to excellent in the ability to supervise white men. Further, 78 percent of the female managers with female bosses, compared to 59 percent of the female managers with male bosses, rate their bosses good to excellent in supervising white women.

Not only do more managers see women as being effective supervisors of various race/sex groups but also female bosses are consistently rated higher than male bosses are in the important areas of career development and performance evaluation. Regardless of the age or race of the bosses, managers at every level, of every race, and of both sexes are more likely to give positive assessments in these areas to female bosses than to male bosses. For example, 74 percent of male managers with female bosses versus 59 percent of male managers with male bosses report that, at least to some extent, their bosses remain open to the managers' interests in career development. Table 7-2 shows the managers' responses.

A final example is shown in table 7-3, which relates to the usefulness of performance appraisals. Both male and female managers report that, at least to some extent, female bosses are more likely to give performance appraisals that are specific, useful, and clear as to what improvements are needed and how they might be effected.

These findings are even more important and profound when one considers the sexist attitudes of male managers, as expressed throughout the study. One can conclude that if sexist attitudes can be excluded from corporate thought, female managers will be much preferred to male managers.

Helen B. Lewis explained the major reasons female bosses may be preferred over male bosses:

> Men, in keeping with the expectation that they will go into the world to earn their livelihood, are trained more frequently than women to understand the workings of inanimate objects or things. But more important, they are expected to accept, without thinking much about it, the idea that people may be treated as if they were things. In the United States, for example, the people who could be mistaken for things were the slaves in the South. The majority of men also often take for granted that they themselves should be treated as if they were things—for example, units in a labor force.
>
> Women, in keeping with the expectation that they will devote their lives to others, are trained—in fact, they train themselves—to understand other people. Men are also expected to understand other people (it's hard to pre-

Table 7-2
Extent to which Bosses Remain Open to Subordinates' Interests for Career Development
(percent)

To What Extent Does Your Boss Remain Open To Your Interests for Career Development?	Men's Responses		Women's Responses	
	Male Bosses (N = 2,229)	*Female Bosses (N = 121)*	*Male Bosses (N = 1,253)*	*Female Bosses (N = 444)*
To a great extent	21.2	32.2	27.5	30.4
To some extent	38.1	41.3	32.2	32
To a slight extent	26.8	14	25	22.1
Not at all	13.9	12.4	15.3	15.5

Table 7-3
Usefulness of Performance Evaluations
(percent)

To What Extent Do You Believe Your Performance Evaluations Are Specific and Useful, Clear as to What Improvements Are Needed, and How They Might Be Effected?	Men's Responses		Women's Responses	
	Male Bosses (N = 2,159)	*Female Bosses (N = 117)*	*Male Bosses (N = 1,187)*	*Female Bosses (N = 424)*
To a great extent	19.5	22.2	26.3	36.6
To some extent	42.7	52.1	40.6	39.2
To a slight extent	25.7	18.8	20.9	17.2
Not at all	12.1	6.8	12.2	7.1

vent). But in our competitive, dehumanized, "business" society, men's dealing with other people are supposed to resemble their dealings with things and very often do.[5]

In short, women seem to be introducing a new, more-open, communicative managerial style, at least in some areas, that may be more functional and productive than is the style men have traditionally used. This is especially true of the new breed of managers with their different value system.

Before concluding this section on bosses, we must state that no relationship appears between race and how managers evaluate their bosses. The one exception is that many more black managers rate black bosses' abilities to supervise minority managers higher than white bosses. This finding is consistent with the black managers' more-critical views about white treatment of minorities than other minority groups.

Age of bosses also is not much of a factor in the managers' responses. Bosses of the "old" and "new" schools apparently do not differ a great deal in managerial style. This finding could be attributed to a manager's strong sense of ethics and corporate style. Those who conform to the corporate operational mode are rewarded more frequently and more lucratively than are those who do not. Thus, good and bad management styles appear to be more a function of values rather than age.

Subordinate Relationships

Another significant member of the work group is the subordinate. Even though bosses have a great deal of power over subordinates, likewise subordinates have a great deal of power over bosses. Surprisingly, however, many subordinates do not recognize their power. Good bosses get good results not by doing the work themselves but by means of their subordinates. More explicitly, the success of the bosses' plans and policies depends directly upon the skills, knowledge, and motivation of those people farther down the ladder who are responsible for applying guidelines or implementing plans. Many occasions have occurred in which subordinates have deliberately sabotaged the work operation in order to get back at unfair, insensitive bosses.

Subordinates' skills and achievements also are very important to bosses who want to move ahead. These bosses must surround themselves with people who can contribute to their job achievement and become part of the bosses' team. In most cases this teamwork will only happen when mutual respect and trust exists between bosses and subordinates. In short, bosses' relationships with subordinates are not only important for the bosses' job performance but also for their advancement chances. Thus, the boss/subordinate relationship is mutually interdependent and not only subordinate dependent.

Demographics of Subordinates

As shown in table 7-4, large variations exist in the percentages of managers who have subordinates who are minority, white, male, and female. The percentages of managers who have white-male subordinates range from 51 percent (Asian women) to 91 percent (white and native-American men). Within each ethnic group, women are less likely than men are to have white-male subordinates. The percentages of managers who have minority-female subordinates range from a low of 53 percent (white men) to a high of 87 percent (black women). Within each race/ethnic group, female managers are more likely than male managers are to have minority-female subordinates. These figures again point out the race/sex occupational segregation in these companies.

Managers' Perceptions of
Subordinate Relationships

The managers usually feel they have satisfactory work relationships with their subordinates. An impressive majority of managers agrees that their subordinates respect their work (98 percent), that their subordinates ask for their ideas and suggestions when problems arise (97 percent), and that their subordinates usually agree with them (95 percent). Considering the negative views of minorities and women illustrated in previous chapters, one would

Table 7-4
Managers Who Have Subordinates in Specific Race/Sex Groups
(percent)

| | Native-American | | Asian | | Black | | Hispanic | | White | | Total |
	Men (N = 144)	Women (N = 104)	Men (N = 122)	Women (N = 135)	Men (N = 474)	Women (N = 433)	Men (N = 387)	Women (N = 286)	Men (N = 1,320)	Women (N = 550)	(N = 3,955)
Subordinates											
White-male	91	66.3	86.9	51.1	84.4	66.3	83.5	66.4	90.9	71.6	70.4
White-female	72.2	93.3	73.8	83	80	91	78.3	90.9	81.2	93	77.3
Minority-male	56.9	46.2	82.8	56.3	66	53.6	67.7	59.1	48.7	46.9	34
Minority-female	57.6	76.9	78.7	85.9	68.8	86.6	58.2	85	52.9	69.9	52.5

expect more-negative views than appear here. In addition, since many bosses receive low ratings by their subordinates and most of these managers have subordinates, these responses might be a reflection of self-congratulations.

Regardless of the satisfactory ratings given by the vast majority of managers, some areas of concern are evident. For example, while 93 percent of the respondents say they can trust their subordinates, noteworthy exceptions appear based on the race of the respondents. Although only 2 percent of the Asian men report that they cannot trust their subordinates, 11 percent of the native-American women and black men and 12 percent of the Hispanic women report lack of trust.

Black managers with a higher percentage of white-male subordinates are more likely to say they cannot trust their subordinates. For example, 29 percent of the black managers who have 81 percent or more white-male subordinates respond that they cannot trust their subordinates, as compared to 7 percent who have between 1 and 20 percent white-male subordinates. Responses of other ethnic groups do not show these relationships.

Another area in which race compounds the findings is in that of informal networks. As noted in chapters 3 and 4, high percentages of managers believe minorities and women are excluded from informal work groups. However, when questions about exclusion by subordinates are presented, much-smaller percentages of managers believe this exclusion to be the case. Overall, 15 percent of the managers agree that their subordinates have a close relationship of which they are not a part. Although more black managers than others believe that minorities and women are excluded from informal work groups, the Asian-male managers, 24 percent, are most likely to feel excluded by their subordinates. Excluding Asian-male managers, between 14 and 17 percent of the other race/sex groups at least agree that their subordinates have a close relationship of which they are not a part.

An *inverse* relationship for black and white men exists between managerial level and alienation, indicating the increasing alienation felt by black men and the increasing security felt by white men as they move up the corporate ladder. White men at lower levels and black men at upper levels are more likely to agree that their subordinates have a close relationship of which they are not a part. Twenty-two percent of the white men and 14 percent of the black men at the second level and below, as compared to 11 percent of the white men and 28 percent of the black men above the second level, agree that their subordinates have such close relationships.

These questions on ability to trust, to share with, and to depend on others are closely linked to the requirements of a managerial position. The managers' job involves planning, coordination, and leadership, which requires that they be able to trust in, depend on, and delegate to others. Leadership means being able to behave in a way that allows others to believe that the leader depends on and trusts in them. It means being able to motivate subordinates by creating a climate that is open enough for them to work and grow. When subordinates have racist and sexist attitudes, the problems that minority and female managers have in being effective bosses are compounded.

Peer Relationships

The final significant part of any work group is the peer group. These relationships are rather fluid, for today's peer may well be tomorrow's boss or subordinate. The secret to successful peer-group interaction is to compete with one's peers without offending or alienating them. As one managerial folk saying goes, "Be nice to everyone on the way up; you'll probably see them on the way down."

Normally, managers must depend on some peers to assist them in meeting their objectives. If peers are alienated for any reason, managers can find themselves with no cooperation, slow and reluctant cooperation, improper or no information, or being left out of the daily running of the business.

Laurie Larwood and Marion M. Wood's comments about women and their peers (co-workers) apply equally well to minorities and their peers:

> Male associates vying with a woman for a single promotion are the most likely to feel threatened by her possible success. While men also react competitively to the success of male colleagues, it is easier for them to single out a woman as invading their territory, to stamp her behavior as unacceptable, and to feel her success is unfair. Although major confrontations are rare, a competitive woman can raise the "masculine consciousness" of her associates, and it is not unusual for her to be frozen from their group conversations and social gatherings. The men's rationales include a woman's lack of understanding of men, lack of experience, likelihood of being offended, or merely of dampening an otherwise freewheeling discussion.[6]

On the positive side, peers can be the most-helpful group in the work-group relationship. They are useful in providing the necessary assistance to accomplish the job, and they provide the understanding of various corporate politics. Managers held in high esteem by their peers are more likely to be promoted than are those who are not. Also, peers fulfill social needs such as friendships, a feeling of identification with formal and informal work groups, and helping others and being helped by them.

Finally, peers, especially those who are working for the same boss, can be very helpful to newcomers in understanding the unique characteristics of that boss. They can help protect one another by exchanging information about a crucial problem of which the boss is aware or unaware. They can be supportive of one another with the boss. Very few bosses overrule the opinions of a majority of his/her subordinates.

Close peer relationships, however, can also be threatening to insecure bosses and can be interpreted as a form of insubordination. For secure bosses, close peer relationships are welcomed as they provide a sense of a united team.

In sum, good peer relationships permit managers the necessary access to informal networks of power and information with relative ease, in addition to providing very important supportive and social needs.

Demographics of Peers

Managers' peers vary a great deal among the various race/sex groups. In table 7-5, the percentages of managers who have white-male peers range from 60 percent of the native-American women to 99 percent of the native-American men. The men of each ethnic group are more likely than are the women to have white-male peers. Another finding is that upper-level female managers are usually more likely than lower-level ones are to have white-male peers. For example, 61 percent of the first-level, 87 percent of the second-level, 96 percent of the third-level, and 100 percent of the fourth-level and above white women have white-male peers. These statistics clearly illustrate the dominant position of white men at higher levels of management.

Managers' Perceptions of Peer Relationships

As was the case with subordinates, the views of minority and female managers in most cases are positive. On the whole, managers are more satisfied with subordinate relationships than they are with peer relationships. This difference may be due to the competition that exists among peers for the few higher-level positions.

A black woman at the second level is representative of the overall positive responses in this section:

> The men I worked with at first level felt that the group was no place for a woman. They don't really feel that way now. They still make comments from time to time, but I feel I have been accepted as part of the team. We also have gained another woman.

Ninety percent of the managers agree both that their peers usually cooperate with them and that their peers respect their work. Ninety percent report that their peers ask for their ideas and suggestions when they have a problem.

Table 7-5
Managers Who Have Peers in Specific Race/Sex Groups
(percent)

Peers	Native-American		Asian		Black		Hispanic		White		Total
	Men (N = 144)	Women (N = 104)	Men (N = 122)	Women (N = 135)	Men (N = 474)	Women (N = 433)	Men (N = 387)	Women (N = 286)	Men (N = 1,320)	Women (N = 786)	(N = 4,191)
White-male	98.6	59.6	86.9	60.7	92.8	63.5	94.8	62.6	97.7	79	83.5
White-female	57.6	83.7	67.2	86.7	59.5	82.4	58.9	81.5	43.3	66.3	57.3
Minority-male	38.2	27.9	45.9	40.7	32.9	27	44.4	35	27.4	25.9	24.2
Minority-female	24.3	42.3	37.7	58.5	31.9	49.9	28.9	55.6	18.8	30.7	24.9

Ninety percent of the managers say that their peers usually do not create work problems for them. Note that 61 percent of the white men at the sixth level, compared to 8 percent of all other white-male managers, agree with this statement. No significant differences exist among the other race/sex groups or by level. Several sixth-level managers explain this difference by commenting that at this level they all have tremendous power and huge egos. This leads them to be much-more critical of any interference by peers in their private, operational domain.

Ten percent of the managers agree that they cannot trust their peers. However, black men, 19 percent, and black women, 17 percent, compared to only 5 to 14 percent of other groups, indicate distrust of peers. A black man at the second level says:

> When I first entered the group I was perceived as a threat to the corporate security of several of my peers. Occasionally, some racial comments are made but glossed over.

A black woman at the first level states:

> Some of my peers can be trusted, mainly the ones 50 and over. Some 35 and under cannot be trusted.

These data and comments have several interpretations, all valid in some cases. One interpretation is that because of pure racist attitudes, many more whites actually distrust blacks than they do other race groups. Another is that whites see blacks as a greater competitive threat because of their numbers—they are more fearful and distrustful of blacks than of others. Still another interpretation is that blacks are more paranoid than others, thus they believe their peers are not trustworthy.

As already discussed, being part of informal groups is very important for survival in the corporate structure. The informal communications network provides an invaluable opportunity for the exchange of ideas and information. The successful executives can be distinguished by their ability to move socially between various race/sex groups. To the extent that a manager is accepted as an equal in the white-male-dominated informal social group, her or his presence defuses sensitivity to sex/race-role differences. As a result, a manager can share the expertise and assistance of the group rather than having it used against her or him.

As was noted, over 50 percent of the managers believe that women are excluded from informal work groups, and more than 40 percent believe that minorities are excluded. Yet overall, only 14 percent of the managers agree that their peers have a close relationship of which they are not a part. For example, a black man at the second level says:

There are three white males and myself in my work group. We normally work well together and support each others' work effort. I have been bypassed on many after-work social affairs, and at first the members of my group were very uncomfortable speaking of these affairs.

As many managers are aware, minorities and women are not the only managers to have peer-relationship problems related to being excluded. A white man at the fourth level says:

My peer group consists of others who report to my boss. Since I am in a skip-level reporting situation most of my "peers" are one level higher than I. I am not included by them in anything they do as a group without the boss, and I feel they are not really interested in me.

The percentage of black men who says that their peers exclude them is more than twice that of male managers of all other ethnic groups, 29 percent versus 8 to 13 percent. In addition, both black men and women at upper levels are more likely than those at lower levels are to feel excluded:

Black women		Black men	
First level	17%	First level	20%
Second level	21%	Second level	30%
Third level	43%	Third level	46%
Fourth level +	N.A.[a]	Fourth level	75%

[a]NA means not applicable.

When white men comprise 81 percent or more of a peer group, larger percentages of black managers report that their peers have a close relationship of which they are not a part. However, when white men comprise 20 percent or less of the peer group, this observation is not true. For example, 36 percent of the black managers with 81 percent or more white men among their peers say they are excluded. This compares to 15 percent of the black managers who feel excluded when they have white men as 20 percent or less of their peers.

Black men and women and Hispanic women who agree that their peers have a close relationship of which they are not a part tend to agree with all of the statements that assess the extent to which minorities are excluded from social interactions. For example, 70 percent of the black men who agree their peers have a close relationship of which they are not a part also agree with all of the following statements:

Many minority workers are excluded from informal work networks by whites.

Many minority managers have a much-harder time finding someone who is particularly interested in their career.

Minority managers are often excluded from many social activities that are beneficial to advancement in corporations.

These statistics reinforce the notion of widespread alienation among a large portion of the black managers, especially the men and those at higher levels.

Female managers with white men comprising 81 percent or more of their peers are more likely than female managers with white men comprising 20 percent or less of their peers to agree that their peers have a close relationship of which they are not a part (26 percent versus 9 percent). Showing the contrasting views of women, a white woman at the third level says:

As a female in a group largely made up of white males, I have always been made to feel an outsider or uncomfortable.

However, a black woman at the second level who has two women, two white men, and one black man as peers says:

I feel I have a good relationship with my work groups. I believe there exists mutual feeling of respect and admiration and cooperation. We have candid discussions on work and employees. We also have disagreements but do not hold grudges.

In addition to other reasons mentioned earlier, a very possible reason many minorities and women do not feel that they are part of their peer groups, especially at higher levels, is that they have not "grown up" with white men in their careers and, in the minority case, their personal lives. A white man at the fourth level describes this type of relationship:

Since I previously worked for most of my present peers, and they were instrumental in one or more of my promotions, they sometimes go out of their way to protect me and make me part of the group.

Conclusion

Bosses, peers, and subordinates are quite clearly enmeshed in interdependent relationships. It is foolhardy for any members of these groups to believe they can be successful in performing their jobs and/or advancing in the corporation without the support of the other two groups and their own group. Equally clear is that managers need to develop managerial skills, especially related to the area of communication. In addition, companies would benefit from developing an atmosphere in which honesty and candidness are premium qualities.

While the work environment appears quite good with regard to peers and subordinates, much room remains for improvement with regard to bosses.

The fact that female managers, even with the sexist attitudes evidenced in these corporations, are rated higher as supervisors than men are by both men and women suggests that female managers provide some functional innovations to manageral style that create an atmosphere more conducive to good work relationships than the old authoritarian style does. Men could benefit by identifying and incorporating these innovations into their own management style.

It is also important to note evidence that since 1975 the views of blacks and whites about their overall relationships with their work group, including bosses, subordinates, and peers, have become more similar. For example, in 1975, 70 percent of the blacks versus 93 percent of the whites were satisfied with their work group.[7] The attitudes of blacks and whites in this study are much-more similar—upward of 90 percent of each group are satisfied. These converging attitudes might indicate a more-sensitive overall treatment of blacks and minorities.

However, much as relations may have improved, women and minorities, especially at higher levels of management, still remain noticeably more alienated. The problems faced by women and minorities, especially blacks, create a very serious malfunction in corporate operations. Minorities and women have yet to be accepted as full members of corporate formal and informal networks. Until they are, not only do they suffer but so does the corporation. The utilization of minorities and women in many, many cases toward corporate effectiveness and efficiency continues to be seriously hampered by behaviors in crucial interpersonal relationships that reflect racist and sexist attitudes.

Part II
Solutions to
Employment Policies
of the 1980s

Part I of this book examined the influences of racism, sexism, and affirmative action on the work situation and treatment of minorities and women in corporations in the late 1970s and the effects of these issues on the careers of all managers. The data vividly demonstrate that racism and sexism still play crucial roles in the corporate environment.

Part II, in addition to examining the attitudes of the new breed of managers, deals with solutions to the problems that have been identified and provides an analysis, by race, sex, and level of the responses, to questions about elements involved in five basic components of an integrated management-employment system, which are listed in the next paragraph.

This writer's conviction is that many, though not all, of the solutions to what have been labeled as race, sex, and EEO/AAP problems are also solutions to basic managerial problems created by the nontraditional styles and values of the new-breed managers. The way to utilize all managerial talent—whether male, female, native-American, Asian, black, Hispanic, or white—is to systematically implement a comprehensive managerial employment system that features the following components:

Work design,
Performance evaluation,
Potential evaluation,
Career planning/training and development.

Specifically, this second part of the book argues that corporations must recognize the need for jobs that offer a sense of wholeness, satisfaction, significance, and autonomy. They must develop hiring, promotion, and performance- and potential-evaluation procedures and practices that are equitable and objective in order to alleviate the insecurity and tensions that white men, minorities, and women are experiencing. They must develop career-planning systems that deal with the new breed's need to have a significant say in their own future.

Managers must, in brief, demonstrate clearly that *no one* is playing with a stacked deck and that employees have valid inputs into their corporate work and careers.

Chapter 12 deals with the primary question of who needs special training to be more-effective corporate managers in the 1980s. This chapter supports the proposition that a more-systematic, integrated management-
employment system would go a long way toward solving employee problems of the 1980s and that this system would be better than special training
programs for any specific race/sex group.

8

Work Design and Job Satisfaction: The First Two Ingredients to the Solution

Social scientists have long recognized that work plays an essential role for humans. The nature of work is crucial and at the center of most adults' lives. It gives them a sense of identity, self-esteem, and order. If an individual's job is unsatisfying and frustrating, serious negative effects can result on all aspects of his or her life. More specifically, the work situation fulfills both egotistic and social needs. (Social needs were discussed with work-group relationships in chapter 7.) The most-important egotistic need is fulfillment in terms of accomplishment—that is, the individual's sense of the importance of his or her own work, rate of progress, completion of work, and productivity. People like to measure their progress, to know whether they are progressing at a satisfactory rate, and to see their assignments completed. Then they can feel they are productive and turning out useful work.

When jobs do not give these kinds of satisfactions, the result is a state of job alienation. Robert Blauner has theorized that job alienation results from certain missing essential elements. Jobs that do not allow the employees to control their immediate work environment result in a sense of powerlessness. Jobs that do not allow for the development of relationships between the actions of an individual in his or her job and the broader corporate objectives fail to create situations in which the individual role is seen as fitting into the overall goals of the organization. In such a situation, the worker develops a feeling of meaninglessness.[1]

Jobs that are boring and monotonous and that prevent opportunities for self-growth provoke feelings of self-estrangement. Such jobs are seen as means rather than fulfilling ends. All these negative aspects can, and too often do, lead to alienation and at times even to aggressive, antisocial behavior.[2]

Some researchers have also noted that a sense of active participation is extremely important in the employee's life. Robert Caplan and John French, Jr. found that a lack of participation in decision-making processes can lead to strain among employees and can adversely affect productivity. Their study of fourteen organizations revealed that high participation was associated with:

> . . . high satisfaction with the job and the organization, high self-esteem, low alienation, high commitment to work and to the organization, more

183

innovation for better ways of doing the job, "doing more extra work," reading more books and magazines related to work, a higher performance evaluation by one's manager, and lower absenteeism.[3]

In *The Conduct of the Corporation,* Wilbert Moore wrote that when all is said and done, the content of the job and the power to act are the best predictors of job behavior.[4]

Expressed job satisfaction was reported to be high for decades in the United States. Ten major studies of job satisfaction from 1935 to 1967 consistently found high levels. No more than 23 percent of the participants ever expressed job dissatisfaction; the average was less than 15 percent.[5] However, data in this area have recently been subjected to challenge. In an article "Work in a New America", published in 1978, Kanter proposed that job satisfaction is neither a valid indicator of how people really feel about their work nor of what they would do if offered an alternative. She cited a recent University of Michigan survey that found that, although few workers (less than 10 percent) expressed direct dissatisfaction with their jobs, a much-higher percentage (up to 60 percent) stated they would seek another occupation if they had a chance.[6] In other words, she argued that independent contextual variables such as expectations, opportunities, reference groups, as well as work content greatly influence the dependent variable of job satisfaction. In the past the overwhelming external variable was probably the economy. When inflation, recession, and high unemployment rates dominated the economy, the pressing need for jobs overshadowed other considerations. As the economy improved and jobs became more plentiful, cultural concerns with the meaning and quality of work life gained prominence. However, in the present cultural atmosphere, regardless of the economic situation, people are seeking and demanding better jobs and working environments.

What are some of the reasons more and more managers are demanding work designed in such a manner that they have challenging and interesting jobs and better work environments? One reason is the higher expectations of a work force that over the past few decades experienced improvement in the overall quality of life. Once having experienced job security and increased concern with the meaning of work, temporary adversities such as the economy have little effect on the needs and concerns of these employees.

Another reason is that the work force is becoming more educated. An educated work force demands not only a good salary and a reasonably secure position but also a challenging, interesting, rewarding job. Door-to-door interviews by the National Opinion Research Center found that white men in the managerial-administrative-sales, white-collar-employment category overwhelmingly preferred important and meaningful work (60 percent) to high income (15 percent), short hours/free time (4 percent), and job security (1 percent).[7]

Still another reason work design has become important is that opportunities for promotion in many industries are steadily declining due to lack of expansion, slow economic growth, and the introduction of new technology. Therefore, many employees' drives and interests can only be sustained if they are given interesting and challenging work in a healthy work atmosphere. This is particularly true of employees such as black and Hispanic men who demonstrate a very high need for advancement (see chapter 5). One of the most-important factors in the participating managers' decision to remain in their company, rather than to seek a new job, is challenging and interesting work. In addition, many people are considering early retirement because they do not like their jobs and their work environment.

The following two managers' comments represent the feelings of many managers about work design and work environment. A white man at the third level says:

> I would take less salary and/or fringe benefits in order to have a job which was interesting and offered more-challenging work. A better work environment would also help.

A first-level black man states:

> The company offers good salary and benefits. I don't feel fair in generalizing about each company's work environment, but mine is not stimulating enough to make me want to stay for a long period of time. Another job in the company may be more suitable. My first impression of the company is not a good one, but I am not idealistic enough to expect Utopia elsewhere.

Douglas Bray has proposed that the type, content, and structure of a job has a strong effect on motivation, which in turn affects job performance and, consequently, an employee's promotability.[8] Support for Bray's position was found in this study. For example, managers who believe that they are performing their jobs as effectively as possible are more likely to respond that their jobs contain desired work-design elements to a larger extent than are those who believe they are not performing their jobs as effectively as possible. Thus, for selfish reasons alone—that is, productivity and efficiency—corporations should be concerned about work design.

A final impetus to improving work design comes from employees' demands for fairer and better performance appraisals, potential evaluation, as well as training-and-development programs and career-planning procedures. The sine qua non for each and every one of these procedures is proper work design. Properly designed work is the basic prerequisite for both the development and utilization of managerial talent.

In sum, work design is becoming increasingly important not only to maintain and improve the morale and health of the employee body but also to maintain the efficiency and productivity of the corporation.

Key Elements to Properly Designed Work

J. Richard Hackman and E.E. Lawler have developed a job model with *core dimensions*. These core dimensions usually include having a large and complete piece of work with an identifiable beginning and end and requiring the utilization of varied tasks and varied skills. The work is performed in a consistent working relationship with an identifiable client, user, customer, geographic area, issue area, or type of equipment. The manager has the authority to make decisions concerning work functions and receives direct, individual, and specific job-performance information that comes through the work itself.[9]

Richard Peterson and Bruce Duffany added that the complete piece of work, "resulting in a product—preferably the largest product possible for the employee . . . is, in effect, the foundation for developing the other characteristics of a well-designed job."[10]

In analyzing Hackman and Lawler, Denis Umstot et al. noted that the data strongly reinforced the fact that employees who have jobs with the core work-design dimensions are more-satisfied and are more-productive producers of high-quality work than those employees who don't have these core dimensions in their jobs.[11]

Participating Managers' Overall Views
of Work-Design Factors in Their Jobs

The findings in this study clearly support the proposition that proper work design is a powerful motivator of managers. In order to analyze the managers' opinions of their work, questions were asked about the extent to which six major work-design components are present in their jobs:

1. Extent to which the job involves doing a whole and identifiable piece of work;
2. Extent to which a variety of skills and talents are needed on the job;
3. Extent to which managers have a consistent relationship with the receivers of their work;
4. Extent to which managers have autonomy on the job;
5. Extent to which the job itself provides feedback about work performance;
6. Extent to which the work is significant or important.

The responses of the vast majority of the managers in the present study indicate moderate to high levels of satisfaction with these basic components. As table 8-1 shows, the percentage of respondents who respond "very much"—that is, 6 or 7—ranges from 46 to 71 percent.

As a composite analysis of the work design, 61 percent of the managers rate their jobs as above average—that is, 6 or 7—on at least five of the six questions. White men (71 percent) are most likely to give high ratings on at least five work-design questions. The level of satisfaction for this group is consistent with its level of satisfaction in other areas with corporate provisions, other than AAP. See figure 8-1 for all race/sex-group responses.

Only among white men do significant level differences exist in response by managerial level. Lower-level white men are less likely than upper-level white men are to answer that their jobs contain, to a large extent, five or more positive work-design elements:

First level	59%
Second level	60%
Third level	73%
Fourth level	80%
Fifth level	88%
Sixth level	100%

White men at lower levels respond similarly to other lower-level managers, while white men at upper levels are much-more satisfied with their work design then their minority and female peers are. Part of this difference can be attributed to the fact that minorities and women at higher levels are much-more likely to be in staff than in line positions. Managers in staff jobs are usually less satisfied about the six factors than managers in line jobs are.

Another interesting finding is that larger percentages of men than women in each ethnic group responded with high ratings—that is, more of them rate their jobs high on at least five of the work-design elements. For example, 58 percent of the black men and 60 percent of the Hispanic men versus 52 percent of both Hispanic and black women rate their jobs high on at least five of the work-design elements. This may reflect the fact that men are more-frequently placed in line jobs and women in staff jobs.

Design quality is reflected in the finding that 56 percent of the managers who hold line jobs versus 36 percent who hold staff jobs rate their job 7, or extremely high, on consistent working relationships. This finding is not surprising since staff managers' products or services are likely to be received by a large, somewhat vaguely identifiable group without much personal interface. In addition, Benson Rosen and Thomas Jerdee have demonstrated that male subjects, given identical background information for a male and

Table 8-1
Managers' Perceptions of Work-Design Features in Their Jobs
(percent)

To What Extent Does Your Job Include Specific Work Design Features? (N = 4,183)	Design Features					
	Significance or Importance of Job	Consistent Work Relationships	Variety in the Job	Information on Work Performance	Autonomy on the Job	Doing a Whole Piece of Work
Very little 1	1.4	6.2	2.9	1.2	2.2	2.3
2	1.8	2.5	2.3	1.3	1.9	2.7
3	3.3	2.6	3.8	2.7	2.8	5.4
Moderate 4	10.1	15.2	13.5	16.3	20.3	23
5	12.4	7.9	12.1	18.4	19.5	20.3
6	22.3	14.4	22.8	28.6	21.2	18.5
Very much 7	48.8	51.2	42.6	31.3	32	27.8

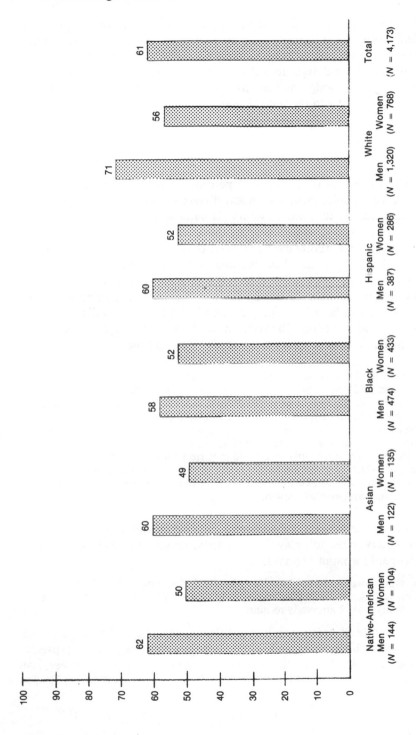

Figure 8-1. Percentage of Managers Who Say Five or Six Work-Design Elements Are Present to a Large Extent in Their Jobs

female candidate for particularly demanding and complex positions, selected women significantly less frequently than men.[12] These more-complex positions are, of course, likely to rate higher on the core dimensions of good work design. In order to understand more completely the key elements of work design and the managers' responses, these elements are discussed more fully in the following sections.

Variety in the Job

Variety in the job ranks high for 65 percent of the respondents. They feel that their jobs require them to do many different things and to use a number of different skills and talents. Twenty-six percent describe their jobs as having moderate variety, while 9 percent think that their jobs require them to do the same routine things over and over. In studying attempts to enrich the variety in jobs, researchers have warned that such efforts might only make work more burdensome rather than more interesting if workers are merely given a greater number of boring tasks.[13] Similarly, assigning additional responsibilities without increasing the breadth of functions will probably increase job dissatisfaction. The relationship between the type of variety and the elements of satisfaction is discussed by Pamela Steen:

> Variety can be built into the work either through functional completeness or direct and consistent situation, or in some cases, both. If it is built in through a functionally large piece of work, more skills will be required, and there will be more opportunity for work-related growth. Learning more of the work in one job will, compared with functionally narrow jobs, facilitate career pathing and upward mobility, particularly for women and/or minorities. The alternative is to build in variety through the second dimension, in which case the job holder might perform a smaller group of tasks for a wider variety of customers, areas, etc. In this case there is less opportunity for work-related growth.[14]

Many of the managers made comments about the important role that proper variety in the job plays in their attitudes and motivation. A second-level Hispanic woman observes:

> Six months ago I told my boss I was dissatisfied with my job. I did not find it interesting or challenging enough. He fixed that! Any lousy project he sends my way. I am ready to quit!

A second-level Asian man had a different experience. During a performance review, his boss asked him his feelings about his job. He expressed concerns that initially the job had tasked all his capabilities. However, now he feels he has mastered the job and is looking for new challenges. He further relates:

My boss and I reviewed the organization chart and the future direction of the design. He decided on certain changes. While maintaining my present responsibilities, I am also the coordinator of our reorganization efforts and how we can better interface with other departments. Since I know very little about other departments, I have a big task ahead of me. I am not complaining. I am just stating a fact. It is a big but challenging task.

A Whole, Identifiable Job

The factor eliciting the most-negative response from the managers surveyed is whether jobs involve doing a whole and identifiable piece of work. This negative response is unfortunate since this dimension is the most-basic element of well-designed work. Table 8-2 indicates that only 46 percent respond that their jobs involve doing a whole piece of work from start to finish. Forty-three percent describe their jobs as a moderate-sized segment of the overall piece of work, indicating that they are responsible for and make decisions about a portion of a work flow for which others are also responsible. Ten percent describe their jobs as only a small part of the overall piece of work and say the results of their activities are not readily identifiable with a final product or service. A first-level Hispanic woman describes the small portion of a work flow for which she is responsible:

My job is not well defined. There is not enough to keep me busy and interested. . . . I plan to discuss the problem with my boss and get him to more-clearly define my job duties and goals so that I can feel I have done something worthwhile with my day.

A third-level white man who is 58 years old says:

I do not know what's happening to me, but my boss is slowly taking away some of my major responsibilities. My job before this process began was complete, now I don't know where it begins or ends. It changes every day. I think my boss figures I am too old to do a complete job. This saddens me, I have many good years left in me, and I want to do the best job I can for the company and myself.

If managers have only a portion of a whole job, how can their performance be determined accurately? How can they accurately get usable feedback from their job, and how does the company determine the skills required for the job? None of these things can be done in an objective fashion because fragmented or narrowly designed work can vary from day to day according to subjective determinants. The managers do not have the opportunities to make valuable contributions and often will be viewed as not very valuable themselves. All of these factors will eventually lead to job dissatisfaction, disengagement, and/or antisocial behavior.

Table 8-2
Job as a Whole and Identifiable Piece of Work
(percent)

To What Extent Does Your Job Involve Doing a Whole and Identifiable Piece of Work?	Native-American Men (N = 143)	Women (N = 103)	Asian Men (N = 121)	Women (N = 133)	Black Men (N = 470)	Women (N = 432)	Hispanic Men (N = 387)	Women (N = 284)	White Men (N = 1,267)	Women (N = 760)	Total (N = 4,124)
Very little 1	1.4	1.9	4.1	1.5	1.9	3.5	2.1	4.6	1.2	3.2	2.3
2	1.4	5.8	1.7	7.5	3	2.8	0.8	4.6	2	3	2.9
3	5.6	3.9	5.8	7.5	4.9	4.6	5.9	4.6	4.9	6.7	5.4
Moderate 4	24.5	34	19.8	20.3	23.4	30.1	22	26.1	19.4	23.3	23
5	24.5	21.4	14.9	26.3	20.9	22.7	16.8	21.5	19	20.7	20.1
6	13.3	15.5	31.4	13.5	18.5	11.1	23	13.7	22.2	16.2	18.4
Very much 7	29.4	17.5	22.3	23.3	27.4	25.2	29.5	25	31.3	27	27.8

Autonomy on the Job

In response to the question of autonomy on the job, table 8-3 shows that 53 percent of the managers respond that they have a great deal of autonomy—that is, the job gives them almost complete responsibility for deciding how and when the work is done. Forty-two percent say they have moderate autonomy. A white man at the fourth level notes:

> Many things are standardized and not under my control, but I can make some decisions about the work.

Seven percent state they have very little autonomy. A black man at the second level says:

> The job gives me almost no personal say about how and when the work is done.

The impression of inadequate decision-making power is not restricted to lower levels of management. For example, a sixth-level white man suggests:

> The company should increase managerial responsibility and restore decision making to lower levels. They should allow managers to manage, reduce paperwork and meet demands, and establish an atmosphere of calm.

A Hispanic man at the second level observes:

> The company is so large that most people are not allowed to use their own initiative to the fullest.

White men are the managers most likely to state that their jobs permit a great deal of autonomy. A larger percentage of men than women in each race group say that their jobs permit decision making to a large extent. For example, 65 percent of white men and 53 percent of Hispanic men as compared with 51 percent of white women and 46 percent of Hispanic women report they have a great deal of autonomy.

This finding may reflect not only that many more men than women are in powerful mainline positions but also that in any given position, men are given more power to act or thus take more power because of the feeling that men are expected to exercise judgment. It is probably still true that some women more than men are not fully confident in their abilities to manage and are thus reluctant to assume much decision making. It also seems still true women are often placed in positions reporting to bosses who are intimidated by female managers' making decisions on their own. They are dis-

Table 8-3
Extent of Autonomy on the Job
(percent)

How Much Autonomy Do You Have in Your Job? To What Extent Does Your Job Permit You to Decide on Your Own How to Go About Doing the Work?	Native-American		Asian		Black		Hispanic		White		Total
	Men (N = 144)	Women (N = 104)	Men (N = 122)	Women (N = 134)	Men (N = 471)	Women (N = 433)	Men (N = 387)	Women (N = 284)	Men (N = 1,314)	Women (N = 766)	(N = 4,159)
Very little 1	0.7	4.8	0	3	2.8	3.5	3.9	3.2	1	2	2.7
2	2.8	0	6.6	1.5	3	2.8	2.1	1.4	1.1	1.8	1.9
3	3.5	1.9	3.3	3	3.8	2.3	2.6	1.8	2.7	2.9	2.8
Moderate 4	22.2	31.7	17.2	28.4	21.9	28.2	18.3	29.2	13.7	20.9	20.2
5	17.4	15.4	23.8	20.1	22.9	21.7	19.9	18.7	16.7	21	19.3
6	16.7	16.3	21.3	16.4	20.6	12.5	20.9	16.2	27.5	20.2	21.1
Very much 7	36.8	29.8	27.9	27.6	25.1	29.1	32.3	29.6	37.2	31.2	32

turbed by women's making decisions without consulting them and more disturbed if female subordinates present positions not in agreement with theirs. The difference between the attitudes of white men and women decreases at upper levels, indicating that women at higher levels take and are permitted to take greater autonomy than are those at lower levels.

White men at lower levels are almost as likely as minorities at lower levels to feel that they have only moderate to very little autonomy on the job. For example, 54 percent of the black men at most levels respond in this manner compared to 47 percent of the white men at lower levels. At the fourth level and above, the figures for managers who feel they have very much autonomy are 53 percent for black men and 82 percent for white men. Thus, as white men move up the corporate ladder, they are more likely than their minority counterparts are to be given more autonomy in doing their job. This is not surprising when one recalls that many white managers, especially those at upper levels, do not believe minorities have the background to be effective managers. A third-level black man points out:

> There are decisions my Anglo peers can make without my boss's approval. However, I must check most of my decisions with him. If I don't, I am in trouble. Frankly, I believe he has problems with blacks. What else can I think, my results are the best of his subordinates.

Regardless of race-sex-level differences, almost half the managers believe they have moderate to very little autonomy in doing their work. These responses are connected to responses on the most-basic dimension—a whole and identifiable piece of work. Without this dimension, managers cannot control a meaningful end result. In many cases, the managers will be viewed as not being able or willing to make decisions, when in fact they have no opportunity. Even with a whole piece of work but without autonomy, they have only minimal to moderate control over a major portion of their daily lives.

Job Provides Feedback

Another dimension of work design is assessed via the question: "Does your job provide you with feedback on your performance, in addition to any feedback co-workers or supervisors may provide?" This question measures whether the job itself is set up so that frequent feedback on individual job performance is available to the manager. This component of work design is, of course, the one that permits the performer to adjust his or her performance in the direction indicated by the feedback before year-end, or major output failure can possibly occur. This component ranks high by 60 percent of the managers, moderate by 35 percent, and low by 5 percent.

While very important to all managers, this aspect of work design can prove particularly critical for minorities and women. Many of the minority and women respondents report feeling that their peers, bosses, and subordinates question their ability to handle their jobs and label them as "quota fillers." These reactions undermine self-confidence and weaken self-images. Work designed to provide objective reinforcement or critical feedback can automatically neutralize the negative subjective effects of labeling by prejudiced and doubtful bosses and co-workers.

Significance and Importance of Work

A larger percentage of managers rated the significance of importance of the job higher than any other work dimension. When asked, "To what extent are the results of your work likely to significantly affect the lives or well-being of other people?", 71 percent of the managers describe their jobs as highly significant and as affecting other people in very important ways. Twenty-three percent say their jobs are moderately significant, and only 6 percent report that their jobs are not very significant. More native-American women (80 percent) and white men (78 percent) rate their jobs higher than other groups. Fewer Asian women (59 percent) and Hispanic women (59 percent) are likely to concur.

Surveys of both college students and working adults have identified this component as one of, if not the most-important, aspects of a job. In the Detroit-area surveys of 1958 and 1971, respondents in both studies named this dimension as being most significant.[15] In another survey of college students in 1975, respondents identified the two major influences on their choice of a career as the "challenge of the job" (77 percent) and the "opportunity to make a meaningful contribution" (72 percent).[16]

It is important to note that the attitude toward the importance of the job is influenced by the extent to which the core dimensions exist in the work as well as by other contextual factors. It is not a directly manipulatable element of design, but it is the element most-directly related to how the worker views him or herself and perhaps because of this, tends to be the most-highly rated aspect of work.

Work Design and Work Performance—
A Direct Relationship

From the standpoint of the corporation, of course, the most-important issue is performance. Effective managerial performance is the desired end result of whatever the company does in the name of meeting its obligations under the unwritten employer/employee contract. Thus, the relationship between work design and performance ought to be a motivating factor for the corporation.

This study produced data that strongly suggest that properly designed work will result in better job performance than poorly designed work will. For example, a relationship exists between the performance ratings of managers and how they rank their jobs on being a whole and identifiable piece of work. Of those managers who say their jobs are a whole and identifiable piece of work, 55 percent receive outstanding performance ratings, 45 percent receive completely satisfactory performance ratings, and 20 percent receive less-than-satisfactory ratings. Conversely, this would mean that 80 percent of the managers who receive a less-than-satisfactory rating do not rank their jobs very high in being a whole and identifiable piece of work. A manager who has responsibility for a whole and identifiable work flow can evaluate his or her job performance and be evaluated more effectively than one who cannot. Thus, he or she is better able to adjust to performance methods, and this in turn leads to better performance for the corporation.

If a manager has responsibility for a whole and identifiable piece of work and high performance ratings, a number of positive benefits accrue to all concerned. Bosses and subordinates can clearly define substantive responsibility, agree on what is expected, and base performance evaluations on meeting significant goals rather than on less-meaningful, less-objective criteria. Of managers reporting their job responsibilities as well defined, 75 percent rate the job high as a whole piece of work. Only 35 percent who rate their job responsibilities as well defined also view their job as not being a whole piece of work.

The positive correlation between performance rating and autonomy was even more pronounced—62 percent of managers who were rated outstanding, 50 percent who were rated completely satisfactory, and 21 percent who were rated less than satisfactory rate their jobs very high on autonomy. Except for those few less-capable managers who are unable to learn to make reasonable decisions, these figures mean that managers who have the autonomy to run their jobs as they see fit are more likely to perform at a high level and to be rated higher than those who do not have the autonomy. When given autonomy to run one's own job, an individual's creativity and unique skills blossom.

Analyzing the managers' responses as to what extent their jobs provide them feedback and whether or not they are performing their jobs as effectively as possible, managers who say their job provides them feedback are evidently more likely to also believe that they are performing their jobs as effectively as possible. For example, approximately 60 percent of the managers who rate their job very high on feedback say they are performing their job as effectively as possible. This compares with 49 percent who rate their jobs moderately high and 40 percent who rate their jobs low in providing feedback who also say they are performing their job as effectively as possible.

Automatic, unfiltered feedback is both more objective and more timely. Whether it results in managers' taking corrective action or pursuing the original course with increased confidence, they are better able to perform with optimal effectiveness.

Conclusions and Recommendations

Several major conclusions can be drawn from this chapter. One conclusion is that women consistently rate their jobs lower on work-design characteristics than do men from the same race group. This information suggests that men, regardless of race, are favored in being placed in well-designed jobs. Another conclusion is that lower-level white men respond quite similarly to their level peers from the other race/sex groups. However, middle- and upper-level white men rate their jobs consistently higher than their minority and female peers do. This information suggests that either minorities and women at middle and upper levels are placed in jobs that are not in the mainstream of the corporate organization or that racist and sexist bosses are not providing those minority and women subordinates in mainline jobs with well-designed work.

A final point is that all of the data presented in this chapter lead to the conclusion that properly designed work definitely affects the managers' motivation to do their jobs as effectively as possible (see table 8-4). The table is made up of the responses of only those managers who indicate that lack of motivation is one of the factors preventing them from doing their job as effectively as possible. A much-higher percentage of managers who rate their jobs low on these factors of variety, whole piece of work, and

Table 8-4
Managers Who Say They Lack Motivation and How They Rate Certain Aspects of Their Job
(percent)

How Managers Rate Their Job for Each Work-Design Dimension	Variety	Whole Piece of Work	Autonomy
Low	54	33	42
Moderate	28	24	22
High	20	19	20

autonomy also indicate that they are not performing their job as effectively as possible, in part because of lack of motivation. For example, 42 percent of the managers who rate their job low on autonomy, compared to 20 percent who rate their jobs high, say their lack of motivation negatively affects their effective job performance. These data support Bray's conclusion that the nature of the job has a strong effect on motivation, which affects job performance, which in turn affects corporate productivity and profitability.

However, properly designed work is not the sole element that makes up the nature of the job. It is simply the beginning. The quality of the work design in terms of core dimensions forms the foundation of a management system. Work design has a relationship not only to performance but also to potential for advancement and the ultimate ability of both the corporation and the employee to meet the shifting terms of their mutual contract.

Figure 8-2 outlines the relationship of work design to the aspects of an integrated management system. Work functions are designed or redesigned into functionally complete entities with consistent relationships (A). The design process is applied layer by layer, from the basic work level to the top of the organization. The power to act (B) is then defined for the functions in each job. These decisions may be phased into the job according to a plan that identifies when the manager is ready. The skills and knowledge (C) necessary to performing each set of functions/decisions will emerge during this process and should be documented. All of this information is essential to the establishment of substantive, measurable objectives (D), by which performance can be evaluated (E), and for which training can be planned (F).

The design of work at each layer of the organization (A) is also essential to determining the skills and abilities to be evaluated (C) as demonstrating potential for advancement. Without this step, the potential to perform at the next level will be based on performance at the current level—in Peter-Principle fashion—and/or on the subjective assessments of managers at the next levels who got to those levels for the same reasons.

Training and development (F) can then be planned for managers' demonstrating the potential to perform at the next level (C), so that the potential can ultimately be realized. With these steps, the foundation will have been laid for a career-planning process (G).

The management system outlined is of course intended to properly utilize managers toward corporate-performance objectives. As the next chapters demonstrate, the effectively developed system fosters the satisfaction to remain with the company, as long as monetary rewards and working conditions are seen as adequate and fair.

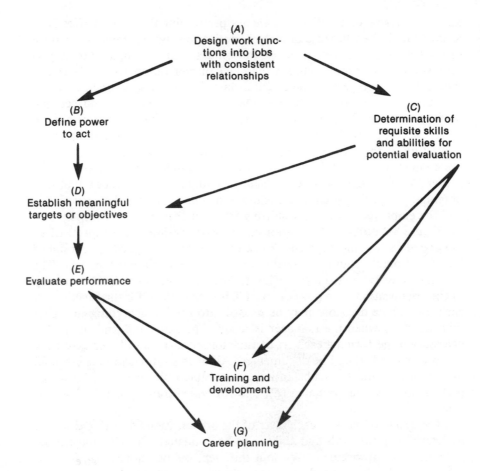

Figure 8-2. A Systematic Managerial-Development System

9

Performance Evaluation

In the past, managers who wished to live at peace in their company would accept, without question, any performance rating their bosses gave them, if they gave any at all, and certainly without complaint. In the present, one prerequisite to the equitable treatment demanded by the new breed of managers is accurate, objective performance evaluations based upon job performance. This performance basis is in contrast with evaluations based on personality, appearance, race, sex, age, managerial level, and other nonobjective criteria.

Performance evaluation is a concept central to effective management and to success as a manager. As such, it has three main functions: (1) to provide adequate feedback to each person about his or her performance, (2) to serve as a basis for modifying or changing behavior when more-effective work habits are desired, and (3) to provide data that bosses may use to plan and estimate future job assignments and compensation.[1]

Unfortunately, these objectives are rarely achieved. First of all, performance evaluations are usually emotionally charged processes for both subordinates and bosses. Thus, in many cases one or the other or both do not enter the process as objectively as they should. Second, it requires formal planning, excellent communications skills, and tact. For managers skilled at the process, it is a time-consuming and potentially stressful experience. Evidence shows that even many skilled managers who think evaluation is a beneficial process would nevertheless avoid it if possible. For managers lacking effective training and the necessary skills, the task can assume nightmarish qualities. These managers find it frustrating, depressing, and threatening to allocate time for an activity for which they feel incompetent. Given the opportunity, they will easily rationalize and indefinitely delay performance evaluations in favor of tackling more-immediate and "urgent" tasks.

Research done on performance appraisals supports these statements. Porter, Lawler, and Hackman found defensiveness by both subordinates and bosses. In many cases they indicated that invalid or misleading data were used in evaluations. They observed bureaucratic behavior—that is, the rules of superiors and subordinates—played out to such an extent that the performance evaluations were just rituals.[2] Paul Thompson and Gene Dalton cited the "performance curve" as an example of how formal procedures are often used in a way that actually subverts the performance-evaluation process, in this instance by fitting people inappropriately to arbitrary standards such as placing limits on how many managers can receive outstanding ratings.[3]

No matter how well defined responsibilities, objectives, and means of measurements are, judgments on performance are usually subjective and impressionistic because information about the manner and difficulty of meeting the objective is inadequate.[4] In addition, different managers apply different standards. What is considered excellent work in one department may be rated unacceptable in another department. Finally, evaluating the performance of managers becomes increasingly difficult as they move up the corporate ladder. The impact of broad, general decisions cannot be accurately perceived or evaluated because of the interactive effect of other decisions. Many of these decisions, the real impact of which cannot be objectively evaluated for years, must be judged on projected results rather than on actual results. Therefore, subjective criteria normally play a more-important role in performance evaluation at higher levels of management than at lower levels.

Despite these problems and pitfalls, the performance-evaluation process is becoming increasingly recognized as having tremendous potential influence on intrinsic and extrinsic work motivations. When implemented correctly, it results in mutually advantageous goal setting between employees and their companies. These goals in turn can be used by bosses as bases for counseling and for helping subordinates improve performance through understanding their strong and weak points. They also assist subordinates in evaluating their own performance. Self-evaluation allows subordinates to make necessary performance corrections without their bosses' input and before their performance reaches any critically negative point.

Performance appraisals are valuable tools for boosting self-esteem and building individual skills. As such, they are valuable for all employees, but particularly for those who may feel isolated or anxious. The split perception of many women and minorities about the legitimacy of their jobs—that they have been given a quota position but also are fully competent to perform the job—causes much anxiety that could be relieved by a precise, objective performance evaluation.

Not only can positive assessments improve self-images, but also they may influence the reaction of co-workers. It has been demonstrated that similar work, regardless of the sex of the worker, receives similar evaluations only when the assessors believe the work has already been sanctioned "a winner" by other judges presumed to be qualified. Without this sanctioning, identical work by a man is rated higher than work performed by a woman. The judgment of implicitly qualified others influences performance appraisal more than the sex of the persons being evaluated does.[5] While this study focused on the role of sex, numerous managers in this study have seen the same interaction with regard to race. A Hispanic man at the second level points out:

> I had the privilege to have an Hispanic boss. He was very understanding about the additional problems Hispanics have in white corporations. However, because of his Anglo bosses' views about his ability, it was very difficult for him to get me a high rating. My new white-male boss, who is viewed as a "comer," has had much more success. After three years of outstanding performance, I finally received an outstanding rating.

Performance-Appraisal Systems in the Participating Companies

What do participating managers believe are the good and bad points about their companies' performance-evaluation procedures? Few differences exist between the responses of managers whose companies are in the process of implementing or had recently implemented new plans and the responses of managers whose companies had performance-appraisal plans that have been used for years. The old plans are very subjective and are not systematic. The new plans are based on Management by Objectives (MBO), which is very systematic and supposedly very objective. The following pages show that lack of systematic, objective implementation causes the similarity in responses to both the old, subjective plans and the new, objective plans.

Seventy-three percent of the managers report that they had received a performance appraisal within the past year. The responses range from 88 percent of Asian women and 82 percent of Asian men to 66 percent of native-American women and 68 percent of white men. Significant differences exist among management levels for the white, Hispanic, and black men. At the upper levels of management, white men are less likely to report that they received a performance appraisal within the past year. For example, 56 percent of white men at the fifth level and above compared to 73 percent at the first level had received a recent appraisal. This could be due to the fact that upper management belongs to the club and club members know where they stand when they get their raises. In addition, to request a formal performance appraisal not voluntarily given by the boss is against club etiquette.

For Hispanic and black men, the opposite is true. A larger percentage of upper-level than of lower-level Hispanic and black men report that they received a recent performance appraisal. For example, 84 percent of Hispanic men at the third level and above, compared to 71 percent below the third level had received an appraisal within the past year. Negative and positive explanations can be suggested for this difference. One possible negative explanation is that Hispanic and black men are more likely to receive formal appraisals because they are not part of the club and thus must be evaluated to justify their rating, which is frequently lower than that of white men. Several positive explanations could be that the companies are more conscientious about giving Hispanic and black men performance evaluations in order to develop them and to make certain they are being treated fairly.

While the overall figure (73 percent) is impressive, it should be pointed out that more than one out of four managers did *not* receive a performance appraisal in the past year. Further, many of those who did receive them are not pleased with their evaluations.

Objectivity of Performance Appraisals

Of those managers who received performance appraisals, 27 percent believe the performance-evaluation procedures used to evaluate them are very objective, 44 percent believe they are somewhat objective, 16 percent state they are not very objective, and 7 percent state they do not know. Black men are least likely (62 percent) and Asian women are most likely (78 percent) to state that the procedures used in evaluating their performance are at least somewhat objective.

While the majority believes the procedures to be at least somewhat objective, further analyses show that the managers are more critical than the previous response might indicate. The explanations that accompanied the somewhat-objective category are often closer in content to the not-very-objective explanations than to the very-objective ones. For example, a first-level black woman who feels her performance appraisals are very objective says:

> The boss uses targets and accomplishments. Speaks to performance only and avoids irrelevant comments. Considers circumstances, improvement in performance, and individual effort, as well as ability to work effectively with subordinates.

A black first-level woman who believes her performance appraisal was somewhat objective comments:

> My boss uses daily performance results in evaluating me. The "figures" speak for themselves, but the circumstances surrounding them are not often taken into consideration or is any guidance given on how to improve. Thus, the appraisals are generally very superficial.

A third-level white woman who says her performance appraisal is not very objective sounds similar:

It is a summary of past accomplishments but does not speak to the quality
of each accomplishment. Gives one total level of performance. Repeats
what I already know. Does not help toward future improvement.

From these comments one can conclude that, while slightly more than
one out of four managers believe that their performance appraisals are very
objective, the majority of managers indicate they are not because of the inclusion of subjective data in their appraisals and/or the exclusion of objective data and constructive criticism.

Table 9-1 shows the managers' responses on the objectivity of the procedures. The two major reasons the managers believe performance-
appraisal procedures are objective are (1) that they are based on clearly
defined objectives, results, and accomplishments that are mutually agreed
upon by boss and subordinate (16 percent), and (2) that they are
characterized by the boss's attempt to overcome his or her personal opinions (14 percent). The major reason the procedures are considered not objective is that subjective opinions of immediate bosses overly influence the
evaluations (23 percent).

Discussing the positive aspects first, the response of a first-level Asian
woman represents reasons for the positive positions:

Each category is discussed fully. I have the opportunity to state how I see
my performance, determine to what extent I met or did not meet company
objectives. Upon completion I have no problem in accepting the final decision because I have had a part in determining my rating from the start.

A second-level Hispanic man concurred by saying:

The first step consists of agreement on job responsibilities, targets, and
measurements to be used. The second step consists of progress reviews and
quarterly discussions. The third step is a formal, job-related appraisal.

Overall, 34 percent of the managers believe that at least to some extent
their bosses follow the three key performance-evaluation elements of MBO.
These elements are (1) performance appraisals based upon meeting
measurable job objectives; (2) specific and useful appraisals, clear as to
what improvements are needed and how they might be affected; and (3)
managers' own estimates of their performance are taken into consideration
by bosses. Black men, who are least likely to believe their performance
evaluations are objective, are also least likely to respond that their bosses
adhere to the MBO criteria (27 percent). Asians, who are most likely to say
their performance evaluations are objective, are most likely to say their
bosses use the three key procedures (46 percent). Between 34 percent and 38
percent of the other race/sex groups respond similarly.

Table 9-1
Objectivity of Performance Evaluations
(percent)

Please Explain Your Opinion of The Degree of Objectivity of the Procedure Your Boss Uses in Evaluating Your Performance.	Total (N = 3,477)
Referring to Boss	
Evaluation is overly influenced by the subjective opinions of the immediate boss.	23
Boss attempts to overcome personal opinions and render an objective appraisal.	13.6
Evaluation is too general. It does not entail specific feedback or explanation.	5.3
Boss is not sufficiently aware of daily working situation or subordinate's particular contributions.	5.3
Boss is sufficiently aware of daily working situation or subordinate's particular contributions.	2.7
Respondent agrees with boss's assessment.	0.9
Referring to Objectives	
Evaluation is based on clearly defined objectives, results, and accomplishments that were mutually agreed upon by boss and subordinate.	15.8
Evaluation is based on meeting objectives, but mitigating circumstances are not taken into account.	5.3
Objectives are not mutually agreed upon, and no specific objectives are set.	4
Nature of the work does not lend itself to clearly defined objectives. Thus, it is difficult to measure accomplishments.	3.4
Referring to Plan/Procedures	
Performance-evaluation procedures are inherently subjective.	5.1
Guidelines are vague and the procedures are not extensive and sufficiently inclusive.	4.2
Objectivity of procedure is severely curtailed by application of the bell curve and its relationship to salary treatment.	4
Respondent is unaware of procedures.	3.4
Other.	4

More-systematic, quantitative data vividly reinforce the view that managers are more likely to believe that their performance evaluations are very objective when they receive explanations and useful feedback on their performance evaluation, are in agreement with their bosses on performance expectations, have communicated their own estimates on performance, and feel their bosses closely follow the company procedures.

Table 9-2 shows the high correlation between the managers' views of objectivity and the extent to which their bosses give useful feedback. On the one hand, 54 percent of the managers who rate the appraisal procedure as very objective say that their bosses give them a great amount of specific and useful feedback that clearly states improvements needed and how they might be affected. On the other hand, 2 percent of the managers who say the performance-evaluation procedure is very objective say their bosses do not give them these types of feedback.

The fact that 77 percent of the managers who rate the appraisal procedure as very objective say that their bosses follow the company procedures very closely, compared to only 37 percent who rate it as somewhat objective and say that their bosses follow the procedure very closely, indicates that the problem may not lie as much in formal company procedures as in how they are implemented. Only about 10 percent of the managers make statements that indicate the procedures themselves are inherently subjective. However, many of them criticize the way the procedures are implemented. A native-American man at the third level observes, "We have an excellent performance-evaluation program on paper, but in practice, few people use it properly."

One major reason many bosses are unable to give objective performance evaluations is not entirely their fault. Many bosses say they are not properly trained in the techniques of performance evaluation, especially in providing constructive criticism. In fact, four in five believe they need training to effectively perform this essential management task. A third-level black man supports the need for training. He says:

> My supervisor has never reviewed objectives. Therefore, he has not modified or revised expectations for each of us. The job responsibilities seem to be all-encompassing and have never been discussed between us. I don't believe he is properly trained to or capable of establishing reasonable objectives or sticking with them if they were established mutually.

Many of the managers who are not properly trained attempt to avoid the process entirely. A second-level white woman makes these comments about her boss's avoidance of giving her an appraisal:

> Upper management should have some way of checking to be sure performance appraisals are being done. I worked for my previous boss for almost two years, and never once did he mention my appraisal, other than a token "nice job you're doing" at raise times. Why didn't I ask? Because two of the four people in our group asked every other month, it seemed, and got the response, "I know I have to do that for all of you, but I just can't find the time."

Table 9-2
Objectivity of Performance Evaluation Compared with Its Usefulness in Assessing Needed Improvements
(percent)

To What Extent Is Your Performance Evaluation Specific and Useful, Clear as to What Improvements Are Needed, and as to How They Might Be Effected?	How Objective Is the Procedure Your Boss Uses to Evaluate Your Performance					
	Very Objective (N = 1,013)	Somewhat Objective (N = 1,621)	Not Very Objective (N = 593)	Not at All Objective (N = 176)	Do Not Know (N = 238)	Total (N = 3,641)
To a great extent	53.6	16.2	3.9	6.8	12.6	23.9
To some extent	37	53.1	30	16.5	41.2	42.3
To a slight extent	7.2	23.7	45.5	29	25.2	23
Not at all	2.2	7	20.6	47.7	21	10.7

Another reason performance-evaluation procedures are not implemented properly is the difficulty in identifying and measuring the
discrete components of job performance in some jobs. A second-level white
woman comments:

> Staff-type jobs in many cases are almost impossible to set objectives for.
> Therefore, the performance is based on the good-will of the boss.

A third-level Hispanic woman who has been on staff jobs for ten years concurs:

> I have tried to establish reasonable objectives with my subordinates based
> on their responsibilities, but is is very difficult because many of our func-
> tions are long term and you might not see the results for a few years. How
> does one accurately measure the results? In addition, we serve so many dif-
> ferent clients with their own game plan, it is hard to tell what impact we are
> having, if any.

One problem managers do have with the specific procedures in some of
the companies is the *forced* distribution of the ratings. Only 25 percent of
the managers can be rated more than satisfactory, and in some cases 15 percent must be rated limited or less than satisfactory. A second-level native-
American man says:

> My main beef is this: If I supervise and evaluate 100 assembly-line workers,
> I have a large subordinate group to consider and can use all the textbook
> techniques of the bell curve. However, this is not often, if ever the case in
> appraising the performance of managers. The imposition of the bell-curve
> concept on small work groups is not fair or meaningful in this context and
> leads to inequities.

One of the major problems that forced distribution creates is that once a
manager is rated outstanding or more than satisfactory, it is very difficult to
have him or her reclassified as performing at less than these ratings. This
difficulty occurs especially for the longer-term employees, many of whom
received their high ratings because of long associations with their bosses or
their bosses' supervisors. An outstanding short-term employee has a very
difficult time breaking the "satisfactory" barrier. Regardless of who gets
what rating, when managers are constrained by the artificial distribution of
the bell curve and are forced to give or accept an inappropriate low rating,
they may become negative or cynical.

One positive aspect of the bell-shaped curve with its forced distribution
is that it makes for more-equitable distribution of performance ratings
among various departments and divisions. As will be seen, this is especially

helpful in giving minorities and women who are concentrated in specific departments or divisions better opportunities for high ratings.

These three factors—lack of training, the problem of establishing targets and measurements on certain jobs, and the forced distribution of ratings—are not the only source of subjective evaluations. Even where these are not problems, subjectivity plays a major role in performance appraisal because of personal values and views. It is apparently difficult for many managers to recognize and admit that all human beings are subjective. Each manager has certain likes and dislikes that influence performance evaluations. A fourth-level white man notes:

> The company procedures are clear as to how to evaluate, but the boss presents a subjective narrative rather than recognizing actual results obtained versus agreed-upon objectives.

A second-level Hispanic man comments:

> On my last appraisal my boss chose to include comments based on rumor (feedback) which were very uncomplimentary, and his boss chose to keep those comments in the appraisal. That was not fair."

A first-level Asian man says:

> Although recently job descriptions were made available, they are seldom used as criteria for evaluation by management. Rather, other areas weigh heavily in ultimate performance ratings . . . specifically if you fall into the good-guy category.

Finally, a fourth-level white man describes his dilemma this way:

> My last appraisal was three-and-a-half years ago. It read like the books of Matthew, Mark, Luke, and John, but the rating came out as if I was Pontius Pilate. His response to my intense question, "How can I improve my rating?" was, "Just keep working hard and we'll see next year." Next year never came.

In brief, this section provided considerable evidence that the main problem with performance evaluations is not with the procedures themselves but with the manner in which they are implemented.

It is crucial for all managers to recognize and admit to the inherent human subjectiveness in the evaluation process. Only by consciously working against personal prejudices and biases will the performance-evaluation process have some semblance of objectivity. Performance-evaluation procedures are only as useful to both the corporation and the employee as their implementation is objective and faithful.

Performance Rating and the Impact of Race

Many times managers receive a performance evaluation and are shocked when they are advised of their actual rating. As table 9-3 shows, of those managers who have had performance appraisals, more than one out of five do not know their rating. Asian women constitute the group of managers with the highest overall performance ratings, and the black men have the lowest overall performance ratings. Illustrative of this point is that 22 percent of the Asian women versus 5 percent of the black men receive outstanding performance ratings.

These findings might indicate that racism is playing a more-crucial role in the black men's evaluations than it does in other race/sex groups, and other data lend substance to this statement. For example, upper-level black men are more likely than lower-level black men are to report receiving ratings of completely satisfactory, satisfactory/fair, or limited/unsatisfactory. Except in one case, second level, the opposite is true of white men:

Black men		White men	
First level	47%	First level	56%
Second level	48%	Second level	45%
Third level	58%	Third level	49%
Fourth level +	66%	Fouth level	47%
		Fifth level	40%
		Sixth level	17%

Another example is that 20 percent of the third-level black men versus 37 percent of the third-level white men are rated more than satisfactory or outstanding. At the fourth level and above, 18 percent of black men were given similar ratings compared to 34 pecent of white men. A third-level black man says:

> I was given a superior rating in October 1976, when formally appraised, but was told in March 1977 that I wouldn't receive an increase based on superior performance because I had a "bad attitude." It was never explained when my attitude turned "bad" or what constituted this state.

A fourth-level black man relates:

> I could and do get the best results of my peer group, but I have never been rated more than completely satisfactory. I guess whites don't believe blacks can be above average.

The differences in ratings between upper- and lower-level black men and between black and white men are consistent with the findings of a

Table 9-3
Managers' Most-Recent Performance Ratings
(percent)

What Was Your Last Performance Rating?	Native-American		Asian		Black		Hispanic		White		Total
	Men (N = 142)	Women (N = 104)	Men (N = 120)	Women (N = 132)	Men (N = 462)	Women (N = 424)	Men (N = 381)	Women (N = 280)	Men (N = 1,279)	Women (N = 756)	(N = 4,080)
Outstanding/ exceptional/superior	11.3	13.5	15	22	5.2	6.6	12.6	7.5	12	10.4	10.6
More than satisfactory	24.6	18.3	23.3	25.8	21.4	26.4	25.2	28.9	24.5	23.7	24.4
Completely satisfactory	35.9	35.6	34.2	33.3	40.9	44.6	31.8	34.3	37.1	43.4	38.9
Satisfactory/fair	8.5	6.7	7.5	0.8	7.8	4.2	3.7	5.7	4.4	3.3	4.8
Limited/unsatisfactory	0	0	0	0	0.4	0	0.8	0	0.3	0	0.2
Do not know	19.7	26	20	18.2	24.2	18.2	26	23.6	21.7	19.2	21.1

1974 study on the effects of race as determinants of ratings by potential employers in a simulated work-sampling task. Findings indicated that homogeneous-worker populations may be necessary for actual production records to be successfully substituted for subjective rating. A systematic bias was found in the higher ratings given to performers of the same race. Blacks received distinctly higher ratings from supervisors of their own ethnic group than from white supervisors, and white employees obtained higher supervisory ratings from white evaluators on overall job performance than did black employees.[6] The possibility of actual differences in objective measures of job performance was ruled out in the study since objective criteria were established.

The fact that blacks received lower ratings than whites did from white raters when performance levels were identical indicates a potentially serious problem in racial bias. In most industrial settings, the supervisors are predominantly white, and therefore, if the results of the laboratory studies are supported by future investigations, it would mean that the use of performance evaluations, if improperly administered, could discriminate unfairly against black employees.

A further finding from a study by Clay Hamner et al., and supported by evidence in this study, was that the differential-criterion bias was especially prevalent from the high-performing black applicant. A statistically significant tendency favors high-performing whites over high-performing blacks, while at the same time favoring low-performing blacks over low-performing whites.[7] Each applicant was rated on a scale of 1 to 15, with 1 being the lowest possible rating. On the overall task-performance scale, low-performing black workers and high-performing black workers were both rated as average workers (7.31 versus 8.89), while low-performing white workers were rated below average (5.63), and high-performing white workers were rated better than average (10.36).

The inability of whites to differentiate among performance levels of blacks, and whites' insistence that few, if any, blacks can be above average, has serious implications. For example, the high-performing black threatens the image held by whites of racial superiority and, therefore, must be overlooked or discredited. The high-performing white who reinforces the stereotype must be acknowledged and generously rewarded. The low-performing black gives whites the opportunity to paternally or benevolently lower the standards. Implicit in the evaluations is the belief, "Considering his or her race, isn't it marvelous that he or she can turn in even a fair job?" The low-performing white, like the high-performing black, threatens the rationalization of white racism. He or she may be subconsciously seen as a traitor to the system: "Since he or she is white, he or she must be performing poorly out of laziness, because we *know* he or she is capable! The low-performing white is harshly dealt with by the assessors. In short, the findings suggest that low-performing blacks are at an advantage and high-performing blacks at a disadvantage, as compared with whites.

Although the studies cited relate to blacks, many of the findings are likely to apply to a lesser extent to certain other minorities, especially those who are of mixed racial heritage, have a close physical resemblance to blacks, and are in nontraditional jobs for that particular minority group. The high percentage of Asian women rated outstanding probably relates to the fact that many of them are in the secretarial/managerial ranks, a traditional female-managerial force. How many bosses want their secretaries to feel unfairly treated?

Performance Rating and the Impact of Sex

In this study, little difference appears in the ratings of men and women. This finding is contrary to a number of studies that show that women are rated lower than men who accomplish the same task. The fact that most women in the participating companies are in traditional female settings and are performing traditional female jobs helps to explain in part why great differences in performance ratings do not appear between men and women. In addition, forced distribution of ratings—that is, only 25 percent in each department or division can be rated above completely satisfactory—makes certain that the distribution of ratings will be given more equally to men and women in this study's companies than to those in the companies in other studies.

Randall Schuller's conclusions support the former proposition. He noted the difficulties women will face as they move into nontraditional female-managerial jobs. He argued that society has classified jobs as "male" or "female." Management is considered a male job and nursing is considered a female job. Men who are managers and women who are nurses are *congruent* types. Female managers and male nurses are *incongruent* types. People who are in the traditional jobs dictated by society—that is, congruent-type jobs—will usually receive better performance evaluations than will those who are in noncongruent types because society perceives congruent-type abilities and skills to do those jobs as better than noncongruent types. Put another way, sex-role socialization has made society believe that men, not women, have the requisite abilities and skills to do managerial jobs. Thus, if a woman is in a managerial job, her performance will not be considered as effective or as good as a man's because of the sexist assumption that she does not possess the necessary skills and abilities. The converse would be true if a man were a nurse.[8]

One of the studies that found sex discrimination in performance appraisals was Kay Deaux and Tim Emswiller's evaluation of male and female ability.[9] They asked male and female college students to evaluate the intelligence and competence of one of four stimulus persons based on taped interviews. The sex of the subject, the sex of the stimulus person, and the level of competence (high or low) of the stimulus person were alternated. Highly competent men were evaluated significantly better than were highly competent women by both sexes.[10] In addition, the researchers found that men anticipated doing better than the person they evaluated on either a masculine or a feminine task, but women predicted a higher score for themselves only on the feminine task.[11] This finding supports the proposition that the rating differences in this book's study are small because the women are largely found in traditionally female jobs within predominantly female departments headed by female bosses.

Mary Cline et al. also produced some interesting findings. Forty-two male and forty-two female subjects selected from a large city, a small town, or a university campus were asked to evaluate four pen-and-ink sketches and four quotations. Two sketches and two quotations were associated with fictitious women's names while the other two were associated with fictitious men's names. Conclusions drawn from these data are pertinent to the current study. First, men devalued work produced by women relative to work produced by men. Second, women tended to devalue work produced by men relative to work produced by women. Third, the cross-sex devaluations were limited to the quotations and did not influence the evaluations of the sketches. Thus, the judges did not generalize prejudices across all types of work produced by the opposite sex. Finally, this patterning of results was found in populations drawn from three very different settings, suggesting that sexism exists in all of society's institutions.[12]

In brief, what these studies suggest is that sexism plays a crucial role in performance evaluation. They also concisely point out how sex-role socialization has not only had a negative effect on men's attitudes about women's performances but also on some women's attitudes toward their own performance and other women's performances. The primary reason the present study finds little difference in the performance evaluation of women is that the vast majority of the women work in female ghettos.

Actual Rating versus Desired Rating

When comparing the manager's responses as to what performance rating they believe they should receive with the ratings they did receive, the difference between the desired ratings and actual ratings of women are smaller than are those of men. Larwood and Wood posit an explanation for this finding. They said that if women are not "supposed" to have expectations in concert with their abilities, one might anticipate that their achievements, which are manifestations of their abilities, are often socially unacceptable.[13] As previously noted, the work of women is normally viewed as second rate compared to that of men, and indisputable achievments by women are thought to be unusual. Therefore, women scale down their opinion of their performance while men do the opposite.

Figure 9-1 shows that black and white men in this study exhibit the widest differences between their desired ratings and their actual ratings—that is, a 32 percent difference for black men, a 28 percent difference for white men. These figures suggest several possible interpretations. In the case of black men, not only are they usually rated lower than they think they merit, but also they are rated lower than any other group of managers. As one of the most-educated groups, and as the group with the highest aspiration, it is distressing that black men should have the greatest differences between anticipated and actual performance ratings. For black men, at the fourth level and above, 75 percent of whom have graduate degrees, 83 percent want to be rated at least more than satisfactory, but only 18 percent are. It may be noteworthy that both Hispanic and Asian men commented in the poststudy-feedback sessions that black men face more prejudice in the work setting because their darker color makes their acceptance into the group more difficult. This notion of a more-virulent and -hostile racial prejudice toward blacks is part of Silberman's hypothesis discussed in chapter 2. If this hypothesis is combined with the proved effects of the assessment bias of white evaluators against nonwhite workers, one would predict blacks to have a larger gap between self-evaluation and assessed evaluation than do other minorities.

The large difference for white men between the expected and actual ratings appears to be some combination of the effects of the impact of the EEO guidelines—that is, fewer outstanding ratings are going to white men than before because of fairer performance-evaluation procedures—and the forced distribution of ratings among the various departments. In other words, white men who are concentrated in departments almost exclusively made up of white men are forced into lower rating categories because of the forced percentage distribution of the performance-rating systems.

Importance of Knowing Performance-Appraisal Content and Rating

The tendency to avoid the presentation of negative but constructive objective feedback contributes to unrealistic expectations, and unfortunately, this avoidance is often rationalized on the unsupportable basis that such

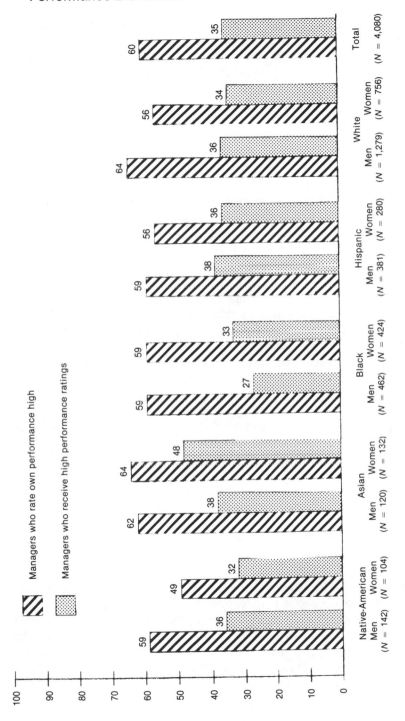

Figure 9-1. Percentage of Managers Who Receive High Performance Ratings and Those Who Rate Their Own Performances High

feedback is not good for the subordinates' psychological health. In this study, at least four out of five managers indicate that it was very important for them to know both their final performance rating and the content of their appraisals. The new breed of managers wants to know where they stand, not only to improve their performance and to be able to judge how fairly they are being treated but also to make reasonably accurate decisions about their work careers and their personalities. Female managers in most ethnic groups are even more likely than male managers are to say this. For example, 88 percent of white women, compared to 74 percent of white men, say it is very important to them to know the content of their appraisal. Out of all the respondents, black women and men are most likely (94 percent each), and white men are least likely (74 percent), to report that knowledge of the content of their appraisal is very important to them. Similar patterns occur between the race/sex groups in response to the question about wanting knowledge of their final performance rating.

The reasons are obvious why ratings and knowing why one received such a rating are more important to women and minorities, especially blacks, than they are to white men. The primary reason is that, overall, women and minorities are less likely than white men are to view the employment system as being fair. They feel that bosses are likely to be fairer if they know they have to discuss ratings and the basis of the appraisal with subordinates. Also, members of oppressed groups experience a certain amount of paranoia, some of which can be alleviated through formal and regular performance appraisals. In addition, women and minorities, being younger than males and particularly white males within corporations and closer to the beginning of their careers, want constructive evaluation, criticism, and direction to formulate goals and expectations. Finally, many more of them than white men are members of the new breed of managers, who want to now where they stand.

Are Managers Performing Jobs as Effectively as Possible?

While 95 percent of the managers who know their job performance is rated at least satisfactory, only 56 percent believe they are performing their jobs as effectively as possible. Figure 9-2 shows that Asian women (70 percent) are most likely and that native-American men (42 percent) are least likely to say they are performing their jobs as effectively as possible. Female managers, except for whites, are more likely than their male counterparts are to indicate they are performing their jobs as effectively as possible. No significant differences appear by levels. In other words, across levels in

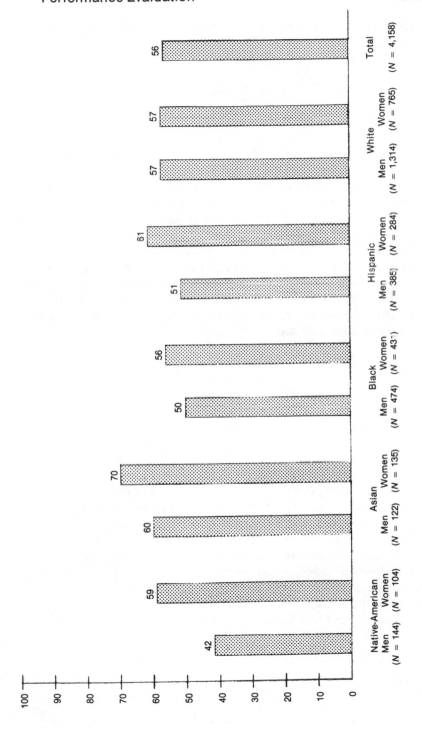

Figure 9-2. Percentage of Managers Who Feel They Perform Their Jobs as Effectively as Possible

every race/sex group, almost equal percentages of managers believe they are not performing their jobs as effectively as possible.

Impact of Education and Age on Job Performance

For managers, regardless of race and sex, as the level of education increases, so does the likelihood that managers will say they are not performing as effectively as they might. For example, among white men under 30 years of age, 17 percent with no college, 40 percent with some college, and 54 percent with college degrees, say they are not performing as well as possible. Age does not have any consistent impact on managers' response—that is, older managers are no more likely than younger managers to believe they are or are not performing their jobs as effectively as possible. As the management work force becomes more educated, the level of job performance may concomitantly decrease because more-educated managers expect better-designed work, more freedom to perform it their way, and a good, healthy atmosphere in which to perform their job. If these criteria are missing, these educated managers are likely to become disenchanted to such an extent that it affects their job performance.

Reasons Why Managers Are Not Performing Their Jobs as Effectively as Possible

During the preliminary-study interviews, a list was developed of factors frequently mentioned by managers that prevent them from doing their jobs as well as they might. The factors most-frequently chosen by respondents are lack of proper information (45 percent), lack of training (44 percent), and lack of experience (40 percent). In addition, 32 percent said too many rules and regulations are in effect, 25 percent mentioned a poor working relationship with their bosses, and 23 percent mentioned a lack of motivation. Table 9-4 shows the distribution of managers' responses. While the study anticipated that many managers would select lack of training, lack of information, and lack of experience as factors hindering effective performance, it did not anticipate that lack of motivation and interest would be cited by 23 percent of the managers as an inhibiting factor, at least to some extent. Note that only 59 percent say lack of motivation is not a factor at all.

Why Managers Lack Motivation to Perform Jobs

Table 9-5 shows that Asian men (38 percent) and Hispanic men (27 percent) are most likely to respond that lack of motivation hinders effective

Table 9-4
Factors that Hinder Managers' Job Performance
(percent)

To What Extent Do the Following Factors Prevent You from Performing Your Job as Well as You Might?	To a Great Extent	To Some Extent	To a Slight Extent	Not at All
Lack of proper information	13.4	31.6	26.7	28.3
Lack of training	11.7	32.3	23.4	32.6
Lack of experience	12.6	27	20.5	39.9
Too many rules and regulations	12.4	19.1	22.6	45.9
Poor working relationship with boss	11.4	13.9	17.8	56.9
Lack of motivation and/or interest	8.5	14.2	18.1	59.2
Poor working relationship with peers	1.8	5.8	14.6	77.8
Poor working relationship with customers	0.6	1.3	4.1	94.1

performance, at least to some extent. White men and women at lower levels are more likely than those at upper levels are to say that lack of motivation hinders performance. For example, 28 percent of the first- and second-level white men versus 14 percent of those at the fourth-level and above cite lack of motivation as more than just a slight factor affecting their performance.

In an attempt to find out why managers in this study say that lack of motivation is a problem in job performance, several important factors were identified. As noted in chapter 8 on work design, job structure greatly influences the managers' motivation to do a good job. Fifty-three percent of the managers who rate their jobs very low as opposed to only 18 percent who rate their jobs very high on autonomy to do their jobs as they see fit say that lack of motivation is more than a slight reason they are not performing their jobs as effectively as possible. A first-level white man says:

> I am trying to get a move into another type of job with different responsibilities and challenges. I am bored now. I have no real say over my job.

A first-level black woman makes related remarks:

> Sometimes I get depressed and disinterested because I'm not in a job where I can use my knowledge and potential to the fullest. It's really not a challenge when it gets to that point. I don't consider myself a genius or whatever, but I do think I could be more productive in a really challenging position.

Table 9-5
Lack of Motivation as a Factor in Ineffective Performance
(percent)

To What Extent Does Lack of Motivation Prevent You from Performing Your Job as Well as You Might?	Native-American		Asian		Black		Hispanic		White		Total
	Men (N = 80)	Women (N = 42)	Men (N = 47)	Women (N = 40)	Men (N = 234)	Women (N = 184)	Men (N = 184)	Women (N = 109)	Men (N = 537)	Women (N = 322)	(N = 1,779)
To a great extent	6.3	9.5	12.8	2.5	11.5	12	12.5	11.9	5.4	6.8	8.5
To some extent	17.5	9.5	25.5	20	10.3	13.6	14.1	11.9	17.3	10.9	14.3
To a slight extent	22.5	26.2	17	17.5	18.8	14.1	17.4	19.3	19.9	15.2	18.2
Not at all	53.8	54.8	44.7	60	59.4	60.3	56	56.9	57.4	67.1	59

Rate of advancement is another motivation factor. Managers, regardless of race or sex, who believe they have advanced slowly at first and then more rapidly, or more rapidly than they had expected, are most likely to say motivation is *not* a problem. For example, those managers who have progressed slowly at first and then rapidly (10 percent), or more rapidly than they expected (19 percent), are least likely to respond that lack of motivation is more than a slight problem. Those who progressed rapidly at first and then slowly (31 percent), or less rapidly than they expected (26 percent), are most likely to respond that lack of motivation is more than a slight problem. Thus, promotional opportunities apparently can have a strong influence on managers' motivation to perform their jobs effectively.

A.P. Raia noted that the anticipation of an objective performance evaluation can have significant influence on performance. He found that a very large percentage of managers interviewed indicated that they perform well just to look good in their performance review because they believe good performance was rewarded.[14]

Support for Raia's findings is found in this study. A definite correlation exists between the objectivity of performance appraisals and motivation. Only 18 percent of the managers who say their bosses are very objective identify lack of motivation and interest as a reason they are not performing their jobs as effectively as possible. Of the other managers who report lack of motivation, 23 percent say their bosses are somewhat objective, 27 percent state not very objective, 34 percent report not at all objective, and 26 percent indicate they do not know. In other words, managers who see their bosses as objective are more likely to be motivated and interested in good performance.

The impact of boss/subordinate relationships on motivation is quite evident in this study. For instance, 14 percent who rate their bosses excellent at explaining why things are done, compared with 34 percent who rate their bosses poor, indicate that lack of motivation is a problem. Another example lies in the fact that 12 percent of the managers who rate their bosses excellent versus 37 percent who rate their bosses poor in giving straight answers to their questions point to motivation as a problem, at least to some extent. A first-level black woman says:

> At the minimum they could at least express that they understand my feelings—and if my supervisor could give me feedback, other than negative, I would probably be more motivated.

A first-level native-American woman comments:

> I must motivate myself and stimulate interest in a job that has become boring due to my boss's lack of interest in the job.

Another reaction is from a second-level white man:

> There is no clear, consistent sense of direction. The rules change constantly, and different superiors in the organization can never agree on what they want. You consequently are caught in the middle and your motivation decreases.

The ultimate dangers from lack of motivation are reflected in the almost-total alienation and disenchantment voiced by a third-level black-male manager:

> The job has become a game of who can do what to whom without suffering any loss. My bosses play games with me and other subordinates in terms of fair ratings and career development. It's silly to be concerned about something which is not in my best interests. Consequently, I opt to *use* the system as much as possible and will only give when forced to or when it appears that the system is treating me fairly. As long as the system continues to operate as it does, I can become political, do nothing, and still get good pay, treatment, and perhaps another promotion.

Several researchers have investigated the relationship of motivation to performance in the present-day work force. Yankelovich has noted that the failure of the old incentive system to catch up with changing motivation has resulted in such deterioration in the workplace that the U.S. position as the foremost industrial nation is threatened. He pointed to the lack of appeal of present-day incentives systems for workers and a growing trend to give less and demand more. However, he also noted that workers often embark on a new job:

> . . . willing to work hard and be productive. But if the job fails to meet their expectations, if it does not give them the incentives they are looking for, then they lose interest. They may use the job to satisfy their own needs but give little in return. The preoccupation with self that is the hallmark of new-breed values places the burden of providing incentives for hard work more squarely on the employer than under the old value system.

> Unaccustomed to this burden, employers are angry and frustrated. Under the old value system employers relied on the carrot-and-stick approach—the carrot being money and success, the stick being the threat of economic insecurity. This combination still works, but not as well as in the past. With the advent of new-breed values, the motivational content has changed drastically. Quality-of-life motivations are not well understood by employers, and even when they are, large organizations do not know how to balance these motivations with their requirements for efficiency and productivity.[15]

Charles Hanson and Donna Hanson concurred that ". . . no single approach will provide the key to motivating all employees' and suggest that

". . . a combination of motivational techiques must be directed toward the needs and desires of the individual":

> It is evident from this survey and from a review of literature that the task of improving work performance—and at the same time contributing to the employee's feelings of satisfaction—is a very difficult one. No single approach will provide the key to motivating all employees toward the ultimate of more and better production. Therefore, since each employee is a unique individual, and since what motivates one will not motivate all, a combination of motivational techniques must be directed toward the needs and desires of the individual.[16]

Conclusions and Recommendations

While performance evaluations can be an important corporate tool to improve performance and motivate managers, they seldom bring about the desired positive effects. The data show that while a company might have a very good performance-appraisal system on paper, it is often not implemented properly by many managers for a number of reasons. One reason is that bosses seem to find that to sit down and honestly discuss strengths and shortcomings with their subordinates is very difficult. Their training in performance-evaluation procedures is lacking, as is their training in providing critical, constructive feedback.

Another reason is that some bosses avoid giving performance appraisals because they do not really believe in the usefulness of the appraisals. Interestingly, many of these bosses criticize their own bosses for not giving them objective performance appraisals. Some bosses avoid doing performance appraisals specifically so that they can be subjective and discriminate against those whom they dislike for reasons of race, sex, appearance, age, personality, or some other factor. All of these excuses lend credence to the observations that the evaluation situation is often an uncomfortable one that managers would prefer to avoid if possible. Unfortunately, many managers who cannot avoid the process perform it superficially and ineptly.

Since no great incentive exists to implement performance-evaluation plans, many bosses do not do so. In these companies no one loses his or her job or receives a lower salary treatment for not doing effective performance evaluations. Managers are paid and promoted for "getting the numbers—that is, meeting their quantitative objectives—and not for if and how they evaluate the performance of their subordinates.

Finally, power plays a role in the avoidance of performance appraisals. A good performance-evaluation system necessarily means the subordinate plays an active, valuable role. However, many bosses see this activity as a threat to their position. Walter Nord and Douglass Durand noted:

[R]esearch shows that the people with power are the ones who are apt to value it the most. A number of articles and books have pointed out that people who rise in modern business organizations tend to have strong interests in and needs for power. Thus, the people whom Human Resource Management proponents expect to run the risks entailed in relinquishing power are the very people who hold power most dear. Strategies that depend on these people giving power away voluntarily are not apt to be implemented.

Therefore, MBO, participative management, and other plans to move power lower in the hierarchy are bound to be subjected to continual counterpressures. When the interests of those near the top of the hierarchy are threatened, controls will be reinstituted and systems will be changed. The research on MBO supports this general prediction. It has shown a tendency for organizations implementing the concept to become overburdened by paperwork, for lower-level participants to feel that top management dominates their goals, and for MBO to be viewed as more form than substance. Similarly, critics of participative management have observed that lower-level participants are seldom able to influence basic goals and structures.[17]

Regardless of the problems in implementing effective performance-evaluation procedures, the data in this study suggest that performance appraisals can have a very positive effect on boss/subordinate relationships, subordinate performance, and subordinate motivation. They can satisfy the ever-increasing need of employees to know where they stand. In addition, minorities and women can benefit greatly because performance appraisals done objectively can aid them to put in perspective the effects of race and sex on their careers.

This study strongly recommends that companies implement a MBO program that should be characterized by an effective training program. Bosses and subordinates should mutually and clearly define responsibilities, determine key objectives, and agree on a means of measurement. The review process should be held quarterly and not be limited to the boss's telling the subordinate how well he or she is doing. Probably the most-crucial aspect of the performance appraisal should be the subordinate's reviewing for the boss how well he or she did and why, and what will be done to improve performance. Bosses cannot have all the knowledge about how and why objectives were or were not met; only the subordinate can have that detailed knowledge. However, bosses can greatly assist subordinates in developing and suggesting solutions to performance problems.

This approach takes the boss out of a godlike position, makes the subordinate feel he or she really has a say in the performance appraisal, and thus increases the likelihood that the subordinate will accept the outcome.

Finally, performance appraisals should be characterized by good monitoring and reward systems as major components of the company's overall strategies.

In conclusion, employees want to be treated fairly and equitably, and they want more knowledge about where they stand than employees have had in the past. Properly designed work is the basis for objective and effective performance appraisals. These two factors not only assist in eliminating overall managerial frustration and lead to better performance but also reduce the impact of race, sex, and other subjective factors on appraisals and ratings.

10 Potential Evaluation

Toward the end of the 1970s, corporate recruiters found that the available pool of talent needed to backfill the wave of retirements was drying up. In a May 1979 article, Frederick A. Harmon suggested that young men and women are turning away from managerial ranks in business because the so-called me generation of the 1970s was not well disposed to subordinate individual needs to implicit corporate needs. According to Harmon, the business community must face up to the reality that its world has changed drastically in the last ten years. No longer can all decisions affecting a company be made in the corporate boardroom. Today, the views of younger employees also must be included in the decision-making process. Many of them will not go along with strict rules of corporate conformity. They tend to be more tolerant and accepting of all types of people, and they expect corporations to keep an equally open mind. These employees hold the key to the future and they cannot be ignored.[1]

Harmon also noted that the problems faced by business in finding good managerial talent are great because of the small pool of good potential managerial talent. Studies have shown that the most-effective managers have above-average intelligence and like to compete, enjoy exercising power and authority, and want to function in a highly responsible position. In addition, managers need the skills and desire to work with and understand people.[2] Unless women and minorities, who make up 63 percent of the population, are evaluated fairly and objectively for their potential, enough good managers will not be available to fill the future needs of corporations. Harmon further pointed out:

> If our corporations are to survive, they must make a concerted effort to find—and keep—their future managers. Every available method should be used to identify potential managerial talent. Once candidates are found, they must be enticed to stay. . . .

> Without competent, dedicated managers, the fabric of the business community could disintegrate. By developing long-range executive search-and-training programs geared to both the needs of the organization and those of the individual, corporations will be taking a solid step into the future.[3]

In addition to what Harmon said, it is crucial for corporations to realize that many of the people who will be selected for management, and many who are already managers, young and old, are developing new-breed attitudes. They want to know where they stand in terms of their potential so that they can make their own career decisions and, thus, decisions about their personal lives. They do not want their futures to be secretly planned by the powers that be. They also expect to have an active role in planning their careers, and this planning requires knowledge about how the corporation evaluates and views their potential.

Potential evaluation has traditionally served to separate the winners from the losers. At the same time, the pyramidal shape of the corporate structure dooms 99 percent of the workers to be labeled as losers at some point in their careers. Time-linked labels are often used in the decimation of ratings, such as "promotable now," "promotable later," or "non-promotable." Many corporations have also created a special category for individuals marked as potential corporate-officer material. These "jet jobs", "water walkers," or "fair-haired boys" are promoted at extremely fast rates. They are given a series of positions chosen to maximize their managerial skills and broaden their knowledge of the corporation. Such "fast tracking" has long been used in the development of selected white men and most recently in the development of an extremely small, select group of female and minority managers. The vast majority of managers, however, will progress at a slower and steadier pace until, at some point in their careers, they are seen as having reached the limit of their abilities or until they lose out in competition with sometimes equally capable people.

All corporations and managers will benefit from valid and reliable programs for potential evaluation because it is a central requisite for maximal utilization of managerial talent. A fair and universally applied potential-evaluation policy is critical to the morale of the managerial force. The criteria of validity, reliability, fairness, and standardization are not as easily built into a potential-evaluation program. While approaches such as MBO have proved both popular and effective in attempts to identify responsibilities and goals achieved, the measurement of job performance cannot be taken as similarly indicative of promotability. They are two quite different issues. A person might be an outstanding performer at one level of management and a poor performer at the next because he or she does not have the requisite managerial skills or abilities for the higher level.

The prevalence of the Peter Principle in corporations results in part from basing promotions almost exclusively on performance evaluations and personal acceptability rather than on objective and systematic potential evaluations. This is not to say that present performance is not a factor to be considered in potential evaluation but that it should not be the only factor.

Performance and potential-evaluation procedures, while used primarily for different purposes, have similar shortcomings. Both functions are complex and involve personal judgment subject to the biases and prejudices of the individual manager. In addition, they are subject to any organizational biases or norms developed over the years. In most organizations, these norms are unconsciously based on the personality characteristics and behavior of white men.[4] All managers are faced with certain personal characteristics that can be liabilities—for example, age, religion, height, weight, looks, and family origins. However, minorities and women have the additional burden of dealing with racism and/or sexism.

Numerous studies have dealt with the impact of racism and sexism on hiring and promotion decisions. In a study that examined the relationship between physical attractiveness in the evaluation of men and women, traditional sex-role differentiation was proposed as the explanation:

> While physical attractiveness functions for women as an indicator of their degree of successful role fulfillment, the indicators of successful fulfillment of a man's role do not include physical attractiveness anywhere as frequently and importantly as women's. It is therefore not surprising that our society values a woman's beauty and that the evaluation of a woman depends so much on her physical attractiveness.[5]

One study in particular helped clarify the nuances of covert sexism in potential evaluations. It found that women were rated as having low potential, particularly when job requirements were less specific, such as for a general managerial job. The explanation given by the researchers was that stereotypes operate more strongly when full information is not available for consideration.[6]

A more-recent study demonstrated that a group of students equally mixed by race and sex evaluated the promotability of a white man higher than that of a black man and a white woman, even though the only information changed for the three study groups was the pictures and names of the candidates.[7] These findings occurred even after the respondents had participated in twelve weeks of intensive study of racism and sexism. Thus, the racist and sexist socialization of young men and women from all five race groups was so deeply embedded that even after carefully studying these phenomenon and expressing great indignation about these evil forces, they subconsciously practiced them themselves. An obvious question then is: What do most corporate managers do who have little or no understanding of how racism and sexism work?

In summing up this introduction, the comments of a fourth-level black man and a fourth-level white man correctly describe the potential-evaluation processes as they have been. The black man says:

> Potential-evaluation procedures! What potential-evaluation procedures? The only one I know about is the good old white-boy network. If you fit their criteria and they like you, you have it made. If you don't, as I don't, you're out in the cold.

The white man says:

Potential for third-level and higher is decided by management-assessment committees, with final decisions made because of "impressions" injected by other than objective evaluation and by "foreign" superiors. Instead of being factual they are subjective, arbitrary, and political as a whole and as a procedure. I say this despite my having promotable ratings all my career.

Participating Companies' Potential-Evaluation Procedures

The companies that participated in this study have just begun to develop a semblance of systematic, universal potential-evaluation procedures. Other than informal potential evaluations based on the subjective opinions of superiors, the only systematic procedure used prior to this study was the assessment process. (See pp. 241-244 for a detailed analysis of the assessment process.) However, the majority of the managers had not participated in the assessment process. Another procedure that is essentially informal and lacks subordinate participation is one in which one level of management formally meets with superiors to discuss their subordinates' potential. Such discussions usually rest on performance evaluations and subjective personal opinions of abilities, likability, appearance, life-style, and other subjective criteria. If this last system is unfair to white men, it is even more unfair to minorities and women. Some of the problems that hurt minorities and women in such discussions are when the manager has had little experience with women and/or minorities in nontraditional jobs or has been pressured into hiring such workers. The manager's inexperience, anxiety, or hostility about affirmative action can cloud his or her objectivity, particularly when a manager feels women or minorities are "different." As noted earlier, managers sometimes judge the same behavior differently, depending on whether men or women are involved and/or whites or minorities.

In short, most managers in the participating companies are still being subjected to an informal potential-evaluation procedure lacking clear and objective measurements and heavily influenced by social nonability factors.

Who Receives Potential Evaluations?

Almost half (49 percent) of all the managers have had a potential evaluation within the past two years. However, 40 percent have never had one. Asian men and Asian women are most likely to report having received a potential evaluation within the last year. Of the managers who received potential evaluations, 55 percent say that their bosses took the managers' own estimation of their potential into account in the evaluation, 62 percent state that their bosses explained the manner in which they arrived at the potential evaluations, and 54 percent indicate that their bosses gave them feedback and recommendations for improvement. Thus, quite clearly, only a small proportion (approximately 27 percent) of the managers have potential evaluations that can be considered useful for career planning and/or self-development.

Who Is Rated Promotable?

Of the 49 percent of managers who have had potential evaluations in the past two years, only 54 percent state that they know their promotability rating. Thus, only one-fourth of the total group of managers surveyed know how they have been classified for future promotions. Native-American managers (51 percent) are most likely to say they are promotable now, and black men and women are least likely (38 percent). Between 39 percent and 46 percent of the other race/sex groups have similar ratings. The high percentage of native-American (24 percent) and white men (36 percent), compared to 14 to 6 percent of the other groups rated not promotable, can be explained partly by the fact that many of them are over 45 years of age.

Managers' Perceptions of the Objectivity of Potential Evaluations

Considering all the previous discussions, it is not surprising that only 19 percent of the managers believe that the procedures their bosses use are very objective. As might be expected, black men are least likely to see their bosses' potential-evaluation procedures as objective. Asians and native-American women are most likely. Table 10-1 illustrates these facts.

As compared to other ethnic groups, Asian-American respondents have consistently more-positive views on the issues of performance, potential, and career planning. The positive views of the Asian-American managers can be explained in part by the fact that the majority of them are employed by the two companies with the most-advanced comprehensive managerial systems of the companies participating in the study. In addition, Asians tend to be less intimidating and more acceptable to whites than are other minorities. White managers who wish to believe themselves sociopolitically moderate to liberal can do so by implementing the employment policies and practices in a fairer manner with Asians than with other minorities. Finally, Asian managers come from a cultural heritage that stresses noncritical, positive outlooks much more so than other cultures do. (See chapter 2 for more discussion about Asian culture and its impact on Asians.)

As was the case with performance-evaluation procedures, most managers who rate these procedures somewhat objective give responses

Table 10-1
Objectivity of Potential-Evaluation Procedures
(percent)

| In Your Opinion, How Objective is the Procedure (Company Procedure or Other) Your Boss Uses in Evaluating Your Potential? | Native-American | | Asian | | Black | | Hispanic | | White | | Total |
	Men (N = 86)	Women (N = 54)	Men (N = 84)	Women (N = 84)	Men (N = 284)	Women (N = 246)	Men (N = 247)	Women (N = 168)	Men (N = 762)	Women (N = 431)	(N = 2,446)
Very objective	14	27.8	17.9	25	15.8	17.9	17.4	17.9	16.5	24.1	18.6
Somewhat objective	39.5	44.4	48.8	42.9	33.5	41.1	44.1	35.7	43	34.1	39.9
Not very objective	16.3	9.3	16.7	15.5	22.9	15.9	16.2	12.5	18.2	14.6	16.9
Not at all objective	3.5	3.7	2.4	2.4	7.7	5.3	4.9	4.8	6.6	3.5	5.3
Do not know	26.7	14.8	14.3	14.3	20.1	19.9	17.4	29.2	15.6	23.7	19.4

similar to those who rate them as not very objective. Thus, the procedures are viewed less positively than the responses in table 10-1 indicate. For example, a white woman who says the plan is somewhat objective notes:

> I feel more and better training is necessary. It is very hard to rate each potential level without strict guideline as to what level of behavior in a particular area is satisfactory as opposed to superior. The process is too subjective.

However, a second-level white man who says the plan is not very objective gives basically the same response:

> It is usually done without the necessary time to do it properly. The new plan was implemented without any formal training in the use of it. Therefore, many mistakes are made which render the program unfair.

These two comments contrast with the very positive statement by a second-level Hispanic man who describes the plan as very objective. He comments:

> My boss was trained in the use of the current procedure utilized in potential evaluation. I received the same training. We shared a mutual understanding of the plan and definition of the dimensions used to evaluate potential. We basically did my evaluation as a joint project.

The most-frequent overall comment managers make about the potential-evaluation procedures is that the procedures are influenced by the bosses' personal opinions (19 percent). Table 10-2 gives the most-frequent explanations that influence the managers' opinions about the objectivity of their companies' potential-evaluation procedures.

A few illustrative comments from the managers add insight to their reasoning about the degree of subjectivity of the potential-evaluation process. A first-level black woman who says the procedures are not very objective says:

> My boss has never shown or explained my potential appraisal to me because he does not believe that one should know this information but that one should wait and see what, if anything, becomes of oneself.

A third-level white man states:

> I found the appraisal process very subjective. Once a career and appraisal pattern is established, whether good or bad, it's very difficult for an individual to change it.

Finally, a second-level Hispanic man and a second-level black man respectively conclude:

Table 10-2

Reasons Potential Evaluations Are Viewed Objective or Subjective
(percent)

Please Explain Your Response Concerning the Degree of Objectivity of the Procedures Your Boss Uses to Appraise Your Potential	*Total (N = 2,146)*
Appraisal is influenced by the personal opinions of the boss.	18.8
Boss tries to be objective, is serious about appraisals, follows procedures.	16.1
Appraisals are always somewhat subjective.	11.1
Respondent is not familiar with procedures used. Plan was too new when used.	10.1
Procedure is too general. The criteria have not been clearly defined.	7.5
Boss uses performance to appraise potential.	7.4
Respondent has not been appraised recently, is not aware of appraisal, not discussed.	7.1
Boss does not, cannot, know my potential.	4.9
Procedures are adequate, cover many areas.	4.7
Potential is mutually agreed upon by the boss and the subordinate.	2.8
Appraisal is affected by curve or quota requirements.	2.7
Other.	6.7

My boss has had only one job with this company since he started working. His views are extremely tunnelized [sic] as to how someone should do his job, dress, what to eat, when to drink, when to go to the toilet, for how long, how much, etc., etc. His approach to management of people is outmoded and pretty close to ass backwards.

Presumably he compares my perceived potential with the job knowledge, competence levels and social "fit" which he sees as necessary or desirable among his own peer groups and then makes a conjectural guess about my future potential. This whole process is necessarily subjective.

In contrast to the managers' views of performance evaluation, of which few managers criticized the actual company procedures but many criticized how the procedures were implemented, table 10-2 shows that both the implementation and potential-evaluation procedures themselves are criticized by many of the managers. These figures support the notion that these companies have only recently begun to develop and implement any semblance of universal, systematic, and objective potential-evaluation procedures.

Any new employment direction—specifically, the implementation of a systematic potential-evaluation procedure—is bound to be fraught with problems. Usually the first attempts are ineffective because the concepts and procedures must be massaged and refined to work out the initial bugs. In addition, many managers oppose drastic changes such as telling their subordinates their potential. These managers will vigorously attack the shortcomings inherent in any new procedure. Other managers will avoid implementing the procedures because they are unfamiliar with them and/or are improperly trained in their use. Finally, as the responses in table 10-2 suggest, when compared with the managers' views on peformance-evaluation procedures, potential evaluation is a much-more subjective process and much harder to systematize and quantify because performance deals with the past and potential deals with the future.

The second most-frequent response managers give about the degree of objectivity of the potential-evaluation procedures is that "the boss tries to be objective, takes the appraisal seriously, and follows the company's procedures very closely" (16 percent). This statement illustrates that while more difficulty exists in making objective potential evaluations, a reasonable job can be done. A second-level Asian man who believes the procedures are very objective says:

> Standardized training to impart a norm for the managerial dimensions gives us for the first time a standard of criteria and a benchmark for each criterion.

A first-level white man agrees:

> I rated my boss very objective. He knows and sees where your weak and strong points are and what is needed to correct the weak points and tells you.

**Factors that Increase Managers' Faith
in Potential Evaluations**

A more-detailed analysis of why managers believe the potential-evaluation procedures are or are not objective reveals that the managers whose bosses closely follow the companies' procedures and take into consideration the subordinates' feedback on their strengths and weaknesses rate the company's procedures as much-more objective than do managers whose bosses do not do these things. For example, 69 percent of the managers who receive feedback on their strengths and weaknesses say their potential evaluations are at least somewhat objective. This figure is four to five times more than the proportions of managers who received such feedback and who rate the potential-evaluation procedures less than somewhat objective. This trend is similar to that of the responses on performance appraisal.

Table 10-3 shows the relationship between the respondents' views of objectivity and whether their bosses take into account their subordinates' own estimates of their potential. The table vividly illustrates that the more the boss takes his or her subordinates' personal opinions into account, the more likely the subordinate is to believe that the procedures are objective.

A final example of the effect of open communications on potential appraisals is that 90 percent of the managers who say that their bosses' procedures are very objective also say that their bosses explain to them how they arrive at the potential appraisals. This figure compares with 33 percent who say that the procedures are not at all objective and that their bosses explain the process.

Do Managers Want to Know Their Potential?

This study dispells a persistent managerial myth that people do not really want to know where they stand or that this knowledge would be too stressful, especially for managers who are told that they have no potential to advance in their company. Three-fourths of the managers indicate that knowledge of both the content of their potential appraisal and their final potential rating is *very* important to them. Black men (86 percent) and black women (88 percent), closely followed by Hispanic men (85 percent) and Hispanic women (84 percent), are most likely to say it is very important to know the content of their potential appraisal. White men (63 percent) are least likely to say this. The same hierarchy occurs with the attitude that knowledge of their final rating is very important—that is, 85 percent of black men and 83 percent of black women versus 60 percent of white men. As pointed out with respect to performance appraisal, newcomers who are attempting to legitimize their managerial identity can reduce uncertainty by

Table 10-3
Subordinate Input in Potential Evaluation and Their View of Objectivity
(percent)

	Input			
Objectivity	*A Great Deal (N = 356)*	*Some (N = 994)*	*A Little (N = 553)*	*Not At All (N = 544)*
Very objective	36.9	43.5	10.6	9.1
Somewhat objective	13.2	51	21.5	14.3
Not very objective	5.3	30.6	33.7	30.4
Not at all objective	5.5	14.1	21.1	59.4
Do not know	6.4	32.2	27	34.3

formal and official endorsements of and constructive feedback about their abilities. White men are the least likely to be concerned about this information probably because of their higher level, their older age, the established tradition of white men in managerial roles, and therefore, the implicit assumption that the system will be beneficial to them unless or until they demonstrate gross incompetence.

Perhaps those bosses who claim that subordinates do not want to know are simply afraid to break the bad news. Obviously no one wants to give any bad news or to receive any. However, truth wins out, and an accepted fact has evolved that psychological well-being is best served in the long run by facing and adapting to disappointments, not by denying them. At some time in their careers, 99 percent of all managers must face the fact that they have had their last promotion. The question is not whether to tell them but how best to tell them. Perhaps, also, managers who claim that subordinates do not want to know their potential feel incapable of effectively communicating with their subordinates about such critical issues.

White-female managers (53 percent) and white-male managers (51 percent) are most likely and black-male managers (35 percent) and black-female managers (39 percent) are least likely to say that advising subordinates that they are not promotable is difficult. The lesser difficulty that minorities, particularly blacks, feel about passing along bad news may be the result of their experience as members of oppressed groups. In order to survive, they have had to honestly and accurately assess their worlds, no matter how painful such assessments might be.

In sum, open, candid discussions and evaluations with active subordinate participation go a long way toward countering subordinates' negative attitudes about potential-evaluation procedures. Harry Levinson supported this conclusion. He wrote:

> When people are provided continuously with verifiable information, including when they have been passed over for promotion and why, they are able to perceive more accurately the nuances of their behavior and their behavioral patterns. Thus, when offered other opportunities, employees are in better positions to weigh their own behavioral configurations against those required by the prospective job. People who know themselves in this way will be more-easily able to say about a given job, "That's not for me." They will see that the next job in the pyramid is not necessarily rightfully theirs. In recognizing their own behavioral limitations, they may save themselves much grief as well as avoid painful difficulty for themselves.[8]

Managers' Self-Ratings on Potential

The managers were asked to rate themselves on sixteen characteristics related to managerial skills and abilities, professional expertise, and behavior. Over one-half rate themselves as very proficient in each area, and no more than 12 percent consider themselves marginal in any characteristic. Table 10-4 shows that managers most-often consider themselves to be very proficient in acceptance of other races in the workplace (94 percent), acceptance of the opposite sex in the workplace (92 percent), and ability to learn (90 percent). The characteristics in which managers are least likely to consider themselves very proficient are tolerance of uncertainty (63 percent), technical skills (62 percent), writing skills (60 percent), and speaking skills (55 percent).

Several interesting race/sex differences occur on some of these ratings. In many but not all cases, a larger percentage of male managers than female are more likely to rate themselves proficient in areas that have traditionally been seen as male characteristic. Some of these areas are technical skills, professional skills, decision making, leadership skills, and decisiveness. It should be emphasized that in most cases the percentage differences between men and women are not great but they are consistent. For example, 91 percent of the white men versus 87 percent of the white women rate themselves proficient in decision making.

Larger percentages of female than male managers from each race group rate themselves proficient in acceptance of the other sex in the workplace.

Table 10-4
Managers' Self-Ratings of Potential
(percent)

Please Rate Yourself on Each of the Following Characteristics. (N = 4,137)	Ratings		
	Marginal	*Average*	*Proficient*
Acceptance of other races in the workplace	0.7	5	94.4
Acceptance of the opposite sex in the workplace	1.7	6.1	92.3
Ability to learn	0.5	9.1	90.4
Decisiveness (whether or not you are willing to make decisions)	1.6	10.1	88.4
Decision making (quality of decisions)	0.9	11.4	87.6
Behavior flexibility	1.1	14.7	84.2
Stability under pressure (resistance to stress)	2.1	14.5	83.4
Leadership skill	2.1	16.8	81.1
Self-objectivity	1.9	19.7	78.5
Organizing and planning	2.8	19.8	77.4
Administrative skills	3.4	23.2	73.5
Professional skills	6.8	25.9	67.3
Tolerance of uncertainty	9	27.6	63.4
Technical skills	12.3	26.2	61.5
Writing skills	9.5	30.1	60.4
Speaking skills	12	33.5	54.6

Approximately equal percentages of male and female managers in each racial category consider themselves proficient in administrative skills, behavior flexibility, and acceptance of the other races in the workplace.

Another finding of interest is that larger percentages of black-male managers than managers from other race/sex groups rate themselves proficient in speaking skills and writing skills, self-objectivity, behavior flexibility, and ability to learn. In the latter area, they are tied with Asian men. These findings present a picture of black men contrary to the stereotypes held by white society.

The managers' overall ratings indicate that they have very high impressions of their abilities and potential that in most cases are not in line with their bosses' views. Because few bosses are communicating effectively with their subordinates about their potential, the subordinates apparently have a much-higher impression of themselves than the company does. Eventually 99 percent of them will be shocked when they find out they are labeled non-promotable. These companies then will be faced with very serious morale problems.

Assessment Centers

An increasingly popular potential-evaluation procedure employed by the companies in this study is the assessment center. As defined by Douglas W. Bray, director of management selection and development research at AT&T, the assessment center is a device "to provide an objective, off-the-job evaluation of developed abilities, potential, strengths and weaknesses, and motivation." This is achieved, he says:

> . . . through the observation of behavior in a variety of standardized performance situations, the rating of that behavior on a number of predetermined dimensions, the drawing of conclusions concerning potential for certain levels and types of work, and the diagnosis of developmental needs.[9]

An individual's evaluation at an assessment center may require one day or several. Typical assessment techniques include an interview, in-basket and group exercises, paper-and-pencil tests of ability and personality, and projective-type personality tests. The assessment staff is usually composed of managers who are one or two levels above the level of the assessee and who have been trained in the administration and scoring of the tests. After the assessment procedure, the staff meets to discuss each candidate and to arrive at an evaluation of his or her performance. The staff then prepares a report that may be used for a variety of purposes including placement, promotion, and early identification of potential and development.

Does the process really provide a sufficiently objective off-the-job evaluation of developed abilities, potential strengths and weaknesses, and motivation? Although the potential exists, a number of shortcomings and problems are evident in the current design and implementation of the process.

In this study, nearly half of all the black-female managers (47 percent) have attended assessment programs, along with 40 percent of the native-American and Hispanic men and women and 39 percent of the black men. In contrast, only 31 percent of white women and 26 percent of white men have attended such programs.

These findings raise questions as to the cause of the disproportionate representation of minorities and women chosen for assessment. Perhaps this representation indicates efforts by companies to be fair to newcomers, tied to a belief that this approach is the most-objective tool available. Perhaps the emphasis on formally assessing female and minority managers is actually a preemptive defensive move to justify decisions not to promote them, to keep them at a lower level of management, or to protect companies from suits for violation of EEO guidelines. A final possibility, in combination with one or more of the others, is that recent EEO legislation has created a demand for minority and female managers beyond normal flow—that is, faster than the rate that would take place based solely on the judgment of superiors.

More than one-third of the managers who had attended an assessment program respond that they do not know their assessment ratings. Half of the managers report receiving promotable ratings, while less than one out of five says they have received nonpromotable ratings. Black women by far are most likely *not* to be recommended for promotion (36 percent). They are followed by black men (26 percent) and native Americans (25 percent). Also, in every race group men are more likely than women are to receive promotable ratings.

These figures are quite possibly indications of race/sex biases in the assessment process. Most of the criteria used to assess potential were identified and defined in the 1940s and 1950s using white men as models. The determination of managerial styles and abilities were based on the traditional white-male value system at the time. This basis has not been significantly altered to encompass effective new styles that female and minority managers, as well as some white men, have brought to corporate management.

Not only can racial or sexual biases exist in the assessment-process criteria but also in the race and/or sex of the assessors. Richard Klimonski and William Strickland, in discussing this possibility, noted:

> . . . another study analyzed data partitioned into two samples of women who had attended a Bell System assessment center during the period 1966-1971. Members of one sample had since been promoted to management positions, while members of the other had not. For both samples,

black women consistently received lower ratings than white women on a variety of criteria. There was no significant difference between black and white women on interpersonal effectiveness, but the white assessees received higher scores than the black assessees on factors relating to administrative skills, sensitivity, and effective intelligence. On overall assessment ratings, blacks in both samples were judged lower.[10]

Another major problem, even for white men, is that the assessment process could be a self-fulfilling prophecy—that is, the company is looking for certain characteristics; the assessors find these characteristics and say people are promotable; because people have been labeled promotable, they are promoted.

Indeed, in the current study a clear relationship exists between the assessment rating received and the level achieved. Managers at lower levels are less likely than those at upper levels to have received promotable ratings. For example, the percentage of white men at various levels who indicate they are rated promotable by the assessment centers are:

First level	33%
Second level	46%
Third level	64%
Fourth level	52%
Fifth level	57%

Klimonski and Strickland argued that "it would be useful to have data that could refute the provocative possibility that obtained assessment-center validity is merely a case of managers [as assessment-center staff] predicting or anticipating how other managers [their colleagues in the organization] will react to a particular candidate in making promotion decisions." They not only recommend that efforts be made to "determine if assessment centers have superior predictive validity for a wider range of criteria than presently investigated" but also advocate research "that goes beyond this to determine how and why they work as effective predictors."[11] They warned against being overly impressed with evidence of assessment-center validity or of making premature generalizations from studies reported and made a number of specific suggestions:

> First, alternative predictors for the typically used criteria need to be identified and evaluated, preferably in comparative studies. Then, there is a need for predictive-validity studies of assessment centers and potential alternatives that use criteria other than those of advancement. We want predictive-validity studies of performance. Ideally, future validity research should include a variety of measures to establish the relationship among the usual advancement measures and the performance indices developed.[12]

Klimonski and Strickland allow that some companies' assessment-center philosophy is sensitive to the factors of a specific product or technology and builds in corrections for these factors. The researchers also wonder if some classes of companies exist for which the concept of the assessment center is inappropriate.

A final point about assessment centers is the way they are used. Earlier, when Bray talks about the purpose of assessment centers, he is speaking solely about benefits and aids to employers that maximally utilize the managerial force as a whole. An equally vital purpose of assessment centers should be to familiarize managers with their own potentials and limitations. Thus, ideally (ideally never happens in many of the companies), the process should not send managers back to their jobs feeling that the experience was a negative one, particularly in the sense that their careers are dead ended in their present companies, but rather with a positive feeling of learning and growth. The procedure should include identification of areas in which improvement is needed, specific suggestions for achieving such improvement, and the option for a manager to request reassessment at some specified time in the future. Furthermore, managers should be reassured that other techniques are employed in assessing their potential. It is both presumptuous and precipitous to write off anyone's potential on the basis of one or two days' performance, particularly when this decision usually is based on the opinion of a group of inexperienced, minimally trained pseudo-psychologists, most of whom are white men.

Conclusions and Recommendations

While 60 percent of the managers in this study have received potential evaluations at some point in their career, many of them rate the procedures as neither particularly objective nor useful.

Potential evaluations present some of the same problems encountered in performance evaluations, including bias and/or inadequacy of bosses' training, poor definitions, and poor measurement methods. However, potential evaluations are even-more subjective because of the time frame involved—that is, bosses are not only analyzing the past but also predicting the career future of their subordinates. The role of prophet is an uncomfortable one, especially when little or no training accompanies the responsibility.

The role of the prophet is more difficult when bosses must evaluate subordinates whose customs, life-style, and value systems may be new or somewhat different from theirs. Women and minorities are frustrated and disturbed when they realize that their futures are being decided by people who they fear have racist and/or sexist attitudes in addition to all the other biases people have, regardless of race and sex. This cognizance of subjectivity undermines the white-male manager's legitimacy when both he and the nonwhite and/or nonmale managers realize that even before minorities and women entered corporate managerial ranks, potential was judged on religion, age, looks, family background, club affiliations, and other similarly subjective criteria.

White men are prone to be upset at being evaluated by any boss, regardless of race and/or sex. They regret that their monopoly on the better management positions is in danger. They are pressured to admit that subjective criteria have been used since the inception of corporations. As Caplow explains:

> The continuity of a group depends upon its ability to enforce its standards upon its members. At each hierarchical level certain secondary qualities determine which of a number of equally intelligent or equally efficient candidates . . . shall be favored. . . . The elders are inclined to select those who are like themselves in general appearance, taste, values, associations and who, in addition, have demonstrated specific ability to conform to hierarchical expectations.[13]

In order to deal with the subjective aspects of potential-evaluation procedures and the fears and frustrations of all groups, companies should develop multifaceted potential-evaluation procedures. Potential should be determined not by a single method but through a combination of techniques. In addition to assessment centers, one excellent but little-used procedure involves temporary or trial assignments of higher-level responsibilities. Also potential-review boards should be established as one part of the review system. These boards should be composed of internal managers and external members such as consultants, reputable members of society, managers from other companies, and so forth. Regardless of who is on the review board, the reviewers should be composed with equal representation of minorities and women who have not themselves evidenced a very high need for approval. This move should counter the previously discussed tendencies of managers to react more positively to other managers of the same sex, race, and cultural background and to make certain that minority and female members will not be easily coerced by the dominant white men.

In conjunction with a reevaluation of the assessment process to make it more valid, assessment centers should not be staffed by part-time managers who are temporarily relieved of their regular jobs. Such assignments are forced, usually upon persons who probably could not pass the test themselves. These should be positions to which high-potential people are sent for a one-to-two-year developmental assignment. This nonprofessional staff should be complemented with professional social scientists.

Regardless of the process, persons' being evaluated should play active roles in their evaluation and the determination of any corrective action. They should be made to feel that their opinions count at least to some extent. This means that both boss and subordinate must clearly understand the potential-evaluation procedures and, where appropriate, be trained in those procedures.

Participation in a potential-evaluation program should be an option available to all managers who request it. It should not be a requirement. Some managers are quite satisfied with their present managerial rankings and should not be subjected to the rigors of a potential-evaluation process.

No matter how objective and useful the procedures are on paper, they are useless unless properly implemented. Left on their own, some managers will not do the evaluations, and others will do them very poorly. When managers are not involved in the actual potential-evaluation process, some are reluctant to send subordinates because of the fear that a negative review will adversely affect the employee's morale. Other managers are reluctant to give up their power to decide their subordinate's potential. Thus, an incentive system should be implemented to reward managers for successfully following the potential-evaluation program, and particularly for developing the potential of their subordinates.

Finally, the procedures that are being implemented should be carefully reviewed, monitored, and revised. The validity of any one assessment technique should be verified through using it in conjunction with at least two other techniques.

11 Career Planning/ Training and Development

A major theme introduced and elaborated upon in the previous three chapters has been the need for the development of a total-management system. A total-management system is an interrelated network of components consisting of work design, performance evaluation, potential evaluation, career planning, and training and development. Bosses and subordinates are only able to effectively discuss and determine career plans and training-and-development needs after they have worked out performance and potential appraisals based on properly designed work. Career planning is the component of this larger system that ties together all of the other components.

In this study, "career planning" refers to a process wherein a boss and subordinate specialize resources to simultaneously maximize the interests of the subordinate and the company. They try to make a match or compromise between the two sets of interests so that the subordinate will have an interesting, challenging career and be a productive, motivated employee. Although the process can occasionally result in a promotion, it will more often result in a lateral job move or a different emphasis within the present job area.

George Thorton accurately described career planning in these terms:

> Career planning is an active attempt of the individual to plan, manage, and influence the direction of one's own career in order to attain long-range personal and professional goals. Career planning, as distinct from manpower planning, implies both an organization and individual responsibility. Career progress does not presume any specific direction of upward mobility or advancement. Progress may be thought of as a better integration of personal, professional, and organizational goals.[1]

The expected benefits of a career-planning system include improved productivity and quality through a better-motivated work force, increased efficiency in training and development, increased employee retention, and more-pragmatic long-range corporate work-force planning.

A Hispanic man at the second level of management reveals the positive effects of career planning:

> Since my career plan was initiated recently and we are working on planning for future job openings and responsibilities, I feel this will have a decided

247

effect on my attitude and my job. I have a positive attitude based on what I know and can expect in the future.

Another advantage of a systematic, properly implemented company career-planning program is that it assists employees in keeping their expectations in line. For the manager whose career plans are out of touch with economic or political realities and/or for the manager whose career plans underestimate or overestimate professional capabilities, frustration is inescapable. A fourth level white man notes:

> Any formalized approach to career planning should take care that employee's promotional expectations are not unrealistically raised. I fear that the company's present approach does promote unrealistic career expectations with the result that "career planning" becomes "career frustration."

However, as career-planning experts, John D. Walker, and Thomas G. Gatteridge noted that heightened expectations are not necessarily bad so long as they have some semblance of reality:

> On the matter of whether career planning raises employee expectations, 82.9 percent of the respondents said that senior management would say that it does. But the implication is not necessarily negative. Raising expectations is an essential step in stimulating individuals to learn new skills and tackle new challenges.[2]

Thus, the career-planning process must be carefully implemented in order to stimulate employees' motivations and interest but not so much that they develop unrealistic expectations and aspirations.

Before analyzing the participating managers' views of career planning, its increasing importance must be noted. Partly as a result of systems implemented in the name of EEO/AAP, and partly because of the greater emphasis employees are placing on controlling their personal destinies, a sensitivity among managers has been growing over this issue. In the early stages of this study (1975), managers' responses to questions on career planning were brief and perfunctory. Most of the discussions focused on EEO/AAP-related topics. Two-and-a-half years later (1978), when the final feedback sessions were held with participants, interest in career planning had greatly intensified, and considerably more time was devoted to this subject in group discussions.

Participating Companies' Career-Planning Systems

The ten companies that participated in this study had a wide range of career-planning systems. A few had somewhat sophisticated, relatively well-developed systems, but most had simple and informal systems developed between bosses and subordinates. In a study done in 1978 of career plans in 225 large and middle-sized companies, Walker and Gutteridge found similar variations:

> The kinds of career-planning activities most-widely touted in published articles are relatively new in application and are not widely utilized. For many of the companies surveyed, career planning remains largely an informal, experimental, and fragmented activity.[3]

Despite the variety of career-planning programs in the ten companies in the present study, the managers' overall impressions of program effectiveness are similar and not wildly enthusiastic. Only 36 percent of the managers rate their company's career-planning system as good or excellent. The responses range from 30 percent of black women to 53 percent of Asian women. Among the other race/sex groups the range is 42 to 31 percent. These responses are fairly similar to those reported by Walker and Gutteridge—namely, that in 225 firms only 32 percent of the managers rated their career-planning programs good.[4] Any attempt to develop and implement improved career-planning programs must first include an analysis of the causes of these low ratings.

Why Do Most Managers Rate Their Company's Career-Planning System Low?

A number of factors contribute to managers' negative opinions about career planning, such as no clear, widely accepted definition of career planning and who participates in the plans; confusion as to what is or is not part of the system; large discrepancies between desired features and actual features; and large discrepancies between managers who desire career plans with active company involvement and those who have them. The following sections examine these factors.

Managers' Definitions of Career Planning and Who Participates

Although a sizable majority (72 percent) of the managers state that their company has a career-planning system for managers, the qualitative response discloses that a great deal of confusion and disagreement exists regarding the system's definition, purpose, and scope.

Definitions for career planning vary from one manager who believes it is a secret, systematic plan that high-level management uses to move employees into different jobs, to another who says it is a person's personal view of what their careers should be like, to still another who says it is a process in which the company and employee work out mutually agreeable career objectives for the employee. In addition, some managers equate career planning only with vertical movement, others refer only to lateral developmental moves, and still others equate it with both lateral and promotional moves.

With regard to who participates, some respondents believe career-planning programs are only for selected managers participating in special programs, especially college hires or a small number of high-potential people being groomed for top-management positions. Others feel that career planning only exists for minorities and women or only for white men.

Lack of Knowledge about the Parts of the Companies'
Career-Planning Systems

As varied as the definitions of career planning are the managers' views about the career-planning system's components. In response to questions about which of the fourteen features listed in table 11-1 are a part of their company's career-planning system, managers who know of the system are most likely to indicate that performance appraisals (95 percent) and MBO or joint target setting (83 percent) are features of it. The components least reported are a personnel data base (25 percent) and a formal organization with counselors and coordinators (22 percent).

This lack of agreement leads to considerably negative views about career planning because some managers, especially those who say they are not sure about a feature, believe that others are benefiting from the feature and they are not. For example, a white man at the third level says:

> I don't know what features are part of the career-planning system. All I know is I am not being helped by any of them and others are. The plan stinks!

In addition to not knowing what features are part of the career-planning system, managers are not well informed about important information needed for them to make intelligent career decisions. Less than half of the managers reported being at least fairly well informed about other jobs that might interest them (47 percent), about knowledge or skills needed for jobs that interest them (47 percent), and about career opportunities available to them in their company (35 percent). As figure 11-1 shows, when the questions are formed into an index, a surprising 45 percent of the managers are not at all informed about any of these three features. One of the main

Table 11-1
Features Included in Company's Career-Planning System

Which of the Following Features Are Included in Your Company's Career-Planning Program? (N = 2,806)	*Included*	*Not Included*	*Do Not Know*
Your performance appraisal	94.9	2.2	2.8
Management by objectives or joint target setting	82.5	7.3	10.1
Your potential appraisal	79.1	12.6	8.3
Opportunity to state what your job or location preferences are	79.1	13.1	7.8
Systematic review sessions with your boss and/or company representative	77.8	16.6	5.5
Assessment programs	75.4	12.3	12.3
Information on present job openings	53.9	35.3	10.8
Provision for planning next job or series of jobs	51.5	30.4	18.1
Published set of management job descriptions	50.1	32.1	17.8
Projection of future job opportunities	45.3	34.6	20.1
Management-transfer plan	43.8	36.4	19.9
Formal training on how the company's plan works	36.6	42.2	21.2
Major parts of the data on your career plan are in a computer (personnel data base)	25.2	22.7	52.1
Formal organization with counselors and coordinators	22.2	50.2	27.6

reasons that managers, regardless of race and sex, are not well informed is the identification of the grapevine as the primary information source regarding career opportunities for managers (27 percent). One-quarter (24 percent) of those who say they depend on the grapevine feel at least fairly well informed about career information and requirements, while 62 percent of those who depend on company communications, and 65 percent of those who say their bosses are their primary source of information, respond that they feel at least fairly well informed.

The fact that, except for Asians, men are by far better informed in these areas then women are suggests that not only is career-planning information poorly disseminated for most managers in general but also that women are at a greater disadvantage than men are in obtaining career information. In addition, out of all male groups, black men are least informed—a response similar to women's.

With specific regard to women, one factor that contributes to their lack of necessary information is the sexist stereotype that women really are not interested in careers, therefore, why waste effort in providing them with information? With specific regard to black men, since they are perceived as the greatest threat to the white-male-dominant position, a greater sub-

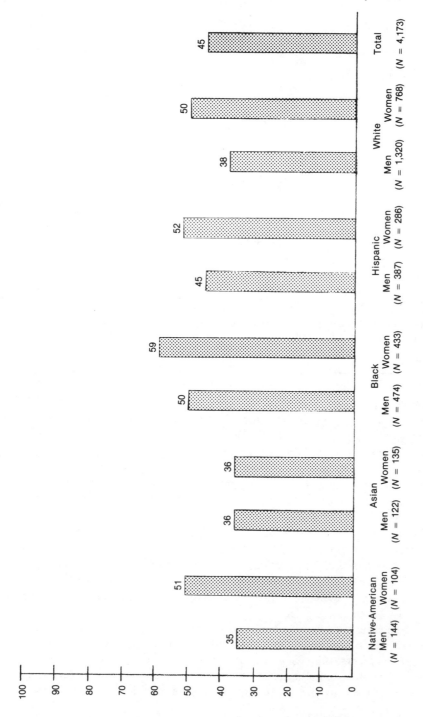

Figure 11.1. Percentage of Managers Who Are Not at all Informed about Internal Career Opportunities and Requirements.

conscious or conscious effort probably exists on the corporation's part to keep them ill informed.

With such wide variations in the responses about some of the features and the lack of career information, one could readily conclude that lack of proper and sufficient information will negatively affect managers' views about career planning. For example, 19 percent of the managers who are not informed on any of these issues versus 59 percent who are informed on all three of them rate their company's plan good or excellent.

Discrepancies between Company Plans and
Desired Plans

When the managers are asked which of the fourteen features listed in table 11-1 should be part of their company's career-planning system, at least 85 percent want to see twelve of the features included, and at least 94 percent want eight of the features included. It is extremely important to note that features that represent formal, systematic, and informational aspects of a career-planning system produced the greatest percentage differences between what managers believe their company plan consists of and what they would like to see included as a feature. These features are listed here with the percentage differences in parentheses:

Formal training on how the company's plan works (52 percent);

Projection of future job opportunities (51 percent);

Formal organization with counselors and coordinators (51 percent);

Management-transfer plan (46 percent);

Published set of management job descriptions (44 percent);

Information on present job openings (43 percent);

Provision for planning the next job or series of jobs (42 percent).

When none of these features is present, 59 percent of the managers rate their companies' plans poor; when four of the features are present, 17 percent rate their company's plan poor; and when all seven are present, only 8 percent rate it poor. Of those managers who rate their company's plans good or excellent, 73 percent say the plan has all of these features, 42 percent say it has four of the seven, and 13 percent say it has none of the seven features. A third-level white-female manager who rates her company's career-planning system poor sums up many managers' feelings:

My personal career plans are highly tentative—partially because of the lack of a company system. I feel neither my boss nor myself have the tools available to realistically map out long-term career plans within this company today.

Types of Career Plans Managers Have

Contributing significantly to the low ratings on career planning is the high percentage of managers who do not have career plans and the lack of active company participation in many managers' career plans. While 55 percent of the managers say they have a career plan within their company, those least likely to say they have a career plan are white men (47 percent) and native-American and white women (53 percent). Most likely to say they have a career plan are Asian men (75 percent) and Asian women (69 percent). Between 58 and 61 percent of the other race/sex groups say this. However, of the 55 percent who have career plans, 51 percent report that it is a personal plan they developed for themselves and have not discussed with anyone else in their company. The types of career plans managers have are shown in table 11-2.

If the personally designed career plans have not been developed in the context of corporate realities, then those managers may well form the core of a group of very dissatisfied managers in the future. A disturbing fact is that half of the managers in these companies who have a career plan developed that plan entirely by themselves, without formal corporate input. While managers should be encouraged to take the initiative in planning their careers, they must also coordinate their planning with corporate realities through their bosses and by negotiating a mutually acceptable compromise.

Although 98 percent of the managers say discussions should take place at least once a year, career-planning discussions have never or almost never taken place for 46 percent of the participants. The more frequently managers have had career-planning discussions with their bosses, the more frequently they believe career-planning discussions should take place. Illustrative of this point is the fact that 66 pecent of the managers who had discussions with their bosses quarterly or more often want them quarterly or more often. However, only 16 percent of those who have never had such discussions want them to occur at least quarterly. Evidently, subordinates who have participated in career planning prefer the give and take that goes on in these sessions that allows them to know where they stand so they can make decisions about their career and personal lives.

Of the managers who have career-planning discussions, 21 percent indicate they initiate the discussions, 33 percent say the discussions are initiated by their bosses, 42 percent respond that both they and their bosses

Table 11-2
Managers' Career Plans
(percent)

What Is Your Own Career Plan?	Native-American		Asian		Black		Hispanic		White		Total
	Men (N = 86)	*Women* (N = 56)	*Men* (N = 91)	*Women* (N = 91)	*Men* (N = 276)	*Women* (N = 250)	*Men* (N = 232)	*Women* (N = 165)	*Men* (N = 584)	*Women* (N = 401)	(N = 2,232)
A personal one developed for yourself	61.6	42.9	45.1	27.5	57.6	54.8	55	45.5	54.8	46.1	51.2
Something you have worked out with your boss but not within the framework of any career-planning system	8.1	28.6	12.1	12.1	7.6	8.8	9.1	13.3	11.1	12.2	11
Something you and your boss have worked out within the framework of your company's career-planning system	19.8	14.3	26.4	46.2	17	19.2	21.6	23	20	26.7	22.3
Something your boss has worked out without any input from you	0	3.6	6.6	4.4	8	6.4	6	8.5	8.2	6.5	6.8
Something you have worked out with someone other than your boss but that your boss supports	1.2	3.6	1.1	4.4	3.3	3.6	1.1	1.2	1.2	1	2
Something the company initiated but left for you and your boss to carry out	9.3	7.1	8.8	5.5	6.5	7.2	7.2	8.5	4.6	7.5	6.8

jointly initiate the discussions, and 5 percent indicate another source of in-
itiation.

Only two out of five managers feel very free to initiate career-planning
discussions with their bosses. Since open communication between bosses
and subordinates is crucial to any successful career-planning process, the
reluctance of many managers to initiate such discussions with their bosses
poses a tremendous potential problem in achieving this goal.

In sum, the vast majority of the participants rate their company's
career-planning system fair or poor primarily because of confusion about
the meaning of career planning, the actual-versus-desired career-planning
systems, and the overall lack of sufficient information and the resultant
lack of career-planning discussions.

Critical Elements for Effective Career Planning

On the basis of the foregoing analysis, three elements appear critical to the
implementation of an effective career-planning system:

Interested subordinates;

Interested bosses;

Viable, company-supported, formalized career-planning system.

Interested Subordinates

The most-basic element of career planning is the subordinate, the manager
whose career plan is to be developed. Over half, 52 percent, of the managers
believe they have the major responsibility for career planning and development. Of the remaining managers, 22 percent believe their bosses have the
responsibility, 13 percent state their department has the responsibility, and
12 percent name their company as the primary responsible agent.

Thorton suggested some reasons why more managers do not say that
they have primary responsibility for their career planning and development:

> Many individuals believe they cannot control their careers. They believe
> that their supervisor or "the organization" will take care of them, that
> "you have to be in the right place at the right time," or that "fate or divine
> providence will direct their careers."[5]

By contrast, it is important to note that many managers in this study are
interested in their careers and are willing to pursue career development if

they believe they have a reasonable chance to do so. Indicative of the level of enthusiasm managers exhibit in pursuit of career growth is a set of responses that centers on the subject of training and development. The vast majority of managers state they are quite willing to pursue training-and-development activities, even in the extreme conditions that would involve being away from home for over a week. Contrary to stereotypical belief, female managers are essentially as likely as their male counterparts are to be willing to take advantage of these opportunities. As shown in table 11-3, 59 percent of white women are very willing and 19 percent are somewhat willing to pursue training away from home for over a week, as compared to 64 and 19 percent of white men. Table 11-3 also confirms the great ambition and drive of black and Hispanic men, 81 and 79 percent respectively, who are very willing to pursue long periods of training for a promotion. Their figures compare to 56 and 69 percent of the other race/sex groups.

While managers are most likely, under most length/location circumstances, to pursue training that prepares them for a possible promotion, four out of five managers (79 percent) are even willing to pursue after-hours training at work to prepare for a lateral assignment.

In response to the question, "Have you pursued, on your own, any developmental or training experiences during the past three years?" Hispanic and black men (70 and 68 percent), are found to be the most likely to have done so, and Hispanic and native-American women and white men are least likely (50 percent in each group). Over half (55 percent) of all managers have independently pursued some kind of training seen as helpful to their careers.

It should be recognized that not all managers are interested in career planning. Wide variations exist in their views. Some managers are content where they are and resent being moved around. This resentment is particularly evident when an individual has realistically accepted the signs that he or she is no longer considered promotable. For example, a second-level white man remarks:

> Why do I have to spend my entire life moving around and changing jobs? Why can't I just stay on a job and just do a good job? I am not going to move up, and I am tired of moving around.

At the other extreme are those managers who not only want to make moves but also initiate career-planning activities themselves. They act on the realization that even the best of bosses have numerous demands that rank more pressing upon their time and energies than developing career plans for their subordinates. A first-level white woman comments on her company's management-appraisal and development program by saying that questions raised or objectives submitted to her boss are never discussed, just pushed aside with the comment, "Yes, we've got to take time to do that

Table 11-3

Willingness to Pursue Training Activities Away from Home for One Week or Longer in Preparation for a Promotion (percent)

To What Extent Are You Willing to Take Advantage of Training and/or Developmental Opportunities, which Would Require You to Be Away from Home for a Period of Time (One Week or Longer), that Would Prepare You for a Possible Promotion?	Native-American		Asian		Black		Hispanic		White		Total
	Men (N = 143)	Women (N = 104)	Men (N = 122)	Women (N = 134)	Men (N = 472)	Women (N = 433)	Men (N = 387)	Women (N = 286)	Men (N = 1,263)	Women (N = 761)	(N = 4,105)
Very willing	66.4	69.2	64.8	56	80.9	69.3	78.6	61.9	63.8	59.1	66.8
Somewhat willing	21	17.3	21.3	22.4	14	17.1	13.7	20.3	19	19.3	18.1
Not very willing	8.4	3.8	7.4	8.2	2.5	6.5	5.4	7	7.4	9.2	6.8
Not at all willing	4.2	9.6	6.6	13.4	2.5	7.2	2.3	10.8	9.7	12.4	8.3

later.'' She says that most of her moves within the company have been self-initiated:

> I've done the research to find out what's available. For a long time, candidate letters were a deep, dark secret—even after a company directive from headquarters said to make them available.

An insightful description of career planning as it is often implemented is given by a third-level white-male manager:

> The success of career planning depends entirely on whether or not you are fortunate enough to work for a boss who is genuinely concerned about you and if that boss happens to work for or know people who are influential in determining moves. This becomes much-more true at third level and above.

The essential point for subordinates is that they must take the primary responsibility for their career plans. Some bosses will be glad to help and will assist their subordinates by redefining careers, providing information, and helping to affect the necessary career steps. Other bosses will do nothing and will become angered, annoyed, and/or threatened if the subordinate should dare to do anything on his or her own behalf. Subordinates must be prepared to deal with a boss who may interpret ambition and initiative as disloyalty and be willing to take all the consequences of such an interpretation. However, the bottom line remains that subordinates' careers depend in large part upon their own initiative.

Interested Bosses

The subordinate, even when willingly, hopefully, and aggressively pursuing career development, will still have great difficulty in furthering his or her career without the involvement of an interested boss.

Walker and Gutteridge found that the greatest difficulty the managers in their 225 companies experienced in implementing career planning was getting the bosses to accept and perform their roles as career counselors. They stated:

> The greatest frustration appeared to be the difficulty of equipping and motivating supervisors and managers to act as career counselors, a factor that is believed to be central to effective career planning. Lack of success in this area seemed to tarnish the overall evaluation.[6]

The company has a responsibility to equip bosses to function in this role. Bosses can effectively use training programs as a tool for career planning only to the extent that they have knowledge of the programs, confidence in the programs, training in how to aid subordinates in career planning, and a belief that the company views career planning as a very important responsibility of the bosses.

A majority of the managers report that they lack the skills and training to handle career planning. In response to the question, "To what extent do you believe you need training in each of twenty-four areas of your job?" the greatest need identified was career-planning procedures. Sixty-three percent of the managers believe they need more than just a little training in this area.

When training needs in career planning and performance- and potential-evaluation procedures are formed into an index, 36 percent of the managers state they need at least some (more than a little) training in all three areas. Twenty-nine percent of white men, 35 percent of Asian women, 37 percent of Hispanic women, and from 41 to 47 percent of other race/sex groups say they need these types of training at least to some extent. This is a crucial finding for corporate training programs. If managers do not have proper and adequate training in conducting performance and potential appraisals, they can neither properly conduct career planning nor determine what training and development would be useful for their subordinates.

The following data illustrate the degree to which bosses in this study are involved in developing and assisting their subordinates. The findings were not expected considering the earlier view of managers in this chapter. Sixty-one percent of the managers believe their bosses assist them in getting developmental experiences on the job, and 60 percent believe their bosses remain open to their career interests. In addition, over half (53 percent) of the managers believe their bosses use their knowledge and abilities to assist subordinates in career development, and almost one-quarter (23 percent) of the managers reported that their bosses assist them in getting developmental experiences off the job.

When these four questions about development are combined to form an index, 58 percent of the managers say their bosses are at least somewhat helpful in two or more of these four areas. However, 25 percent believe their bosses do not assist them, even to some extent, in any of the four developmental areas. Figure 11-2 shows the managers' responses by race and sex.

Not only do bosses not implement career planning because of lack of training but also many bosses are not interested in implementing career planning because of the demands upon their time. Some managers say, rather defensively, that of course they should assist in career planning for their subordinates and that they want to, but they despair of finding the necessary time for the task. They point out that when they are evaluated by their superiors, their performance is measured for a wide range of responsibilities but that very little, if any, weight is given to how conscientiously or effectively they attend to career counseling for their subordinates.

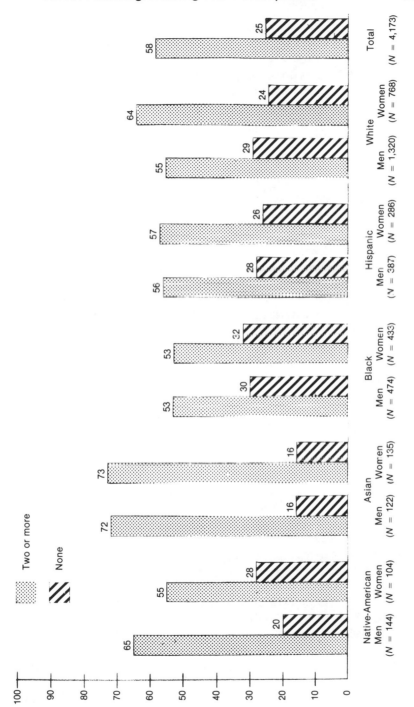

Figure 11-2. Percentage of Managers Who Believe Bosses Are at Least Somewhat Helpful in Two or More or No Areas of Career Development

A third-level white woman states that a boss "would have more incentive to spend time on career planning for his or her employees if that aspect of his or her job were encouraged by upper management."

Another reason bosses do not implement career planning is simple self-interest. As noted previously, minority managers sometimes feel that affirmative-action programs operate against their individual best interests. Their bosses refuse to let them move on because their work is satisfactory or better, and the bosses do not want to search for another minority member to fill a quota. White managers also complain that "once a department gets a trained management person, it becomes selfish and wants to keep that person. Thus it will shield other department's openings from him or her."

Despite all the legitimate reasons and irrational excuses bosses give to avoid career planning with their subordinates, the greatest obstacle to that activity appears to be the bosses' discomfort and reluctance to sit down to a frank and honest discussion with a subordinate. The fact that such discussions have not been in the corporate tradition is the major reason so many employees are forced to depend upon grapevines, distortion, and innuendo for information. In the corporate world, as elsewhere, information is a form of power. The tendency is to hoard it. Even if that tendency could be neutralized, many bosses are insecure about how to proceed. They are uncomfortable with the whole process, particularly with those parts of it requiring them to help subordinates to scale down unrealistic expectations or to give critical construction feedback.

Viable, Company-Supported Career-Planning System

Some overlap occurs between the second and third elements—the interested boss and the viable, company-supported career-planning system. The charge is repeatedly made by managers that a company career plan on paper does not imply its implementation. Some bosses consider time spent on career planning as a waste because upper management denies them the power to move subordinates around in any systematic fashion. Subordinates seem to be aware of this attitude, since only half of the participating managers believe their bosses have the power to advance their career.

Other charges are that upper management is not committed to career planning because it would lose the power it has to make decisions on personnel moves. A first-level white man states that career planning is "an ideal which in reality is a facade unless there is an individual high enough in the company's organization to 'sponsor' your upward mobility." This charge that upper-level managers are unwilling to give up power is supported by a more-careful analysis of the managers' responses about career planning. For example, while 86 percent of the managers want a systematic career-planning system, important and significant differences occur by level. Upper levels of managers, regardless of race and sex, express the least interest in a systematic plan. Illustrative of this point are white men who have the biggest differences in views between upper and lower management:

First level	89%
Second level	82%
Third level	71%
Fourth level	62%
Fifth level	43%
Sixth level	38%

The history of industrial management provides a partial explanation for this finding. When the managerial class came into existence in the nine-teenth century, its members were very concerned about establishing the legitimacy of their authority. As Reinhart Bendix pointed out in *Work and Authority in Industry,* they were neither owners nor part of a traditional "ruling class."[7] Daniel Bell argued that with the end of family capitalism, managers sought to legitimatize their position through the development of an ideology that awarded control of a large group of workers to a small and exclusive group of men.[8] This ideology also separated the viewpoint of managers from that of owner/entrepreneurs. Wilbert Moore agreed with earlier works when he commented that without the power of property to back them, the new managers created and relied upon a claim of "efficiency" in order to "justify the unilateral exercise of power by management."[9]

Thus, those managers who have risen to the upper levels through a loosely structured career-planning system would think most positively about maintaining this system since they have risen through it and now operate it. Such savvy types may realize that fluid opportunities to move informally through the company's informal networks may be more beneficial to their personal career-planning strategy than changing to a formal plan. A fifth-level white-male manager, while admitting that measured performance and potential would be the fairest criteria for career-planning programs, stated that "personalities and highly subjective judgments cloud this issue. Personal relationships still dominate career programs." These personal relationships are, de facto, the framework upon which the informal networks depend. In short, the more informal career planning is, the more control and power remains in the hands of higher-level management.

Conclusions and Recommendations

A substantial majority of the managers in this study rates their companies' career-planning systems low for several reasons. One reason is the confusion in the definition of purpose and scope. Another is the lack of necessary information for managers to effectively plan their careers. Still another reason is the large discrepancy between what managers believe *should* be components of the plan and what they believe *are* components of it. Finally, managers are very critical because of the usually poor implementation by bosses of even the best plans.

Many bosses, if not most, do not put much time and energy into career planning. One of the main reasons for this lack is the inability of many of them to effectively communicate with their subordinates. Another reason is a matter of perception. Whether career planning is perceived by bosses as beneficial, burdensome, or costly to themselves depends on how they perceive their own job and how their company values and rewards such activities. With so many pressing demands upon their time, many managers are naturally going to match their priorities to their companies' priorities as evidenced by the reward system that emphasizes various types of numerical results and not employee-development results.

The most-probable explanations as to why even the best career-planning systems have not been very successful is the lack of real commitment from top management. Most of the upper-level managers in this study are really opposed to any systematic career-planning system because they will lose the power they have acquired in the informal career-planning process.

While many problems exist with career-planning procedures, such procedures are becoming increasingly important for corporations' survival. Considering the lack of economic growth, the pyramidal nature of the hierarchy, and the attitude of the new-breed managers, the vast majority of managers at some time could become very dissatisfied with their careers. Nevertheless, corporations can minimize this dissatisfaction by providing managers with opportunities for growth by restructuring organizational values, providing alternative or additional rewards and recognition, redesigning work, and redirecting people into different and interesting jobs. All of this needs to be done by means of, and tied in with, career planning. The first step is for top management and personnel departments to be totally committed to the process. Secondly, they must be more honest and straightforward with managers about their career plans and allow managers to be active participants in the planning process. Corporations should not promise more than they can deliver. They must accomplish this lowering of expectations for promotion to a realistic level through substituting alternative incentives without creating a pendulum effect and depressing expectations of job satisfaction below a functional level. While corporations should not promise more than they can deliver, they should make certain what they deliver is done fairly and equitably. Specific steps companies should take are as follows:

1. Make a policy decision at the corporate level to develop the central and systematic components that managers want but do not have. Integrate all appropriate components into a career-planning system, with an organization possessing the power and authority to enforce the plan at all levels of management.
2. Distribute to all management personnel a publication describing all the career-planning features it now provides and how these features are applied and implemented. It should be reissued whenever components are added, deleted, or altered. It may be supplemented with other media.
3. Make policy and practice decisions at the corporate level that make accessible to *all* managers the information on job openings and job descriptions that have been previously available only to some managers.
4. Provide extensive training for bosses in implementing the system. Subordinates should also have training in the system. Bosses and subordinates should receive much of this training together because career planning should be a joint venture.
5. Provide counselors and coordinators to assist both bosses and subordinates in communicating with each other—a major feature of the system.
6. Establish a process to evaluate the impact of selection processes on such elements as race/sex groups. This process should include all aspects of the selection process, including but not limited to, qualifications.
7. Evaluate the effectiveness of all components of career planning. Monitor programs or processes related to transfer and promotion in order to detect any differential impact.
8. Institute a reward system that motivates managers to pay sufficient attention to career planning.

The purposes of these specific recommendations are to diminish the negative attitude spawned by the inequitable distribution of career information, to enhance the likelihood that career planning will be more-evenly applied, and to take one step toward an integrated managerial system.

In conclusion, most managers agree with the advantages of career planning. Nevertheless, it remains a system fraught with problems. The problems exist basically because career planning takes some of the secrecy and power from the corporate kingmakers and gives it to employees. To belabor the obvious, today's corporations are too complex and facing too many difficult issues to continue staffing in an uneven, unfair, unsophisticated, and unsystematic manner because of big egos. Too much is at stake.

Jane Miller expertly sums up the need for career planning and what would be the ultimate result if corporations do not take the initiative and make it successful:

. . . if corporations do not address themselves to the current need for a career-planning program, they will continue to lose some of their best employees. Furthermore, it is my opinion that the government will some-day require some form of career-planning program as it has previously required other programs such as OSHA and EEO.[10]

12 Who Needs Special Training?

A major question has not yet been answered: Do minorities and women need special training? As noted in the chapter 1, the impetus for conducting this study was to determine whether minorities and women need special training to become successful managers. Many scholars, managers, and government officials—the majority of them white men—have claimed that the primary reason greater numbers of women and minorities have not been placed in middle- and upper-management positions is their different cultural backgrounds and/or socialization patterns. The most-frequently discussed solution to this problem, or any problems encountered by minorities and/or women in corporations, has been special training.

Specially designed programs for women and minorities are not unusual these days. One of the most-frequently used reasons for the establishment of these special training programs is that minorities and women have not developed the necessary managerial skills and attitudes to be effective managers. Underlining this reason is the sexist assumption that women inheritently lack these skills.

Even though no one has clearly demonstrated the effectiveness and usefulness of special training for women, it has become big business. The *Wall Street Journal,* on 31 August 1979, did not fail to mention that special training for women has become a very large and profitable business. Not only private companies but also colleges and universities have formed departments to provide such training. The article suggested that many of the people who have entered this training area are self-styled—that is, they have little skill and knowledge about the real problems confronting working women.[1]

These same comments hold true for minorities. Dr. George Neely, a consultant on black managers in corporations, has pointed out that the same arguments and assumptions used to justify special training for women are used for minorities. He wrote that numerous managerial-consultant firms have been created, and departments of established firms have developed sections to deal with special training for minoirites. The money some of these firms make is incredible. However, the results of their programs do not justify the cost. He believes that the special training is being directed toward the wrong groups and that the reason it is not effective in most cases is that the people who need special training are the white men and not the minorities and women. However, a few consulting firms have developed an expertise to assist white men with their special-training needs with regard to dealing effectively with minorities and women. Those firms that have are not being sought out by the white-male-dominated corporate leadership.[2] Neely's views receive a great deal of support from this study.

Most minority and female managers, and many white-male managers participating in this study, suggest that the concept of special training be enlarged to include white men and be primarily for them. They believe that white men have a lot to learn about their own racist and sexist prejudices and stereotyped views and that they could benefit mightily from some awareness-generating experiences. Illustrative of this fact is that one-third of all the managers (35 percent) in this study believe most minorities and women need special training to be successful managers. However, almost one out of two (47 percent) of all the managers believes that white men need special training to work more effectively with women and minorities.

The statements from a white man and a black woman exemplify the opposite sides of this issue as it relates to minorities and women. The white man at the third level says:

> Minorities and women must learn about profit-making methods and motivating factors. Cultural backgrounds often inhibit their progress. They need to learn how to stress hard work, diligence, etc.

However, the black woman at the first level does not believe this to be the case. She notes:

> This special-training issue allows companies to make excuses as to why minorities and women are relatively rare in middle and upper management (lower management too) . . . they try to say we are culturally different and socialized differently. I can interact effectively with whites and males but can they interact effectively with me? Most cannot as far as I am concerned.

Special Training for Female Managers

Figure 12-1 illustrates that approximately one-third of the managers (35 percent) believe that most women need special training to be successful in management. Responses vary greatly among different race/sex groups. Native-American men (51 percent) and white men (42 percent) are most likely to believe that women need special training. Asian women (23 percent) are least likely to believe this. Within each ethnic group, male managers are more likely than their female counterparts are to believe that women need special training. For example, 42 percent of white men versus 30 percent of white women believe women need this training. No significant differences occur by level within any race/sex group.

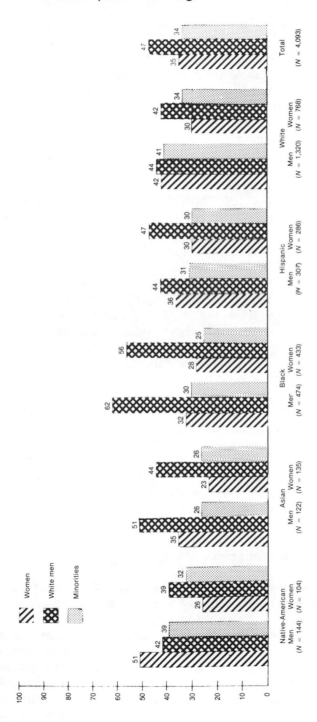

Figure 12-1. Percentage of Managers Who Believe Special Training Needs Exist for Minorities, Women, and White Men.

Stereotypes and Special Training for Women

The number of female peers or subordinates a manager has does not influence his or her opinions about the need for special training for women.
This finding, along with the responses to several other questions, indicates
that many managers who believe that women need special training believe
so not because of personal experiences but because of stereotypical views they
have about women. For example, 70 percent of the male managers who
agree that women are too emotional to be competent managers say that
women need special training, while only 35 percent of the male managers
who disagree or strongly disagree with this stereotype feel that women need
special training. This pattern also is found among the responses of female
managers—that is, 39 percent of those who at least agree with the
stereotyped view versus 18 percent of those who disagree or strongly
disagree say that women need special training.

Managers who feel that women use sex as an alibi for the difficulties
they have on the job and that they are not serious about a professional
career are more likely to feel that female managers need special training.
Looking at the responses of third- and fourth-level men who have the most
impact and influence on women's careers, since most women are at the first
and second levels, one finds that 65 percent of the third- and fourth-level
men who believe that women are not serious about a professional career say
that women need special training.

Probably the most-important finding, which suggests that the sexist attitudes of managers rather than their personal work-related experiences
with female managers are primarily responsible for their beliefs, is the
managers' self-rating on acceptance of opposite-sex groups. Male managers
who rate themselves low in their ability to accept women in the workplace
are more likely than are those who rate themselves high to feel that women
need special training. This information casts serious doubts on the objectivity of those who say women need special training.

Types of Special Training for Female Managers

When managers are given the opportunity to explain the types of special
training they believe women need, they identify three main areas: (1)
managerial/supervisory, (2) work-group relationships, and (3)
technical/educational. Table 12-1 shows the managers' responses. An important overall observation from the table is that many of the special-
training categories are really not very special in the sense that they are only
unique for women. What many of these managers are saying is that women
need more training in traditional areas than men do. This additional

Table 12-1
Special Training for Female Managers
(percent)

What Type of Special Training Do You Believe Female Managers Need?	*Total*
Managerial/Supervisory Training	(N = 526)
Understanding political aspects of management	23
Leadership	18.6
Administration	17.7
Decision making	17.3
Handling stress/emotional issues	11.4
Corporate issues and financial trends	5.3
Other	6.7
Peer/Subordinate-Relationship Training	(N = 555)
Dealing with male subordinates and peers	48
Assertiveness	17.7
Objectivity to people	11.4
Building self-confidence	9.2
Learning how to be successful (accepted) in a white-male organization	7.7
Competition	1.6
Other	4.4
Technical/Educational Training	(N = 686)
Technical skills	59
Overcoming lack of previous work experience	32.5
Courses in general	3.1
Language skills, communication	2.3
Basic education/writing skills	1.2
Understanding of technical problems	1
Other	0.9

training they consider special. These comments also apply to the minority section. In addition, many of the comments made about a particular area of special training in the sections on women apply for the same training in the sections on minorities and vice versa.

Training in Corporate Politics

An analysis of several of the most-frequently selected categories illustrates the questionableness of many of these "special" training areas that women are thought to need. In the managerial/supervisory area, the most-frequent response managers give is that women need training to understand the political aspects of management (23 percent). What is interesting about this response is that white women (33 percent), Asian women (33 percent), and black women (31 percent) are most likely to say that women need training in understanding the political aspects of management. As a white women at the fifth level says:

> I believe that women do not understand the political operations of the corporate world—they are too naive.

A second-level white woman comments:

> Most women and minorities lack experience in business and the difficulties of coping with company business politics. Males also tend to exclude women and minorities from the business world.

A number of social scientists such as Harragan have endorsed this view. She has argued that the only qualification some women are lacking is the correct perspective—that is, organizational management must be thought of in game terms. The conduct of business is subject to specific rules that shape the nature of the game and ordain the resulting patterns, traditions, and operating procedures. "Corporate politics is the x factor, the missing component in the female-'qualified' equation."[3]

Some women (and some men) may truly be naive about corporate politics, but the belief that special training is the only, or the most-effective, solution to women's corporate problems is not necessarily supportable. Harragan's position is based on the assumption that only one corporate game exists when, in reality, there are thousands, and the game changes as the actors change. The rules, patterns, and traditions are modified by the actors in different departments and areas of a corporation. Therefore, while similarities might exist among corporate games, so may many differences. Training to be effective under such varying circumstances would have to involve learning how to optimize the use of personal qualities in the differing contexts. The skills involved are highly individualized and, as training experts will recognize, do not lend themselves to cost-effective acquisition through training courses. Rather, experience is the best teacher, requiring, of course, on-job opportunities.

What actually happens is that, willingly and/or unwillingly, men block women from participating in corporate politics. Thus, women are labeled as naive about this issue. In addition, some women might decide not to participate in corporate politics. More specifically, the new breed of managers, many of whom are women, are less willing to make the personal compromises necessary to assimilate into the corporate political system. They are less interested in the nonfinancial rewards of successfully doing so. They expect to be evaluated and rewarded objectively, without playing subtle games, and often seek and achieve personal fulfillment outside the corporate day rather than participate.

None of these comments is to dismiss the importance of understanding corporate politics. This understanding is a reality that probably affects most employees' careers, sometimes more than others. In this study, 57 percent of the managers believe that their corporate political skills will affect their achieving their desired positions. However, remember that one learns corporate games not through formal training but through informal training by being given the opportunity to be a full corporate member. The most-important skills a person, male or female, needs in order to understand the corporate political game are an understanding of people and of him- or herself and the opportunity to demonstrate these skills.

Training for Dealing with the Male Work Group

In the area of work-group relationships, the type of training most-frequently mentioned (48 percent) is training to deal with male subordinates, peers, and bosses. Interestingly, larger percentages of men than women in each ethnic group state that women need training in coping with male subordinates, peers, and bosses. For example, 73 percent of Asian men compared with 33 percent of Asian women say that such training is needed. A predominant view of managers who believe women do need such training is typified by a white woman at the third level who says:

> In order to overcome male peers', subordinates', and bosses' resentment and resistance to female authority, sex-discrimination training is needed to help cope with this discrimination when it is encountered.

A white man at the third level supports this view:

> There is a built-in resentment by many males to working for a woman. Women should be trained in how to cope with this and how to recognize it.

A white man at the fourth level registers a long-held male view:

> The traditional environment and role of women has not been in the business world. Training and supervision of males, basic problem-solving and decision-making courses would help females in these areas.

A Hispanic man at the second level sums up the sexist view held by many men and some women:

Women are usually biased and emotion rules. Therefore, they require a course in personnel management and objectivity.

Managers who believe that women need special training to deal with male subordinates and peers, and who base this belief on the view that women are somehow inadequate, are blaming the victim. The real issue is not that female managers are so different from male managers and/or lacking some specific skills but that the sexist attitudes and stereotyped behavior of many male managers makes life very difficult for female managers. That many women are adept at on-the-job interpersonal relations and able to overcome sexist obstacles is evident in the fact that both male and female respondents in this study rate female bosses higher than male bosses on a number of important qualities essential to effective management.

Assertiveness Training

Another type of training managers frequently suggest for career women is assertiveness training (18 percent). With the exception of native-American managers, the women of each racial group are more likely than are their male counterparts to indicate a need for assertiveness training. For example, 32 percent of black women compared with 11 percent of black men say that women need assertiveness training. Some of these women believe that unless they are as aggressive as men they will not be accepted in the corporate world. A Hispanic woman at the first level says:

> I believe women need assertiveness training. Women are not taught in the Latino culture to be aggressive. There are many times I wish I was more aggressive like the men. I might be much further along in my career.

However, a question women should consider is whether they should try to emulate aggressive male behavior or whether men should be urged to modify their own aggressive behavior. The fact that aggressive behavior in men has been linked to major health problems might strongly suggest the latter. (See the appendix for greater detail about male behavior and its relationship to heart attacks.) Also, considering the fact that female bosses receive higher ratings from their subordinates than do male bosses, modification of aggressive male behavior might be more beneficial to corporate functioning than assertiveness training for women would be.

Another problem with the belief that women need assertiveness training is related to how women who attempt to assert themselves are interpreted. More specifically, assertive behavior on the part of women is usually interpreted negatively by most men and some women, while a man's exhibiting

the same behavior is usually interpreted positively by the same people. In fact, for some managers, women's behaviors are never correct.
A white man at the fifth level says:

> Most career women I know are either too aggressive or too passive. They are intimidated by the male-dominated environment or they try to run over it.

Larwood and Wood, elaborating on this viewpoint, wrote:

> Women make threats [serious ones] less frequently than men. When a woman does begin to assert herself . . . [in this manner], she is unlikely to be believed or taken seriously by men. When her aggressive intentions are established beyond a doubt, however, the woman is a double threat—not only is she as aggressive as a man, but she also behaves unpredictably and inappropriately. At this point, others have license both to "counteraggress" to maintain their own positions and to enforce social norms for appropriate behavior against the woman. The double threat is most likely to occur when an assertive woman encounters a man. In contrast, men anticipate appropriate assertiveness from each other. They have developed cue-and-bargaining strategies to assess and deal with the assertiveness and are unlikely to provoke overreaction from such behavior. In interactions between two women, either can readily justify allowing the other to assert herself.[4]

All of these comments strongly indicate that to say all women need assertiveness training is a broad generalization with little foundation. Some women, because of sexist socialization, may not be assertive enough to be effective managers in the present authoritarian, macho mode of many corporations. However, many men also are not assertive enough to be effective in the same corporate environment. In addition, the new-breed managers are demanding a work atmosphere that is less authoritarian and aggressive and more democratic and humane.

Special Technical Training

The third area of special training suggested in this study is technical/educational needs, and in this area 59 percent of the managers indicate a belief that women do need technical training to be effective managers. A white man at the second level says:

> I feel many good women managers are promoted from clerical jobs, and they need both technical training and management training to get off to a good start and a fair break.

A Hispanic woman at the first level notes:

> Most women managers come up from the ranks and many "old-time" women managers tend to be workers, not administrators or managers. There should be classes to assist in the transition, especially in the technical areas.

Legitimate reasons exist as to why some women need technical training, but these are often the same reasons that some men need technical training. A black woman at the third level says:

> Women managers only need technical knowledge that would also be needed for males. Generally, females who advance are well rounded in interests, job knowledge, and interpersonal relations.

Women traditionally have been excluded from technical areas because, unlike men, they were not socialized from childhood into technical areas and because the better-paying jobs, many in technical areas, have been reserved for men. As this occupational segregation is brought to an end, an initial period will occur during which more women than men will need training as they transfer in from less-technical areas. The important point is that all managers need technical training, especially at the lower levels, and many more will need it as technology becomes more complex. A danger exists that women might be required to have much-more formal technical training than men will in order to compete with men of average skills.

Special Training for Minority Managers

Figure 12-1 shows that one-third of the respondents (34 percent) believe that most minority managers need special training in order to be successful. White men (41 percent) and native-American men (39 percent) are most likely to say that minorities need special training, and black women (25 percent) are least likely. Male managers within each race group (with the exception of Asians) are more likely than female managers are to believe that minority managers need special training. For example, 41 percent of white men compared to 34 percent of white women believe this.

Of the 41 percent of white men who report that minorities need special training to become successful managers, managers at the upper levels are more likely than those at the lower levels to make this response:

First level	33%
Second level	39%
Third level	43%
Fourth level	48%
Fifth level	45%
Sixth level	49%

For white men, the larger percentage of higher-level managers who believe minorities need special training could reflect several causes. It may reveal an attempt by upper-level managers to justify the nearly total exclusion of minorities from their ranks. Lower-level white men may be more cognizant of the comparable skill levels of minority managers due to the larger numbers of minorities at these lower levels. However, lower-level white men's opinions might also reflect their concern that any special training for minorities will show preferential treatment that provides what they believe to be an unfair advantage for minorities.

The data from this study support the latter view. Approximately 10 percent more white men, most at lower levels, believe some deficiencies are evident in minority managers, but they do not believe the company should provide any special training. They view such training at best as favoritism and at worst as reverse discrimination. A white man at the second level comments, "I don't believe the company should have special training for minorities—they want everything. This is reverse discrimination."

Stereotypes and Special Training for Minorities

As noted earlier, more managers who rate themselves low, then high, on acceptance of women in the workplace believe that women need special training. This tendency is not evident for managers who rate themselves high or low on acceptance of minorities in the workplace. This may indicate that managers are more aware of and open about their views about accepting women than minorities in the workplace. This follows the societal position that the verdict on minorities is in—it is not acceptable to be a racist. However, the verdict is still out on women—a sexist attitude is still acceptable in many societal circles.

Opinions about special training for minorities is not affected by percentages of minority peers or subordinates of managers. This is also the case with special training for women. The fact that the number of minorities in the work group do not influence views about special training for minorities indicates that white managers may be basing their views not on personal experiences but on assumptions and stereotypes. This conclusion is supported by the managers' attitudes concerning minorities; use of race as an alibi for their present job difficulties. Seventy-one percent of the white managers who strongly agree that minority managers use their race as an alibi also believe minorities need special training. This compared with 48 percent who agree, 30 percent who disagree, and 23 percent who strongly disagree. In sum, what these facts demonstrate is that managers who have stereotypic views of minorities, regardless of their work-related contacts, are much more likely than are those who do not to believe minorities need special training.

Types of Special Training for Minority Managers

Training in Corporate Politics

Table 12-2 shows that the main area in the managerial/supervisory category in which managers believe minorities need special training is understanding the politics of the corporations (28 percent). While observations put forth in the section on women also apply here, additional considerations are related to minority cultures, particularly black culture. Considerable numbers of

Table 12-2
Special Training for Minority Managers
(percent)

What Type of Special Training Do You Believe Minority Managers Need?	*Total*
Managerial/Supervisory Training	(N = 448)
Understanding political aspects of management	27.9
Administration	24.6
Leadership	20.3
Decision making	10.3
Corporate issues and financial trends	7.4
Handling stress/emotional issues	3.6
Other	6
Peer/Subordinate-Relationship Training	(N = 608)
Learning how to be successful (accepted) in a white-male organization	30.8
Dealing with white subordinates and peers	26.6
Building self-confidence	13.2
Objectivity to people	11
Assertiveness	6.6
Dealing with white-male subordinates and peers	2.8
Dealing with minority subordinates and peers	1.6
Other	7.4
Technical/Educational Training	(N = 678)
Overcoming lack of previous work experience	37
Technical skills	27.7
Language skills, communication	18.1
Courses in general	8.3
Basic educational/writing skills	7.2
Other	1.6

minorities believe that their open, candid, operational style and lack of concern about strict hierarchial leadership is threatening to white men. Therefore, many white men, especially at the upper levels, see minorities as lacking political know-how.

Other minorities may appear to be lacking in political skills because of cultural values that place more importance on who is in the position rather than on actual position.[5] Interviewers in this study frequently heard comments similar to the following by a fifth-level black man.

> In white culture, the respect, deference, and dependency is not to the person in the position but to the position. This is totally opposite the black views of things. If I can't respect the person in the position, I can't respect the position.

Minority managers who adopt these views might then be considered to be in need of special training.

Administrative and Leadership Training

Administrative (25 percent) and leadership (20 percent) training are two additional categories in the managerial/supervisory areas for which training is needed in the view of the managers who say that minorities need special training. A black man at the first level comments:

> Due to lack of exposure to certain facets of professional, technical, and administrative areas, minorities will need additional training. Another problem minorities will experience is communicating with peers and also lack of desire from whites to help them achieve on their jobs.

A white woman at the fourth level notes:

> Problem solving. In my experience the minority managers have difficulty recognizing a problem but even more in determining how to solve it. They tend to shy away from problems. They lack leadership.

Many managers lack leadership and administrative skills either because they have not had the opportunity to develop them or do not have the basic ability. What happens too frequently in corporations is that when a minority or female manager lacks these qualities, many white and/or male managers generalize these deficiencies to all women and/or minorities. Further, they attribute the lack to a deficiency in basic ability. These generalizations do not happen when white men are seen as lacking in such qualities. In addition, minorities and women with superior leadership abilities in a normal, healthy atmosphere could have problems in a hostile, sexist/racist climate in which they receive little support from subordinates, peers, and superiors. Superior white men can also fail in hostile, nonsupportive environments.

Finally, racist and sexist attitudes get in the way of defining good leadership and administrative skills, especially since these skills are difficult to evaluate and are basically judgmental, as was pointed out in chapter 10.

Rather than condemning any nonautomatic deference to authoritarian or traditional leadership styles, the corporation and its managers have more to gain from encouraging those whose approach is varied, thoughtful, and open. Corporations should begin to develop leadership-training sessions that teach such positive qualities, and they should recognize these qualities through promotions, pay incentives, and the like, rather than through special training for perceived minority and female deficiencies.

Training for Acceptance in White Corporations

In the work-group-relations area, 31 percent of the managers believe minorities need special training in learning how to be accepted in a white-male organization. A white man at the fourth level says:

> In general, minorities appear to have some personality hang-ups which seem to interfere with development.

A Hispanic man at the second level comments:

> They need to be oriented to white-male, middle-class "traditional" thinking so they will be able to communicate with upper managers.

Attempting to teach minorities (or women) how to be accepted in a white-male organization may very well be an exercise in futility. No matter how much minority (female) managers strive to become what the white-male-dominated corporations wants them to be, they will never succeed because they cannot change the most-critical factors for acceptance—their race and/or sex. Even if women or minority men could become white men in mind and spirit, it would not mean acceptance but instead would invoke reactions like "Look at her, she's trying to act like a man" or "He or she is trying to be white."

Moreover, qualities such as ambition, assertiveness, and self-confidence in a woman may cause many men to characterize her as a "pushy broad," and such qualities in a minority may inspire many whites to apply the label of "uppity nigger," "uppity red," "uppity Spic," "uppity Jap," and so on. However, similar qualities in a white man are likely to earn him recognition as "a comer." Such stereotypes die hard in some quarters.

A 1975 study determined that many of the managers, both minority and white, were aware of an ironic inconsistency in the attitudes of a large number of the white managers. At times they complained that minorities are lazy and have little or no ambition, initiative, and aggressiveness. At other times, however, these same white managers were heard to accuse the minorities of being too ambitious, independent, and aggressive. A young black woman, a lower-level manager at one of the companies, observed: "They always find a problem with the minorities, such as their personality, aggressiveness, appearance, etc." A white middle-level manager from a different company corroborated this view: "Minorities are stereotyped. When people are looking for a reason to find fault, they will use anything. In other words, some whites will never be satisfied."

Probably the best advice for minorities and women is to know themselves and be themselves because success is not guaranteed, no matter what approach is taken.

Training for Dealing with Whites

In the work-group area, the second most-common type of training managers feel minorities need is in dealing with whites and/or white men (27 percent). Interestingly, black men (30 percent) and white men (30 percent) are most likely to state that minority managers need special training in dealing with white men as peers and subordinates. Black women (17 percent) are least likely to give this response. A white woman at the second level says:

> Minority managers need special training in how to handle problems that might occur because of racial problems of work-group members who might see themselves as passed up for promotion.

While this type of training can be helpful to those minorities who believe they need it, it will not be very useful unless whites are also given training to deal with minorities. Because minorities have had to learn to survive in the white world and are bicultural, training for whites would be more beneficial because of their greater deficiency in dealing with minorities. Chapter 3 goes into great detail about the concept of the biculturalism of minorities and the cultural deficiencies of whites.

Training in Technical/Educational Areas

In the technical/educational area, more work experience (37 percent) and technical training (28 percent) are the most-frequent types of special training suggested. As an Asian man at the first level says:

To satisfy AAP targets, minorities are often thrown into a demanding situation without the benefit of training. Type of training depends on the job. However, in most instances, managerial skills and technical training are badly needed. Had minorities been developed all along, of course, and shared acceptance, instant skills would not be an issue.

A white woman at the third level comments:

> If they are managing in an environment which is largely technical and/or nonminority and their technical background is limited, they may need crash courses in technical matters and/or in relating to white-male superior, peers, and subordinates.

As is the case with women, many minorities are excluded from the higher-paying technical jobs. As a result, more of these managers are lacking technical experience than white men are. The question as it was put to women is: How much training are they really lacking?

The issues of minorities; needing more technical experience is debatable. Many white men say that minorities and women need more experience, especially in a variety of departments, to give them a better view of the overall operations of the company. Yet this variety of experiences is not required of most white men. The job histories of white men who have made it to upper-middle management and above revealed that most of them had advanced to their present levels within the same department. Thus, the need for a variety of departmental experiences for advancement is more of a myth than a reality.

Another conflict with regard to minorities; needing additional experience is the so-called Catch 22 in which many of them find themselves. A Hispanic woman at the first level clearly illustrates the Catch 22. She wants to get into a supervisory position because she was told that in order to get promoted to the third level, she needs to have supervisory experience. On numerous occasions, she requested a transfer to a supervisory job but was told she could not get the position because it required previous supervisory experience!

Once again, corporations must be certain that they have not established two sets of experience requirements—one for white men and another for minorities and women. They also must be certain that they do not place women and minorities in Catch-22 situations.

Special Training for White-Male Managers

While a lot of discussion has gone on here about special training for women and minorities inside and outside the corporations, very little discussion has occurred about special training for white men. This section represents one of the first attempts to quantify managers' views on this subject made in any previous study.

Figure 12-1 shows that almost one out of two managers (47 percent) believes that white men need special training in order to work more effectively with women and minorities. Predictably, differences in responses occur among the race/sex groups. Black men (62 percent) and black women (56 percent) are more likely to respond affirmatively. Native-American women (39 percent) and native-American men and white women (42 percent each) are least likely to respond affirmatively. Note that white men, white women, and black women at upper levels are more likely than those at lower levels are to believe that white men need special training. For example, 49 percent of white-male managers at the fourth level and above versus 35 percent at the first level believe white men need special training. Sixty-five percent of white-female managers at the fourth level and above, as compared to 33 percent at the first level, agree that white men need special training.

Several explanations are possible for these level differences in responses. Many women at the lower levels are in a predominantly female environment. Perhaps they are less likely to encounter overt sexist attitudes from white men and thus are less inclined to say that white men need special training. Among white men, quite possibly those at upper levels recognize the difficulty and resistance put forth by lower-level white men who are most affected and threatened by AAP/EEO. Another explanation could be that upper-level managers are not condemning themselves when they say white men need special training because they do not have to work directly with minorities and women. Lower-level white men must work directly with these groups, and to say that they need special training is to criticize their own fairness and managerial skills.

As figure 12-1 poignantly displays, managers from every race/sex group, with the exception of native-American males, are more likely to say that white men need special training than they are to say that women or minorities need it. College-graduated black and white managers, regardless of age, are more likely than nongraduates are to believe white men need special training. The responses among the other minority groups are somewhat mixed. Black-male and -female graduates over 30 years of age are most likely to believe that special training is needed for white men—69 percent and 76 percent respectively. This finding can be traced to blacks' experiences during the civil rights struggles of the 1960s. Their earlier optimism has dimmed as they see a conservative trend in the country begin to erode the gains they worked so hard to achieve. They have done what society required—"Get an education and work hard"—but they see very few results for their efforts because of racism. In addition, they are competing more with white men and present a greater threat to the white-male monopoly positions than younger and less-educated blacks do. Thus, this group of black managers is probably confronted with more-hostile racist and sexist attitudes than is the younger and less-educated group.

Another interesting point is that white men over age 40 are usually more likely than those in the younger age group with similar education are to say white men need special training. For example, 49 percent of white men over age 40 with a college degree, 45 percent between the ages of 30+ to 40, and 42 percent of those age 30 and under believe white men should have training to deal more effectively with minorities and women. An obvious reason for these views is that older white men may be less likely to feel that their career prospects are threatened by minorities and women. Having had fewer contacts with them and feeling less threatened, older white men may be freer to recognize the effects of racist attitudes from interactions between whites and minority men and women.

A white man at the fifth level has some constructive views on why white men need special training:

> White males need to be confronted with and recognize the racism and sexism minorities and women face and encouraged to coach and counsel to the degree we claim we do for all but don't really do for everyone. Coaching of minorities and women is essential if we're going to maximize opportunity for success.

Types of Special Training for White-Male Managers

The most-frequent response to the question of type of special training needed by white men is training to overcome biases and stereotypes about women and minorities (33 percent). As table 12-3 shows, most answers to this question include a need for training in areas related to understanding minorities and/or women. The managers who believe white men need special training are basically saying that white men do not have the experience and knowledge to overcome the racist and sexist attitudes that are part of the fabric of our society. The following comments clearly illustrate this problem. A black woman at the third level says:

> They have closed minds because of limited experiences. There is no special training to care for that. Remembering to act in a professional way might help.

A black man at the third level has a similar comment:

> A course in race relations or sexism would be helpful. Often these managers turn people off because they insult them with their narrow-minded views and behavior.

A white woman at the fourth level mentions:

> They need to be able to recognize that talent exists in women and to learn to utilize it—learn to deal with women on an equal basis. They tend to look down on women's ability to do a job as well as a man.

A black man at the first level sees white men as having "problems with treating anybody as equal." A white man at the fourth level feels that upper-level managers need more help in understanding bigotry. He says:

> They must learn what a bigot is so they can understand when they are acting like one. The higher the level, the more true this is.

Similarly, a white woman at the second level states:

> My experience indicates that most white-male managers are somewhat fearful of dealing with women and minorities. Perhaps this stems from their own insecurities. The training I would suggest would deal with looking at women and minorities as people and not as threats.

A black woman at the second level expresses the views frequently heard

Table 12-3
Special Training for White-Male Managers
(percent)

If You Believe White Men Need Special Training, Please Indicate What Type.	*Total (N = 1,882)*
Overcoming bias and stereotypes toward women and minorities	32.7
Understanding problems specific to women and minorities	14.3
Human relations	13.8
Overcoming bias toward women	5.6
Understanding EEO/AAP policies	5.4
Understanding cultural backgrounds of women and minorities	5.1
Understanding cultural backgrounds of minorities	3.9
Honest communications	2.8
Understanding problems specific to minorities	2.7
Leadership skills	2.6
Understanding problems specific to women	2.6
Recognizing potential of individual subordinates	2.4
Overcoming bias toward minorities	2.4
Technical skills	1
Other	2.7

from black groups and some women's groups in the pre- and post-interview sessions. She concludes:

> They need training in personal relations. Their superior attitudes need to be deflated. Their super egos need to be brought back into the realm of reality. Their insecurities need to be explained and responded to.

Most of these suggestions indirectly recognize that white men are a product of this society. Since their early youth they have been socialized in racist and sexist attitudes. Many of them do not recognize on a conscious level their negative feelings and perceptions and thus have never made any attempt to change and correct them.

Effectiveness of Training for White Men

When considering the responses of managers who believe that white men do not need special training, we see that the vast majority of the reasons stems from a belief that training would not be effective in changing existing white-male racist and sexist attitudes. A white man at the fourth level concludes:

> If a man's work habits with others are going to be affected by matters of race or sex, no amount of training is going to change that.

A fifth-level white man made these Utopian comments:

> Training will not change prejudice. I feel that an open mind which will allow communication of ideas between human beings is the only positive way to ensure more-effective working between the sexes and minorities.

Finally, a white woman at the second level expresses an opinion of a small but vocal group of white managers:

> For heaven's sake—let's give the white-male managers a break. I think there's no problem in those I deal with.

Conclusions and Recommendations

This chapter established that the need of minorities and women for special training to assist them in being effective managers is more questionable than is the need of white men for special training. This result is somewhat encouraging since blaming minority and female managers for problems they may have is a form of neoracism/neosexism. This blaming of the victims allows the white man to assume no part of the solution. Since white men control most of the universities, publishing houses, and the news media, we should not be surprised that the concept that minorities' and women's supposed cultural and social deficiencies are the main reason for their lack of representation in the managerial ranks has been widely accepted. Other points of view are seldom heard. That some minorities and women have adopted this position is understandable. As adults, people receive reinforcement and rewards from the white-male power structure for espousing views that do not challenge the existing power structure.

Minorities who live in a society in which they have little control of the institutions are inculcated with the dominant white culture's views and attitudes about aspects of life such as work, success, drive, and the functioning of organizations. In addition, minorities must understand and know the dominant culture in order to survive. This does not mean that understanding necessarily translates into a compliance with and adoption of dominant cultures. No such survival pressures are forcing white society to understand the minorities' cultures.

The truth is not that minorities, especially those aspiring to become managers, possess cultural differences that would hinder their becoming a part of the business world but that they are being stopped because of racial barriers and are given little chance to disprove the white attribution of undesirable characteristics. The truth is not that minorities are unable to interact with whites—they are forced to do so every day—but that many whites will not or cannot admit that minorities can interact successfully if given the slightest opportunity. The many whites who isolate themselves from minorities and are unable or unwilling, or both, to interact successfully with them are the ones in need of special training.

Women, having been oppressed and kept in subordinate positions, have had to understand men to survive. The opposite, however, is not true. More explicitly, women as workers, mothers, wives, and girlfriends, have had to deal with and really understand men because of the men's dominant position. Again, women's understanding does not necessarily mean compliance with an adoption of male views and values.

Most of the minority and female managers in the corporations, especially those who have attended colleges and/or have long experiences in corporate life, have had to develop skills to cope and survive. Put another way, even though women and minorities *are* socialized differently to varying degrees and some minorities *do* have different cultural backgrounds, the fact remains many more similarities than differences exist between men and women and among minorities and whites. As a black man says:

> I do not subscribe to the theory that there is something different or special about females and minorities other than the obvious—physical characteristics and numbers. They only become special when an organization

allows a climate to persist which treats them differently. A large corporation like my company quite naturally reflects the society as a whole, but because of its likeness to the military and because of past discriminatory practices in this country, it's difficult for females and minorities to make gains into management. Special training is not required to work with female managers—50 percent of the world population is female. Therefore, in my opinion any such training is a waste. I suggest training for white males who resent having a female/minority manager.

An important point that should not be dismissed is the possibility that the socialization and cultural differences of women and minorities have produced positive characteristics that can prove valuable in the operation of corporations in the 1980s. Carol Hymowitz, a writer for the *Wall Street Journal,* noted that women who attempt to become men in word, deed, and action will hurt themselves and will be seen as servilely compliant by men. She strongly suggests that women recognize that their uniqueness can assist corporations in adjusting and being successful in the 1980s.[6]

A managerial work force made up of heterogeneous rather than homogeneous groups leads to a variety of questions, views, and positions that will ultimately produce better results. Put another way, homogeneous managerial force tends to replenish itself with noncritical "yes men" who concern themselves with driving independent and original minds out of the company.

With specific regard to the concept of special training, Pamela Steen, an opponent of programs aimed at the maintenance of homogeneous management styles, made the following comments. Her remarks also apply to special training programs for minority managers.

> The need to establish special management-development programs for women is questioned. This is especially true of programs whose purpose is to "condition" women so that they will feel more at home in business. It is recommended that a more-effective change strategy would be to modify the beliefs of those persons who do not think that women are capable of managing, rather than to change the attitudes of women about their roles at work. Special training programs may be in order, but not for the group for which they were originally intended.[7]

While criticisms have been leveled against special training for women and minorities, reasons can be found to advocate such training in many cases. It seems fair to suggest that training should be available to give all managers a foundation for an understanding of the complexities of racism and sexism. If white men understand how racism and sexism operate, they will have a better understanding of their own subconscious biases and thus be able to treat minorities and women more equitably. Such training would provide women and minorities with better means of dealing with prejudiced whites and men and a better understanding of the effects of discriminatory treatment on their personal development.

Another reasonable suggestion is that all managers, regardless of race and sex, should be provided with proper training in those areas in which they are deficient. True, many women and minorities are moving into more-technical jobs, thus more of them will need technical training than will the white men who have dominated these technical areas. It is also true that many mechanically oriented white-male managers who are moving into nontechnical managerial jobs need nontechnical training. This is not special training but necessary training that would be important for all managers.

Finally, for those managers who feel they need special training to deal with new environments because of their socialization and cultural backgrounds, such training should be provided. However, this training will be of limited value if it is not held in conjunction with the training of the managers with whom they will be working in their new environment.

In sum, racism clearly has negative psychological effects on both minorities and whites, and sexism clearly has negative psychological effects on both women and men. In addition, recent research has shown the male role model to be detrimental to the health of men. For these reasons it seems imperative that corporations do not formulate special training directed at any one group. Rather, they should provide training on racism and sexism for all groups. Only by exposing the extent of these two destructive forces in our society in general, and in the business world specifically, will corporate managers work together at their highest level of efficiency and effectiveness.

13 Conclusion

The Industrial Revolution, evolving technology, the rise of labor unions, and the diminishing work ethic in modern society all are blamed, with varying frequency, for the problems corporations are facing today. Two factors, however, probably surpass all these in producing employee stress and conflict—the changing value system of our society and the combined effects of EEO/AAP that have changed the makeup of the corporate work force from a relatively homogeneous to a heterogeneous employee body.

Corporations have long recognized the economic advantage of resources expended to develop and train employees. In more-recent years, they have become much-more aware of the need to maintain a satisfied, motivated work force in order to increase efficiency and productivity. This task is much-more difficult than in the past. The rapid expansion of the American economy during and after World War II created vast opportunities for employment, and because racial and sexual discrimination excluded large numbers of minorities and women from the competition for jobs, existing employees essentially had a corner on most employment markets. These employees were company men—men who place loyalty to the corporation above personal goals and desires. It was, in many ways, an ideal situation for the corporation—a thriving economy and a dedicated, homogeneous work force that asked little more than a day's pay for a day's work—and no hard questions for the corporate bosses.

The changes of the 1960s and 1970s brought increasing uneasiness to the executive suites. Today the combination of an ailing economy and a diversified, vocal employee work force with strong personal expectations and demands is presenting new problems that will not be solved by old answers. The corporations that will survive will be those that provide all employees with fair and equal treatment and that capitalize on the opportunity the new breed of employee presents for creativity, individualism, and diversity.

The New Breed and Corporate Conflict

Few members of society have escaped the impact of the radical social changes of the last three decades on their value systems. The new value system of employees is exemplified by the demand for more recognition by employers of personal needs, both inside and outside the workplace.

Employees are no longer willing to totally subordinate their needs to corporate dictates. They are saying, "We appreciate the opportunity to work in this corporation, and we recognize and try to fulfill the corporation's needs and goals." However, they are also saying,

> While we recognize the corporation's needs and goals, the corporation must recognize our goals, needs, and contributions. We want interesting, challenging, fulfilling jobs that we control. We want to be treated fairly and equally. We want a say in the evaluation of our performance and potential. We want to play an active role in determining our career plans and our training and development needs. We want to be recognized for our individuality and uniqueness. Our personal lives and beliefs should be of no concern to the corporation unless they affect our job performance.

In other words, the new-breed employees want to be heard. They are no longer likely to accept corporate decisions, policies, and practices without questioning the whys, whens and hows. They believe in individualism and oppose conformity. They do not believe in one right style of management; they believe in many different styles of management so long as the foundation of that style is based on such concepts as openness, honesty, and humaneness. They also expect their individual life-styles to be accepted, so long as those life-styles do not interfere with actual job performance and, in some cases, even if they do.

Not surprisingly, these new values have created increasing conflict, particularly in corporations that have been run like military organizations, in which orders are given and followed without question, in which the organization is first and the individual is second (or last), and in which the tried and proved way of doing things is greatly favored over taking risks and moving in new directions. Lou O'Leary, vice president at AT&T, accurately wrote:

> The pluralism of values is significant for us as managers. My management generation was more of a piece. Even where we had very obvious individual differences, there still was an agreed-upon model of values and beliefs, an ideal person—employee and manager—who exemplified them. Norman Rockwell could have painted such an ideal; in fact, he did—a number of times. Today, we are faced with burgeoning pluralism. Our people are coming from a lot of different places. We simply can't manage everyone the way we were managed, and expect it, and them, to work. Observers predict this will hold true well into the future. This, then, seems to us—to me—to be our central problem. In a company metamorphosing in the 80s, many of us are managing people who grew up in the 60s, and we are managing them with the management style and techniques we learned in the 50s. To the extent that the style of those techniques are based on eternal verities of the human condition, fine. To the extent that they are based on values that have changed and are changing, we are in trouble.[9]

In short, corporations are faced with a work force that is becoming increasingly vocal and concerned about the treatment of workers as human beings. Corporations will no longer have the luxury of overlooking the impact of their actions upon the personal and work life of their employees. To do so will be to create a work force with so much stress and conflict that corporations will cease to be effective, productive, economic institutions.

Impact of Race and Sex on Corporate Conflict

The impact of the new breed of manager on corporate conflict has been receiving increasing attention. However, the impact of racism, sexism, the increasing numbers of minorities' and women's entering corporate managerial ranks increasingly has been downplayed. A major reason is that racism and, to a lesser extent, sexism have taken on new forms that are not as frequently overt as they were in the past. However, they still exist and are still powerful forces in this society. The major difference between old and new racism and sexism is that the new forms have been institutionalized or have gone underground. Corporate managers must recognize that they must now deal primarily with neoracism and neosexism and institutional racism and sexism. The former are more-sophisticated, -subtle, -indirect forms of racism and sexism. The latter forms use traditional rules, regulations, procedures, and standards that, while not originally designed to exclude minorities and women from full participation in society's institutions and life, in reality do exclude them.

Another important problem complicating the understanding of racism is that the effects of racism encountered by the four different minority groups in this society in general and in corporations in particular differ in kind and degree. The extent of sustained white-racist attitudes toward blacks is greatest. Minorities other than blacks have sometimes been viewed negatively, and at other times positively, depending on the political and economic situation. Blacks, however, have always been viewed negatively. Because of the ambiguous feelings about other minorities and the clear-cut feelings about blacks, whites have attempted to keep as much social, economic, and political distance as possible between themselves and blacks. In many surveys on social distance, the order of acceptance of minorities by white society is: American (U.S. whites), native Americans, Asians, Mexican-Americans, and blacks. An important illustration of this point is that the Iranian government refused to allow 51 white men and women to leave the U.S. embassy there. Two of these people were Hispanic and one was native American. Thus, even in the international area, Hispanics and native Americans are considered whites.

In addition to unambiguous negative attitudes about blacks, whites' negative feelings are exacerbated by the fact that blacks pose the greatest threat to their dominant position because of the blacks' large representation in the U.S. population and their lack of geographic concentration. Since blacks present the greatest threat, elaborate stereotypes have been developed to justify the denial to blacks of their full equal rights in this society.

An important problem complicating the understanding of sexism is that while the society as a whole has come out, at least in word, against racism, sexism is still an issue of great debate. Society has not yet determined, even in word, never mind deed, the role women should play in society. Therefore, many men and some women hold sexist attitudes and behave in sexist manners that they deem appropriate.

In the past thirty years, minorities, especially blacks, and women have been in the forefront of many of the most-radical social changes that have occurred and are occurring in this society. Their inclusion in the corporate managerial ranks has not only created a new conflict centered primarily around a power struggle for the more-desirable jobs but also has greatly influenced the new values of managers.

With regard to the former, until recently, white men have been able, because of their control of society's institutions, to effectively define and dictate the roles that minorities and women would play in corporate America. With new laws and executive orders, the white man's power to completely define and dictate minorities' and women's positions in corporations has become limited. What has ensued is a power struggle between white men, who make up 37 percent of the population and who have dominated 95 percent of the lucrative managerial positions for hundreds of years, and minorities and women, who make up 63 percent of the population and who have been given only 5 percent of these positions.

White men are not likely to just say, "Well, the law says we must share these positions with minorities and women, so let's do it." Most believe they have dominated these positions for years, not because their corporations discriminated against minorities and women but because white men had the ability, qualifications, and desire to work for these positions. They are likely to see the smallest steps toward equal-employment opportunities for minorities and women as tremendous movement. Many will cry gross denials of their rights. The realities of the white man's situation in corporate America is that they are at a disadvantage in the present environment because they only represent 37 percent of the population. The crucial question is, "Are white men being treated unfairly because of this new competition?"

While white men believe they are increasingly becoming victims of reverse discrimination, minorities and women are strongly arguing that white men are still by far the most-favored group. Many people recognize that those in a dominant position, regardless of race and/or sex, will not give up much of their power unless they are convinced that to do so would be more advantageous than not to do so. They argue that even though the laws have been passed to provide minorities and women with equal opportunities, the consequences to corporations for disobeying the laws are not great enough for most corporate executives to sincerely attempt to provide minorities and women with similar opportunities to white men. Some point out that even though a number of firms such as AT&T have been brought to court and have had settlements to rectify discriminatory employment policies and practices, the settlements do not go far enough. They reason that, until these settlements force corporations to promote specific numbers of minorities and women to upper-middle- and upper-level managerial positions where the real power to bring about change exists, true equality of opportunity will not occur.

Two main reasons why minorities and women believe the government must increase sanctions to force the inclusion of minorities and women not only at the lower and middle levels of management but also, and probably more so, at higher levels of management require elaboration. One reason, as noted in chapter 5, is that studies have clearly demonstrated that managers tend to select employees who resemble themselves. Since white men control 95 percent of the power positions in corporations, most are looking for white men who fit their image. Another reason is that these powerful positions will be the last ones that white men will give up because to do so would directly affect the power brokers themselves. They would directly suffer from any advancement of minorities and women. It is much easier for the upper levels to tell the lower levels that their opportunities are limited than it is to limit their own opportunities.

One must conclude then that, yes, white men are at a numerical disadvantage if they have to equally and fairly compete with minorities and women. However, one must also conclude that white men, because they represent a minority of the population and must now compete with the majority, are not being treated unfairly. If anything, white men are still at a great advantage for the two reasons mentioned in the previous paragraph. In addition, many of the white men who claim that their group is at a great disadvantage because of EEO/AAP seem not to recognize that many of them would not have been in their present positions over the past forty years if they had had to compete on an equal basis with minorities and women.

From the point of view of many white men, not only are minorities and women unfairly taking away their opportunities but also are bringing with them different values that are, to say the least, disconcerting to many of them. As oppressed people and, in the case of minorities, people from different cultural backgrounds, they have developed operating and survival behaviors that conflict at times with the traditional corporate value systems and modes of operation. They are much more likely than white men are to be forthright in their corporate dealings and to be more critical of corporate policies. Many will openly challenge supervisors, a practice traditional managers find to be a sign of disloyalty. They are more likely to take risks and to seek new directions—both essential survival techniques for oppressed people. By contrast, many white men, as O'Leary and others have noted, are more likely to be indirect, more conforming, set in their ways, and less likely to take risks.

Other characteristics that many of these minorities and women bring to the corporation, such as an ability to communicate well with subordinates, a more-open management style, and a greater orientation toward people, go against many traditional corporate-managerial values. However, they are more conducive to new types of management demanded by the new-breed managers. Illustrative of this point is the fact that female managers as bosses are rated higher than male bosses by both men and women, despite the sexist attitudes evident in the corporations studied.

An outlook that seems to be especially characteristic of blacks and that strongly goes against traditional corporate values, is lack of respect for the position when respect for the person in the position is absent. The fact that black managers are most critical of their bosses' overall managerial and supervisory style might be an indication of this conflict in values.

In sum, the inclusion of minorities and women into the managerial ranks has created a power struggle between white men and these groups for the lucrative managerial positions. Each side presently considers the other as having favorable advantages. In addition, minorities and women are bringing some values into the corporate world that are in direct conflict with those of the white-male traditions but that are more in line with what the new-breed managers are demanding from their corporate bosses.

Conflict and Managerial Retention

If corporations do not deal effectively with these new conflicts, they will begin to lose large numbers of educated, high-potential managers. A significant number of younger, educated managers in this study are considering leaving their companies for reasons other than retirement. Table 13-1 shows the managers' responses by race, sex, age, and education. More than one out of five of all managers between the ages of 30 + and 40 who hold college degrees and more than one in three who are 30 and under are thinking of leaving their company. While similarities are evident among the reasons managers give for seriously considering a change of employer, some differences of emphasis also appear between groups of managers. The general reasons given relate to both the new value systems generated by the sociopolitical forces of the last two decades and to the problems of race and sex in corporate management. The following summaries show the most-important concerns for the managers in each group who are seriously considering leaving their companies.

Table 13-1
Managers Who Are Considering Leaving Their Companies, by Race, Sex, Age, and Education
(percent)

Age and Education	Other Minority		Black		White	
	Men	Women	Men	Women	Men	Women
30 years or less						
No college	10.5 (21)	11.7 (60)	16.7 (12)	14.3 (28)	16.7 (6)	17.6 (34)
Some college	18.4 (38)	20.3 (59)	22.9 (35)	16.3 (49)	5 (20)	18.4 (38)
College graduates	34.7 (124)	37.3 (67)	35.1 (111)	33.9 (62)	42.4 (33)	40.3 (67)
30+ to 40 years						
No college	33.3 (27)	6.7 (90)	0 (18)	2.6 (38)	13.6 (44)	4.4 (91)
Some college	13.2 (106)	17.6 (68)	17.1 (70)	7.6 (79)	30 (60)	2.2 (45)
College graduates	30.8 (120)	23.1 (26)	30.3 (109)	21.9 (32)	26.3 (159)	28 (82)
40+ years						
No college	1.8 (76)	1.1 (90)	8.3 (24)	1.4 (71)	3.5 (257)	2.7 (259)
Some college	4.4 (90)	2.2 (45)	3.9 (51)	3.6 (56)	8.7 (229)	3.6 (83)
College graduates	4.2 (48)	0 (10)	16.2 (37)	20 (10)	9.7 (494)	11.9 (59)

Note: Numbers in parentheses indicate number of managers by group.

1. Native-American men will probably leave their companies if advancement opportunities are not improved, if their companies do not reduce the emphasis placed on EEO/AAP, and if salaries do not become better.

2. Native-American and Asian women will probably leave their companies if they are not given more-interesting and -challenging jobs with better career-development and advancement opportunities. They also want a better atmosphere for female managers. Family reasons are a final consideration for some of them.

3. Asian men are likely to leave if they are not given more-challenging and -interesting jobs with better career development. Lack of job security is another factor that would influence their decision.

4. Black men not surprisingly, are most likely to terminate employment with their present companies if they do not have better advancement opportunities and if the overall treatment and work atmospheres for minorities do not improve greatly.

5. Black women place emphasis on the three factors the black men mention but also want more-interesting and -challenging jobs tied in with better development and training. They also emphasize money as a factor that would influence their remaining with their company.

6. Hispanic men will remain with their firms if they have better advancement opportunities and fairer employment policies, not necessarily directed toward all minorities and women but specifically for Hispanic men. They want better work relationships, especially with their bosses. In addition, more-interesting and -challenging work is important to their decision to remain with their companies.

7. Hispanic women emphasize better advancement opportunities with appropriate training and development and a better atmosphere for women. In addition, family reasons could make them leave their companies.

8. White men primarily want better advancement opportunities and less emphasis on EEO/AAP in order to remain with their companies.

9. White women emphasize that a decision to remain with their companies would require more-interesting and -challenging work and a better atmosphere for women. Family responsibilities might require some of them to leave.

From these summaries, we can see that the major reasons managers will consider leaving their companies are lack of advancement opportunities; lack of challenging, interesting work; no improvement in training and development; no improvement in work atmosphere and treatment, especially for minorities and women; and, depending on one's race and sex, the emphasis or deemphasis, as may be the case, on EEO/AAP.

While the previous data give some idea of the reasons why managers consider leaving their companies, corporations do not have the necessary information to determine how to keep many of the managers, who will not leave their firms, from slowly becoming disillusioned and nonproductive. Chapter 9 presented considerable information that illustrates the fact that a number of managers are losing motivation to do their jobs effectively because of their perceptions of their treatment and work in their companies. Corporations have solutions to deal with these conflicts and problems. What is required is a willingness to put the time, effort, resources, and commitment behind the solutions.

Major Solution to Many Personnel Problems Confronting Corporations in the 1980s

The implementation of objective, systematic employment processes and systems is one means of alleviating some of the conflicts and stresses that have resulted from differing value systems and from race/sex issues. Some problems managers attribute to their race and/or sex in fulfilling their goals and aspirations in the corporation are really not race and/or sex problems. They are related to the fact that only in recent years have corporations begun to develop employment practices and processes that have attempted to be fair, equitable, objective, and systematic. The managerial problems that are a function of the differing value systems can also be solved in large part if companies implement a systematic process for developing and utilizing managers, with its major components being work design, performance- and potential-evaluation procedures, career planning, and training and development programs.

The implementation of this management system will be difficult because its viability depends upon properly designed work—a concept and process few corporations have recognized as the basis for an effective management-utilization and -development system. Corporations that have recognized the usefulness of work design have had difficulty in implementing it because the concept basically gives the subordinates more power over their work than most traditional bosses feel comfortable in giving up. Work, when properly designed, is whole with an identifiable beginning and end, offers variety, provides subordinates with automatic and direct feedback, gives subordinates sufficient autonomy to make decisions about the job, and has a specific user and receiver.

Once work is properly designed, the other components of the system can be implemented. Responsibilities can be defined by bosses and subordinates, and clear objectives and means of measurement can be established. With clearly defined responsibilities, objectives, and means of measurement, agreed upon by both bosses and subordinates, performance evaluations will more likely be based on the job done and not on subjective criteria such as race, sex, age, or political connection.

Since properly designed work produces a clearer picture of the skills and abilities needed to perform jobs, potential evaluations will be more effective, especially if a variety of potential-evaluation procedures are used to check and balance one another. Evaluating past performance is much easier than evaluating future performance.

In order to be most useful to subordinates, performance and potential evaluations should provide useful and specific feedback on subordinates' strengths and weaknesses. They should take into consideration subordinates' views about their performance and potential. With these two evaluations properly done, bosses and subordinates will be able to effectively determine career plans and needs for training and development. This, of course, is providing the company has given both the manager and subordinate proper training and sufficient information to develop such plans.

It is imperative, if this managerial system is to be effective, that subordinate participation is active and that this participation exists in all aspects of the process. Many bosses are very reluctant to include subordinates for both personal and practical reasons. On the personal side, they view such a managerial system as denying them exclusive traditional authority. Some view it as revolutionary—since they usually oppose minor procedural changes, they are bound to resist drastic changes in managerial methods.

On the practical side, managers are reluctant to implement systems in which they are not properly trained. Critical communication with subordinates is difficult for many bosses (even in areas in which they are comfortable and well trained). Communication is much-more difficult when no proper training has occurred. Bosses not only lack training in the basic content and function of these system parts but also in methods for providing constructive and critical feedback to their subordinates, especially about negative issues. Also, since managers are paid for meeting numerical objectives, not human objectives, the necessity of priorities encourages bosses to place less emphasis on how to handle, evaluate, develop, and motivate people than on meeting targets. Managers are not paid for human objectives. They view this role as something in addition to their jobs, rather than as an integral part of them, and tend to avoid it.

Corporations must make certain that this managerial system is implemented equitably and fairly for all managers. Many managers find it difficult to recognize and admit that all human beings are subjective. They have certain likes and dislikes that will always influence their use of this or any other system and must consciously work against personal prejudices and biases. *All* managers are faced with personal characteristics that can be liabilities: age, religion, height, weight, looks, and family origins. Minorities and women have the additional burden of dealing with racism and/or sexism. Thus, corporations must develop a strong EEO/AAP program to protect the rights of all employees, including white men, to equitable and fair treatment. In addition, they should develop training in understanding racism and sexism for all managers. This training should not be a one-shot deal. Since racism and sexism are developed throughout life, a one-day or one-week seminar on the subjects is not sufficient to understand these concepts. Corporations must develop simple to complex courses that all managers must attend over a number of years.

The components of this managerial system already exist in the participating corporations in some fashion. They do not have to develop entirely new ones or greatly refine the ones that exist. What they must do is to make certain the plans are properly implemented by competent, secure managers. Millions of dollars can be, and have been spent on developing new managerial systems, but unless the managers are motivated to properly implement and support them, this money is wasted.

To sum up the recommendations of this book in concise terms, corporations should begin to:

Develop an employment atmosphere that has as its main tenets individuality, creativity, honesty, openness, and acceptance of diversity;

Recognize the crucial, destructive, and costly roles that racism and sexism play in corporations;

Develop programs to educate managers not only on racism and sexism but also on cultural and value differences of the increasingly heterogeneous corporate employee body;

Develop a managerial system that has as its main components work design, performance- and potential-evaluation procedures, career planning, and training and development;

Provide special training programs for managers; especially those who believe these programs will be helpful to their corporate success;

Provide a strong EEO/AAP emphasis and programs with specific immediate sanctions against those who violate its philosophies and tenets.

While these suggestions will not resolve all the corporate conflicts created by the entrance of minorities and women and by the value systems of the new-breed managers, the ideas and concepts can go a long way toward helping corporations develop a satisfied, motivated, high-performing work force able to compete with the best. If corporations do not effectively implement such a managerial utilization and development system, the conflicts will increase. Minorities and women are becoming more aggressive in pursuing their rights to be treated equally, and they want their fair share of corporate rewards. White men are going through a very serious psychological readjustment as they see their dominant position slowly slip away toward a more-equitable one. Finally, the conflict between traditional corporate values and the new values will also increase. Increasingly, new-breed managers are turning away from the impersonal, dictatorial corporate environments and are attempting to seek their individuality in more-receptive environments.

Since the corporate raison d'être is the provision of goods and services at a reasonable profit, corporations' compelling motive should be the elimination of conflicts that interfere with production and that threaten the return on investment. If corporations do not effectively deal with these new conflicts, their work force will become increasingly nonproductive, and employees will turn to an ever-eager government to assist them in their drive to equality and treatment as human beings.

Appendix:
What Are Racism
and Sexism?

A white woman at the third level of management, who received the B.A. in business administration in 1959, was refused a job when she first applied to several major corporations because they had no female managers, but they wanted to know if she could type! Today, this type of treatment is, of course, a violation of Title VII. After several disappointing experiences, she was quite happy and grateful to land a managerial job with her present employer, even though it was in a female-ghetto department. After several promotions in the course of the next ten years, she was still in a female ghetto, and her career seemed to be at a dead end. When she began to express her wish for a career path into a mainstream department—that is, a traditionally male department—she was told her experience and technical background to be a manager in such a department were inadequate. Fortunately, after years of effort she got a job in her desired department and at a higher level because of governmental action against her company.

A young black man at the second level of management, with a B.S. in engineering, who joined his company in 1973 was not faced with overt discrimination in applying for a job. He was vigorously recruited by a number of firms. Nevertheless, he has been confronted with on-the-job problems related to his race. For example, he complained vehemently that while his white work group did not evidence any overt racist attitudes and behaviors, his "training period was much longer than his white peers'!" He believed small mistakes on his part were blown out of proportion compared to those of his white peers. Finally, he felt he was not an integral member of his work group and was excluded.

These case histories emphasize various forms of racism and sexism. Sometimes they are hard to spot, sometimes easy.

Racism and Sexism Defined

In this study racism and sexism are defined as basic cultural ideologies that state that whites and men are inherently superior to minorities and women, solely on the basis of race and sex, and that whites and men have the power over societal institutions to develop, evolve, nurture, spread, impose, and enforce the very myths and stereotypes that are the basic foundations of racism and sexism. These myths and stereotypes are used to maintain and justify the whites' and men's dominant social, economic, and political position.

The underlying bases of racism and sexism are power struggles between the dominant white men who want to maintain their privileged positions in society and the minorities and women who are determined to change the status quo. Even with their total control over all of society's institutions, the power struggles in which the whites and men find themselves create great fear. This fear of loss of their privileged positions has driven whites and men to develop myths and stereotypes in order to preserve these positions.

During the past 100 years, new political and social values have taken hold in the United States. A steady progression of laws has challenged the whites' and men's preferred positions and monopoly on power. Although these laws contain the devices for putting some of the new values into practice, they cannot eradicate the pervasive, unconscious ideologies that have a tremendously negative effect on all people, both morally and psychologically.

Thus, racism and sexism are still two of the most-powerful and -complex social forces affecting every institution in American society and most aspects of Americans' lives. However, the form of these forces has changed drastically, especially since 1964. Our present laws are trying to correct the obvious forms of racial and sexual discrimination that are called *overt* racism and sexism. The subtle forms have to do with policies, practices, and patterns of decision making, and they are called *institutional* racism and sexism. Finally, the even subtler covert forms of racism and sexism are called *neoracism* and *neosexism*.

In order to understand racism and sexism, a brief discussion of their evolution is presented. This overview does not trace the entire evolution of sexism and racism since the beginning of civilization, but it outlines the impacts of religious beliefs, legal thought, and language usage in America on the perpetuation of racism and sexism in this society. In addition, the negative psychological consequences of racism and sexism and their new forms will be discussed. Readers interested in pursuing these topics in more detail will find sources in the bibliography.

Historical Aspects of Racism

Racism is an old problem that divides people into superior races and inferior races. A number of writers have argued that racism had its origins among Western Europeans during the sixteenth century with the rise of nationalism and that it was applied first to class conflicts and then to national conflicts. Other researchers find evidence of racism much farther back in man's history.

The Bible story of Noah and his son Ham was used as an early justification of racism. Ham saw Noah lying naked and asleep in his tent, and Noah, upon discovery of this, put a curse on Ham's son Canaan: "Cursed be Canaan, a slave of slaves shall he be to his brothers." Canaan, according to the old Testament, was the progenitor of the early Egyptians and other African tribes. So although no reference to skin color occurs in this passage, the phrase "a slave of slaves" was used as righteous justification of the enslavement of black Africans, the supposed descendants of Canaan.[1] This view was supported by interpreters of the Bible who associated the blackness of people with things that mean evil, sin, death, despair, and ugliness. Barry Schwartz and Robert Disch stated that the English colonists brought to the New World a large number of associations connected to the word *black* that:

> . . . became important as men put language to use in first defining and later justifying the status they desired for the nonwhite. Before the close of the fifteenth century, the words *soiled* and *dirty* first became linked with *black*. By 1536, black connoted *dark purposes, malignant, deadly*; by 1581, *foul, iniquitous*; by 1588, *baneful, disastrous*, and *sinister*.[2]

Winthrop Jordan agreed that these negative associations with the word *black* preceded any contact between the English and black Africa.[3]

With such negative definitions of blackness and positive definitions of whiteness such as those symbolizing purity, goodness, and holiness, the English had no difficulty in justifying the enslavement of black-skinned people.

Racist ideology in America is not only aimed at blacks. While Europeans were encountering the "uncivilized," non-Christian culture of Africans, a similar type of meeting occurred between the Puritans and native Americans with similar attitudinal results. As the Puritan population increased and the demand for land and resources grew, the Puritan's intolerance of native Americans increased. This led to the development of racist attitudes and behaviors toward native Americans culminating with the view that the only good Indian is a dead Indian.[4]

Using the Bible as a justification, early legislators in this country passed laws to make racism a reality, not only in thought but also in practice. The preamble to South Carolina's code of 1712 said that "blacks were of barbarous, wild, savage natures, and . . . wholly unqualified to be governed by the laws, customs, and practices of this province. They must be governed by special laws as may restrain the disorders . . . and inhumanity to which they are naturally prone and inclined."[5] Sixty years later, when the U.S. Constitution was first written, a black man could be counted as only three-fifths of a white man for apportionment purposes. Black women, of course, were not considered to be even three-fifths of a person. Almost a century later, Chief Justice Roger B. Taney concurred and wrote in his opinion of the *Dred Scott* v. *Sanford* case (1857):

> The question before us is whether the class of persons described in the plea for abatement compose a portion of this people and are constituent members of this sovereignty. We think they are not, and that they are not included, and were not intended to be included, under the words "citizens" in the Constitution, and can therefore claim none of the rights and privileges which that instrument provides for and contrary, they were at that time considered as a subordinate and inferior class of beings, who had been subjugated by the dominant race, and whether emancipated or not, yet remained subject to their authority and had no rights or privileges but such as those who held the power and the government might choose to grant them.[6]

This antiblack trend continued through the 1860s until the Thirteenth, Fourteenth, and Fifteenth Amendments to the Constitution granted blacks equal rights of freedom, due process, and the vote. Yet, legal discrimination against blacks and other minorities, especially Asians, did not stop. Thirty years after the Civil War, in *Plessy* v. *Fergusson*, the U.S. Supreme Court ruled that "separate but equal" facilities were permissible. This precedent was not reversed until 1954 in *Brown* v. *Board of Education*.[7]

Article XIX of the California Constitution, passed in 1879 and in effect until 1952, extended legal racism to include the Chinese. The article prohibited the hiring of Chinese by corporations and by "any state, county, municipal, or other public work, except in punishment for crime."[8]

The American resentment of the Japanese culminated in the Johnson Immigration Act of 1924, passed by Congress, banning the immigration of persons "ineligible for citizenship." This act was directed against the Japanese and was not repealed until 1952.[9]

Finally, only fifteen years ago nonwhites were guaranteed the right to public accommodations, and twelve years ago interracial marriages and cohabition ceased to be illegal in the fifteen states with laws against miscegenation in *Loving* v. *Virginia*. These laws were originally directed against blacks, and in many cases, Asians.

Historical Aspects of Sexism

Sexism is not a new social phenomenon. Sexist attitudes originated tens of thousands of years ago, as noted by Marvin Harris:

> Male-supremacist institutions arose as a byproduct of warfare, of the male monopoly over weapons, and of the use of sex for the nurturance of aggressive male personalities. And warfare . . . is not the expression of human nature but a response to reproductive and economical pressures. Therefore, male supremacy is no more natural than warfare.[10]

Long ago, war was conducted with hand-held weapons whose effectiveness was a function of physical strength. The less-rugged anatomy and child bearing duties of women rendered them less physically powerful, so males dominated in war and food gathering. Male babies were preferred since they added to the defensive team, and they had first choice of available resources. Drudge work was assigned to women, and their subordination and devaluation followed automatically from the need to reward men at the expense of women and to provide supernatural justifications for the whole male-supremacist complex. Thus, the origins of sexism are tied to the exigencies of cave and village life. In later years sexism became culturally induced, made permanent by laws, and when necessary, rationalized with religion.[11]

A biblical passage used to show that men were superior to women is 1 Corinthians 11:3-9:

> But I would have you know that the head of the woman is the man, and the head of Christ is God. For a man indeed ought not to cover his head forasmuch as he is the image and glory of God, but the woman is the glory of the man. For the man is not of the woman, but the woman is of the man. Neither was the man created for the woman but the woman for the man.[12]

Notice that here the ideological distortion has woman only of man and created for man, and the man is not of woman but of God.

This definition of woman as inferior and subservient to men was reflected in early English law. The oldest written English law, Ethelbert's Dooms of 600 A.D., and the laws that followed it in Western civilization were developed, written, and interpreted by men who subscribed to this definition of women and who used the Bible to justify their sexist outlook.

Even 1,273 years later in 1873, the U.S. Supreme Court found that the State of Illinois could deny a woman a license to practice law in the state. Notice the biblical influence on Supreme Court Justice Joseph Bradley's words:

> . . . the civil law, as well as nature herself, has always recognized wide differences in the respective spheres and destinies of man and woman. Man is, or should be, woman's protector and defender. The natural and proper timidity and delicacy which belongs to the female sex evidently unfits it for many of the occupants of civil life. The constitution of the family organization, which is founded in the divine ordinance, as well as in the nature of things, indicates the domestic sphere as that which properly belongs to the domain and functions of womanhood. . . .
>
> It is true that many women are unmarried and not affected by any of the duties, complications, and incapacities arising out of the married state, but these are exceptions to the general rule. The paramount destiny and mission of women are to fulfill the noble and benign offices of wife and mother. This is the law of the Creator. And the rules of civil society must be adapted to the general constitution of things and cannot be based upon exceptional cases.[13]

The attitude conveyed by Bradley in "noble and benign offices of wife and mother" was still in effect in 1961 when the Earl Warren Court upheld a Florida law (many other states had similar laws) that had given women special immunity from jury duty in order that they be allowed to remain at "the center of home and family life."[14] This decision was overturned by the Warren E. Burger Court.

A well-known fact is that the Civil Rights Act of 1964 included women only because some southern congressmen thought such a ridiculous idea would easily defeat the bill. However, their strategy backfired. During the 1970s, many state laws that discriminated against women were challenged and often upheld at the state level and sometimes overturned at the federal level. Idaho provides an excellent illustration.

In the 1970 case of *Reed* v. *Reed*, a woman challenged an Idaho statute that stipulated that men must be given preference over women as administrators of estates of persons dying intestate (who have made no will). The Idaho Supreme Court found the statute constitutional and, calling upon nature, gave this feeble opinion:

> Philosophically it can be argued with some degree of logic that the provisions of I.C. 15-314 do discriminate against women on the basis of sex. However, nature itself has established the distinction, and this statute is not designed to discriminate but is only designed to alleviate the problem of holding hearings by the Court to determine eligibility to administer. . . . The legislature, when it enacted this statute, evidently concluded that in general men are better qualified to act as an administrator that are women.[15]

The most-recent legislation—and the most-important—pertaining to the rights of women is the Equal Rights Amendment to the U.S. Constitution. This amendment states simply and succinctly, "Equality of rights under the law shall not be abridged or denied by the United States or by any state on account of sex." Not only men but also millions of women are against the passage of this amendment. Years of pro-male socialization are preventing women themselves from seeking legal protection of their right to equality, should they choose to exercise that right.

Legislators have had not only the Bible but also the dictionary to assist them in justifying their sexist positions. Like other textbooks and instructions, the dictionary contains words that apply sex-role stereotypes to both sexes. Gershuny H. Lee found numerous examples of this cited in *Sexism and Language*.

She burst into tears upon hearing of his death, but it was only a grandstand play.

She always wears a crazy hat.

He is the pivot of her life.

She depends on her father for money.

Women with shrill voices get on his nerves.

You could see him turn off as she kept up her chatter.[16]

While dealing with the daily expressions of sexism in a legal system that designates her a "he" and recognizes her by the husband's surname, women come up against still more frustrations when dealing with the societal institutions that have given her labels and definitions, relegated her to an inferior position, and reduced her to a second-class status. It is one thing to cope with the men in the office who call her "doll," or "toots," or "baby" and quite another thing to get rid of the stereotypes when the courts and legislatures of the land make them a part of their judicial opinions and legislations.[17]

In sum, this nurturing and legitimizing of the inferiority of minorities and women by law, religion, and language is not new. Ruth Benedict aptly summed up the historical perspective of the power struggle that is the cause of racism and sexism when she observed:

> Persecution was an old, old story before racism was thought of. Social change is inevitable, and it is always fought by those whose ties are to the old order. Those who have these ties will consciously or unconsciously ferret out reasons for believing that their group is supremely valuable and that the new claimants threaten the achievements of civilization. They will raise a cry of rights of inheritance, or divine right of kings, or religious orthodoxy, or racial purity, or manifest destiny. These cries reflect the temporary conditions of the moment, and all the efforts of the slogan makers need not convince us that any one of them is based on external verities.[18]

Development of Racist and Sexist Attitudes and Behaviors

Racism and sexism are developed and nurtured by all societal institutions controlled by the dominant white-male group. Children learn racist and sexist attitudes and behaviors at a very early age. Families, schools, churches, other social groups, government, and the media socialize the population by communicating what is "good" behavior and what is "bad" behavior. They teach humans what to expect of themselves, their friends, and their families. They teach people what relationships they should have with society. Governments influence people through public education institutions. Governments also resolve conflicts within the society in accordance with prevailing values.

As a result of their socialization, children learn how to be minorities or whites, men or women. They acquire a picture about the worth of their social group and of self from their earliest contacts with other members of their family and with peers and teachers; in what they see in the movies, on television, and in advertisements; in what they read; in the conversations they overhear; and from their daily observations. Some social scientists argue that children acquire racist and sexist attitudes indirectly, mostly through parental instructions or admonitions, and through conversations designed to transmit prejudicial attitudes.[19]

Innumerable studies have explored the development of racist attitudes in white children at very early ages. One study found that very young children have a strong preference for the color white over black and that their regard for the color black is transferred to their perception of black people.[20] Another study found very young black children well on their way to developing negative concepts about their blackness.[21]

These studies were done after the "Black is Beautiful" movement reached its peak (1974). A study done before the movement (1964) came up with similar findings—specifically, that white children, age four, had already internalized feelings of superiority to blacks.[22] These three studies clearly show that the control of society's institutions by whites dominates children's perceptions. No matter how strongly the black community says "Black is Beautiful," the Hispanic community says, "Brown is Beautiful," or the native-American community says "Red is Beautiful," few of society's members will believe it unless most of society's institutions support these propositions.

With regard to sexual socialization, as early as the age of two, little boys are aware of their sex role, according to Helen Lewis. She observed that they must show that they are different from their mothers and must renounce all characteristics that may be considered unmanly. She wrote:

> No wonder they have more trouble with their gender identity than little girls. And no wonder men are more prone than women to obsessional neurosis and schizophrenia.[23]

Experimenting with the role of the opposite sex is much-more acceptable for little girls than for little boys. Girls learn at a young age that the male role is to be envied and imitated. Girls are free to dress in boys' clothes but certainly not the other way around. At some stage in a girl's life, some parents are amused if they have a daughter who is a tomboy, but they are genuinely distressed if they have a son who is a "sissy."[24]

The result of these role-modeling techniques is that the woman's need to achieve is, ever so gently, sublimated into a need to nurture and serve:

> She is discouraged and protected from taking risks by her parents. At the same time she is subjected to peer pressure to fit the mold. "If you take

chemistry, you won't have time to date"; "If you really swim your hair will look a fright and your muscles will bulge"; If you get good grades you're a drag"; "If you always win at tennis, no one will want to play with you"; and on and on.[25]

The result of all of this is that she follows tradition:

> She doesn't plan for the long range and doesn't recognize choice points but begins to back into or avoid decision making. She becomes more dependent on others because it is easy and comfortable. She ceases her formal education, takes a job, finds a man, and becomes the role model.[26]

Impact of Racism and Sexism on Society

With such strong forces operating to socialize people, many people believe that a racist and sexist society is the natural consequence of human behavior. This is because when someone receives a universal, consistent message about race and sex from the church, family, peers, schools, newspapers, and television, the consequence is an unconscious or conscious ideology, a set of beliefs and attitudes that he or she accepts implicitly as the natural state of the universe. Everyone has heard a family member, schoolmate, co-worker, friend, or political, social, or economic leader say, "Of course I have racist/sexist attitudes, everyone has them. One cannot help it. We were brought up this way."

Racism and sexism as unconscious ideologies have debilitating effects on people's psychological and physical health. For example, the U.S. Commission on Mental Health declared in 1965 that Americans' racist attitudes, which causes and perpetuates tension, is a most-compelling health hazard, severely crippling the growth and development of millions of young and old citizens. The commission diagnosed racism as a form of schizophrenia, "in that there is a large group gap between what whites believe in and actually practice."[27]

Put another way, a white-centered superior attitude leaves the people who adopt it both confused and mentally underdeveloped. Judy Katz pinpointed this by declaring that "racism has deluded whites into a false sense of superiority that has left them in a pathological and schizophrenic state." Further, it has produced "miseducation about the realities of history, the contributions of Third-World people, and the role of white people in present-day culture. In short, it has limited the growth potential of whites.[28]

James Harrison stated that the socially prescribed male role requires men to be uncommunicative, competitive, nongiving, inexpressive, and to evaluate success in terms of external achievements, rather than personal and interpersonal fulfillment. A man is caught in a double bind because if he fulfills the prescribed role requirements, he has to deny his human needs. If he meets these needs, he could be considered unmanly.[29]

The negative consequences of the male sex-role stereotype on the male life expectancy have been increasing for some time. In 1900, life expectancy in the United States was 48.3 years for women and 46.3 years for men. In 1975, it was 76.5 years for women and 68.7 years for men. During this 75-year period, the life expectancy for both men and women increased by more than 20 years, but the difference between their respective life expectancies increased substantially, from 2 years in 1900 to 7.8 years in 1975.[30] In 1980 the gap increased to 10 years.

Harrison also cites the higher mortality rate of men and evidence that points the finger at male-role socialization for these early deaths:

> Recognizing the multiplicity of variables within the chain of casuality . . . three-fourths of the difference in life expectancy can be accounted for by sex-role-related behaviors which contribute to the greater mortality of men . . . one-third of the differences can be accounted for by smoking, another one-sixth by coronary-prone behavior, and the remainder by a variety of causes.[31]

Dominant groups, of course, are not the only ones to suffer the far-reaching effects of racist/sexist attitudes. Blacks show symptoms of disturbances resulting from the arduous emotional conditions under which blacks in America are obliged to live. Researchers have observed that even four-year-old patients were able to perceive themselves as black, different from white, and that they were also displaying signs of some emotional disturbance as evidenced by the vagueness of responses to the "Who am I" question.[32]

A number of black social scientists have stressed the negative effect of racism on blacks' not being allowed to compete successfully as adults. Some psychological results are aggressive behavior, professional anxiety, and escape from reality through alcohol and drugs. Some negative physical effects of racism are higher rates of hypertension, high blood pressure, and suicide among blacks than whites.[33] Racism's negative effects of the mental and physical health of native Americans has also been well documented.

A greater incidence of mental illness among women has been reported, Some researchers attribute it to the greater stress of women's role. They also report an interaction between sex and marital status, which suggests that marriage is related to a decreased risk of mental illness for men but an increased risk for women.[34]

In these few pages we see quite clearly that racism and sexism have created severe physical and mental problems, not only for the oppressed minorities and women but also for the dominant whites and men.

Neoracism and Neosexism

Clearly, racism and sexism continue to be powerful negative forces in American life. While some progress has been made toward ousting these negative forces, like all social change it is slow and just now beginning to make a limited impact. In addition, the character of racism and sexism have in large part changed. The new forms are in most cases subtle, devious, and more sophisticated than in the past. They can be labeled *neoracism* and *neosexism*.

A very good example of neoracism occurs in a field in which blacks have been very successful—football. Raymond Rainville and Edward Mc-Cormick conducted a study in which they found that announcers build a positive reputation for white players and a comparatively negative reputation for black players. Although announcers are probably not consciously producing the negative effect, Rainville and McCormick pointed out that in describing the play, the announcers more-frequently praised the white players and pointed special focus toward them by depicting them as aggressors. By contrast, the announcers depicted the black players as the recipients of aggression, compared them negatively to other players, and made negative references to the black players' past achievements.

> The negative elements built into the black players' reputations probably have a greater impact on the listener than do the positive components. We base this judgment on the fact that Jones and Davis have demonstrated that one piece of socially undesirable information has much-greater impact on reputation than an equivalent amount of socially desirable information would have.[35]

Neosexist views clearly can be seen in the obstacles women face in obtaining faculty positions and in advancing through the faculty hierarchy. In evaluating the candidacy of a female faculty member, the caliber of the school she attended is the first consideration. Most women must have attended a prestigious university or college to obtain a faculty appointent in a four-year institution. If she passes that test, the next consideration is her grades, which must be outstanding. If she passes this test, a female candidate must then have earned her degree in the correct fields of study. Next, she must have solid and reasonable publications in established journals and with reputable book publishers. If she passes all these tests, then *maybe* she will get the job or the promotion. However, major fields, reputable publishers, and relevant, well-written topics are all factors in which neosexist attitudes can play a role. Numerous studies have shown that the same performance by women is evaluated lower than men's on most occasions. This is apparently due to the subconscious, neosexist views held by the evaluators.[36]

An article in *The New York Times*, 22 April 1979, noted how neoracism and neosexism can effectively hinder highly qualified minorities and women from pursuing professional careers in the private sector. The article pointed out that Dr. Patience Claybon, the only black-female psychiatrist in Birmingham, Alabama, was refused staff privileges at the Baptist Medical Center in Princeton on the grounds that her field of specialization was overcrowded. This neoracist/neosexist tactic is similar to that of universities refusing a woman a faculty position because of overcrowding or lack of relevance of her specialty to the overall position of the department.[37]

Another example of neosexism/neoracism is that aggressive, confident, ambitious minorities and women are seen as being too aggressive, too confident, and too ambitious, while their white-male peers' exhibiting the same characteristics are viewed favorably. Depending on who is doing the acting and who is doing the interpreting, identical behavior is often construed and described differently.

One of the main indications of this type of neosexism lies in a stereotype developed over the years by psychologists and psychiatrists. This stereotype defines mentally healthy women as dependent, emotional, and passive. Women who display male characteristics like independence, stoicism, and aggressiveness are considered mentally unhealthy.

This stereotype was explored in three studies that investigated the relationships between sex-role standards and the psychiatric referral process. Would children who exhibited inappropriate behavioral characteristics for their sex be referred to psychiatric facilities more frequently than children who exhibited appropriate behavior characteristics? Based on records of an out-patient child-guidance clinic, the first study found that a larger number of boys than girls were referred for being emotional and passive, and a larger number of girls than boys were referred for being defiant and verbally aggressive. In two subsequent studies, hypothetical case histories were read by samples of parents and graduate students in clinical and school psychology. In these case histories, identical behavior problems were attributed either to a boy or a girl. The child seen as exhibiting inappropriate behavior for his or her sex was classified as more-severely disturbed, more in need of treatment, and less likely to have a successful future.[38]

Women are caught in somewhat of a double bind. They learn that to be attractive to a male partner, they must develop certain characteristics traditionally identified as feminine. They also learn increasingly that to have successful careers and/or independent self-identities that command respect for self and others, they must develop characteristics that have not traditionally been encouraged in women. So, because of the sexist definition of a healthy woman and the conflict that evolves during the socialization process, more women have sought and been advised to seek mental-health assistance. These factors create the illusion that women are the more emotionally unstable sex and reinforce that stereotype.

Institutional Racism and Sexism

Inertia or, at best, the reluctance to change tends to pervade organizations. Their rate of change is naturally slower than that of the individuals who comprise the organizations or the groups of individuals who maintain them. Institutions tend to captivate these groups and use them in a way that defies individual influence—that is, they become systems or entities somewhat apart from the people whom they serve. Institutional racism and sexism are based on these systems.

Harold Baron believes that people do not have to exercise a choice to perpetuate a racist or sexist act. The organizational rules and procedures have already prestructured the choice against minorities and women. An individual only has to conform to the operating norms and values of the organization, and it will do the discriminating for him or her.[39] This idea is supported by Robert Blauner, who terms the procedures used to exclude or restrict as "conventional, part of the bureaucratic system of rules and regulations. Thus, there is little need for individual prejudice as a motivating force."[40] Well-meaning individuals inadvertently perpetuate an unjust system:

> The people of goodwill and tolerance who identify racism with prejudice can therefore exempt themselves from responsibility and involvement in our system of racial injustice and inequality by taking comfort in their own "favorable" attitudes toward minority groups. . . . The error in this point of view is revealed by the fact that such individuals of goodwill and tolerance help maintain the racism of American society and in some cases even profit from it.[41]

A good example of institutional racism and sexism is seen in the old-boy network, a system that works for its members in ways that include finding candidates for the higher-level jobs in public and private institutions. The network's composition is almost exclusively white male. Therefore, by using the network as the primary-selection agent, chances are the candidates will be white men.

Another stronghold of institutional racism and sexism exists in the "publish-or-perish" syndrome of the academic world. Since publishing in academic journals greatly depends on the placement of friends in the professional organizations controlling these journals, minorities' and women's opportunities to be published are greatly diminished because few of them can count as part of their network of friends the members of review boards.

Also, an imbalance exists in teaching loads that would appear to have a significant impact on the publishing capability, which is a qualification for promotion in academia. Forty-nine percent of the male and 63 percent of the female faculty have full teaching loads, defined as nine or more class hours per week.[42] Thus, women have considerably less time to engage in research and, subsequently, to publish. The effect of this teaching-load practice seems to contribute to discrimination. In fact, female faculty compared with male faculty publish less than could be explained by their proportionate representation in various specialities.[43] However, married women with doctorates who work full time publish slightly more than either men or unmarried women. This last fact weakens the argument that the home role detracts from women's ability to publish.[44]

President Jimmy Carter was confronted with institutional racism and sexism in selecting 152 new federal judges. The criteria that many senators used were traditional requirements such as previous service in the state court systems or twenty years of experience in a distinguished law firm. Since few, if any, qualified minority and female lawyers have had the opportunity to meet either of these criteria because of past race and sex discrimination, obviously few of them would be acceptable to the senators. Thus, the senators do not have to be racist and/or sexist to exclude minorities and women—all they have to do is adhere to the traditional standards.

The phenomenon of women's moving into nontraditional jobs illustrates still another example of institutional sexism. One of the stereotypic beliefs is that some of the equipment and tools used in "men's" work are not appropriate for a woman's physical makeup. Therefore, she might not be able to do the job or might not do it as well as a man. However, most, if not all, equipment and tools can be slightly modified for use by a woman, if necessary. A few determined women have demonstrated that if selected, and if not prevented by their work group, they can perform these jobs at least as well as men.

Still another form of institutional racism is exemplified by zoning laws. The U.S. Civil Rights Commission noted that discrimination remains the prime factor in containing minorities in their own neighborhoods, in which poor housing, minimal public services, and resultant serious social problems exist. Exclusionary zoning and other local government and/or banking actions have prevented minorities from obtaining decent housing and have reinforced patterns of racial and economic segregation.

Conclusion

This appendix attempted to give the reader a basic understanding of racism and sexism and its various new forms. It is important to remember that many people believe racism and sexism are no longer important influences in our society's institutions. However, these evils have only gone underground, which makes them more difficult to see but no less destructive.

In terms of mental health, racism and sexism, regardless of their forms, are more-pervasive and far more-serious threats than "childhood schizophrenia, mental retardation, psychoneurosis, or any other emotional derangement."[45] Their destructive forces severely cripple the growth and development of millions of Americans regardless of age, race, and sex. Yearly, they directly and indirectly cause more fatalities, disabilities, and economic loss than any other single factor.[46]

Endnotes

Chapter 1

1. Douglas T. Hall and Francine S. Hale, "Career Development: How Organizations Put Their Fingerprints on People," in Lee Dyer, ed., *Careers in Organizations: Individual Planning and Organizational Development* (Ithaca, N.Y.: New York State School of Industrial and Labor Relations, Cornell University, 1976), p. 6.

2. Daniel Yankelovich, "Work, Values, and the New Breed," in Clark Kerr and Jerome M. Rosow, eds., *Work in America: The Decade Ahead* (New York: Van Nostrand Reinhold, 1979), p. 10.

3. Hall and Hale, "Career Development," p. 198.

4. Rogene A. Buckholz, "An Empirical Study of Contemporary Beliefs about Work in American Society," *Journal of Applied Psychology* 63:2 (1978):219-27.

5. Steven H. Applebaum, "Attitudes and Values: Concerns of Middle Managers," *Training and Development Journal* (October 1978), pp. 52-58.

6. M.R. Cooper et al., "Changing Employees Values: Deepening Discontents?" *Harvard Business Review* (January/February 1979), pp. 117-25.

7. Kathryn Welds, "It's a Question of Stereotypes vs. Reality, Limits vs. Potential," *Personnel Journal* (June 1979), pp. 380-83. Used with permission.

Chapter 2

1. Melvin Steinfield, *Cracks in the Melting Pot: Racism and Discrimination in American History* (Beverly Hills: Glencoe Press, 1970), p. xxiv. Copyright © 1970 by Melvin Steinfield. Reprinted with permission.

2. Vine Deloria, Jr., *Custer Died for Your Sins* (New York: Avon Books, 1970), p. 172. Copyright © 1969 by Vine Deloria, Jr. Reprinted with permission.

3. James Wilfred Vander Zanden, *American Minority Relations: The Sociology of Race and Ethnic Groups* (New York: John Wiley & Sons, 1963), p. 52. Reprinted with permission.

4. Judith Caditz, *White Liberals in Transition* (New York: Spectrum, 1976), p. 113.

5. Ibid., pp. 91-92.

6. Doris Y. Wilkinson et al., *The Black Male in America: Perspective on His Status in Contemporary Society* (Chicago: Nelson-Hall, 1977), p. 228.

7. Philip L. Berg, "Racism and the Puritan Mind," *Phylon* 36 (March 1975):1-7.

8. Steinfeld, *Cracks in the Melting Pot,* p. 73.

9. S.J. Makielski, Jr., *Beleagued Minorities: Cultural Politics in America* (San Francisco: W.H. Freeman, 1973), p. 53.

10. David M. Reimers et al., *Natives and Strangers: Ethnic Groups and the Building of America* (New York: Oxford University Press, 1979), p. 228.

11. Michael Knight, "Gains Affirm Indian Rights Demands," *The New York Times,* 9 July 1979, p. 10.

12. Elizabeth Almquist, *Minorities, Gender and Work* (Lexington, Mass.: Lexington Books, D.C. Heath and Company, 1979), p. 43.

13. Zanden, American Minority Relations, p. 207.

14. Reimers et al., *Natives and Strangers,* p. 194.

15. Steinfeld, *Cracks in the Melting Pot,* p. 130.

16. William Wong, "Chinese Americans Help U.S. Employees Bridge the Language Gap in China," *Wall Street Journal,* 3 July 1979, p. 30.

17. Charles F. Marden and Gladys Meyer, *Minorities in American Society* (New York: Van Nostrand, 1973), p. 200. Reprinted with permission.

18. Ibid., p. 201.

19. Steinfeld, *Cracks in the Melting Pot,* p. 141.

20. Marden and Meyer, *Minorities in American Society,* p. 202.

21. Donald Keith Fellows, *A Mosaic of America's Ethnic Minorities* (New York: John Wiley & Sons, 1972), p. 137. Reprinted with permission.

22. Reimers et al., *Natives and Strangers,* p. 247.

23. Fellows, *Mosaic of America's Ethnic Minorities,* p. 141.

24. Dr. Chalsa Loo's comments are from an analysis of data commissioned by the author in June 1978. Reprinted with permission.

25. Zanden, *American Minority Relations,* p. 201.

26. Steinfeld, *Cracks in the Melting Pot,* p. 80.

27. Almquist, *Minorities, Gender and Work,* pp. 73-74.

28. Zanden, *American Minority Relations,* pp. 205-206.

29. Stan Steiner, *La Roza: The Mexican Americans* (New York: Harper and Row, 1968), pp. 233-234.

30. Matt S. Meier and Feliciano Riviera, *The Chicanos: A History of Mexican Americans* (New York: Hill and Wang, 1972), p. 190.

31. John M. Crewdson, "Hispanics Angered as U.S. Bars Brutality Charges against Police," *The New York Times,* 10 July 1979, pp. 11-12.

32. Almquist, *Minorities, Gender and Work,* p. 90.

33. Zander, *American Minority Relations,* p. 196.

34. Almquist, *Minorities, Gender and Work,* p. 80.

35. Clara Garcia, "Hispanic Managers in Corporations" (Unpublished paper, 1975), pp. 1-20.

36. Ibid.

37. Almquist, *Minorities, Gender and Work,* p. 83.

38. Joel Kovel, *White Racism: A Psychohistory* (New York: Vintage Press, 1971), pp. 13-14.

39. Thomas Sowell, *Race and Economics* (New York: David McKay Company, 1975).

40. See Robert Blauner, *Racial Oppression in America* (New York: Harper & Row, 1972). Reprinted with permission; and Charles Silberman, *Criminal Violence, Criminal Justice* (New York: Random House, 1978). Reprinted with permission.

41. William Julius Wilson, *The Declining Significance of Race, Blacks and Changing American Institutions* (Chicago: University of Chicago Press, 1978), p. 61. Reprinted with permission.

42. "Special *Ebony* Poll: Survey Queries of 4,500 Black Elected Officials," *Ebony* (May 1979), pp. 183-85.

43. Thurgood Marshall in speech at Howard University, June 1978.

Chapter 3

1. Robert M. Jobu, "Earnings Differences of White and Ethnic Minorities: The Case of Asians, Americans, the Blacks and Chicanos," *Sociology and Social Research* 66:1 (October 1976):24-38.

2. John P. Fernandez, *Black Managers in White Corporations* (New York: John Wiley & Sons, 1975), pp. 91-92.

3. Elizabeth Almquist, *Minorities, Gender and Work* (Lexington, Mass.: Lexington Books, D.C. Heath and Company, 1979), p. 154.

4. Fernandez, *Black Managers,* pp. 94-116.

5. Ibid., p. 97.

6. Judith Caditz, *White Liberals in Transition* (New York: Spectrum, 1976), pp. 53-87.

7. Charles A. Valentine, *Black Studies and Anthropology: Scholarly and Political Interests in Afro-American Culture* (Reading, Mass.: Addison-Wesley, 1972), p. 33. Reprinted with permission.

8. Margaret Hennig and Anne Jardim, *The Managerial Woman* (New York: Doubleday, 1976), p. 14. Copyright © 1976 by Margaret Hennig and Anne Jardim. Reprinted by permission of Doubleday and Company.

9. Doris Y. Wilkinson et al., *The Black Male in America: Perspectives on His Status in Contemporary Society* (Chicago: Nelson-Hall, 1977).

10. Harold Wilensky, "Measures and Effects of Social Mobility," in

Neil J. Smelser and Seymour M. Lipset, eds., *Social Structure and Mobility in Economic Development* (Chicago: Aldine, 1966), pp. 98-140.

11. William H. Grier and Price M. Cobbs, *Black Rage* (New York: Basic Books, 1968), pp. 154-161. Reprinted with permission.

12. Ibid., p. 161.

Chapter 4

1. Juliet Mitchell, *Woman's Estate* (New York: Pantheon Books, 1971), p. 52.

2. Helen B. Lewis, *Psychic War in Men and Women* (New York: New York University Press, 1976), pp. 123-24. Reprinted by permission of New York University Press.

3. Elizabeth Janeway, *Man's World, Woman's Place* (New York: Dell, 1971), pp. 163-67. Reprinted with permission.

4. Barbara Ehrenreich and English Deidre, *Complaints and Disorders* (New York: Faculty Press, 1973), p. 16.

5. Upton Sinclair, *The Jungle* (New York: New American Library, 1906).

6. Sheila M. Rothman, *Woman's Proper Place: A History of Changing Ideals and Practices, 1870 to the Present* (New York: Basic Books, 1978), p. 22. Reprinted with permission.

7. Ibid., pp. 47-48.

8. Ibid., pp. 42-48.

9. Ibid., p 42.

10. Ibid., pp. 221-22.

11. Ibid., p. 224.

12. Mary P. Ryan, *Womanhood in America: From Colonial Times to the Present* (New York: New Viewpoints, 1975), p. 403. Reprinted with permission.

13. Rothman, *Woman's Proper Place*, p. 229.

14. Rachel A. Rosenfeld, "Women's Intergenerational Occupational Mobility," *American Sociological Review* 43 (February 1978):36-46. Reprinted with permission.

15. Paul Burstein, "Legislation and the Income of Women and Non-whites," *American Sociological Review* 44 (June 1979):367-91.

16. Larry Suter and Henry Mitler, "Income Difference Between Men and Career Women," *American Journal of Sociology* 78 (January 1973):962-74.

17. David L. Featherman and H. Robert M. Hauser, "Sexual Inequalities and Socioeconomic Achievement in the United States, 1962-1973," *American Sociological Review* 41 (June 1976):462-83. Reprinted with permission.

18. See Gerda Lerner, ed., *Black Women in White America: A Documentary History* (New York: Vintage, 1973) and Robert Staples, *The Black Woman in America* (Chicago: Nelson-Hall, 1978).

19. Dr. Gloria Lindsey Alibrahou's comments are from an analysis of data commissioned by the author in September 1977.

20. Elizabeth Almquist, *Minorities, Gender and Work* (Lexington, Mass.: Lexington Books, D.C. Heath and Company, 1979), p. 79.

21. Ann Nieto Gomez, "Heritage of LaHembra," in Sue Cox, ed., *Female Psychology: The Emerging Self* (Chicago: Science Research Associates, 1976):226-34.

22. Stanley L.M. Fong and H. Peskin, "Sex Role Strain and Personality Adjustment of China-Born Students in America," *Journal of Abnormal Psychology* 74 (October 1969):563-67.

23. Almquist, *Minorities, Gender and Work*, p. 121.

24. Dr. Chelsa Loo's comments are from an analysis of data commissioned by the author in June 1978.

25. Diane K. Lewis, "The Black Family: Socialization and Sex Roles," *Phylon* 36:3 (September 1975):221-37.

26. Dr. Gloria Lindsey Alibrahou's comments are from an analysis of data commissioned by the author in September 1977.

27. Donald Keith Fellows, *A Mosaic of America's Ethnic Minorities* (New York: John Wiley & Sons, 1972), p. 59.

28. See, for example, R. Brooke Jacobsen, "Changes in the Chinese Family," *Social Science* 51 (Winter 1976):26-31; and Marshall Jung and Reiko Homma-True, "Characteristics of Contrasting Chinatowns: Philadelphia, Pennsylvania, and Oakland, California," *Social Casework* 5 (March 1976):149-59.

29. Irene Fujitomi and Diane Wong, "The New Asian-American Woman," in S. Sue and N. Wagner, eds., *Asian Americans: Psychological Perspective* (Palo Alto, Calif.: Science and Behavior Books, 1973), pp. 252-263.

30. Dr. Hardy Frye's comments are from an analysis of data commissioned by the author in June 1978. Used with permission.

31. V.E. Schein, "The Relationship between Sex Role Stereotypes and Requisite Management Characteristics," *Journal of Applied Psychology* 57 (1973):95-100; Schein, "Relationships between Sex Role Stereotypes and Requisite Management Characteristics among Female Managers," *Journal of Applied Psychology* 60 (1975):340-44; and R.L. Thorndike, *Personnel Selection* (New York: John Wiley & Sons, 1966).

32. David McClelland, *The Achieving Society* (New York: Free Press, 1961).

33. Elizabeth Janeway, *Man's World, Woman's Place: A Study in Social Mythology* (New York: Morrow, 1971), p. 305.

34. Margaret Hennig and Anne Jardim, *The Managerial Woman* (New York: Doubleday, 1976), pp. 205-07. Reprinted by permission of Doubleday and Company.

35. June Kronholz, "Women at Work: Management Practices Change to Reflect Role of Women Employees," *Wall Street Journal*, 3 September 1978, p. 1.

36. Allen Pace Nilsen et al., *Sexism and Language* (Urbana, Ill.: National Council of Teachers of English, 1977), p. 143.

37. From *Games Mother Never Taught You*; Betty Lehan Harragan. (New York: Warner, 1977), pp. 368-69. Copyright © 1977. Reprinted by permission of Rawson, Wade Publishers.

38. Rosabeth Moss Kanter, *Men and Women of the Corporation* (New York: Basic Books, 1977), pp. 233-37.

39. Ibid.

40. Ibid.

41. Harragan, *Games Mother Never Taught You*, p. 355.

42. Robert Seidenberg, *Corporate Wives—Corporate Casualties?* (New York: AMACOM, a division of American Management Associates, 1973), p. 129. Reprinted with permission.

43. Cynthia Epstein, *Woman's Place* (Berkley: University of California Press, 1970), pp. 16-17.

44. Hennig and Jardim, *Managerial Woman*, pp. 37-38.

45. Donald C. Pelz, "Influence: A Key to Effective Leadership in the First-Line Supervisor," *Personnel* 29 (1952):3-11. (New York: American Management Associated, Inc.) Reprinted with permission.

Chapter 5

1. George Ritzer, *Working: Conflict and Change* (Englewood Cliffs, N.J.: Prentice-Hall, 1977), p. 114.

2. Theodore Caplow, *The Sociology of Work* (New York: McGraw-Hill, 1954), pp. 71-72. Used with the permission of the McGraw-Hill Book Company.

3. Melville Dalton, *Men Who Manage* (New York: John Wiley & Sons, 1959), pp. 269-70; Garda W. Bowman, "The Image of a Promotable Person in Business Enterprise," (Ph.d. diss. New York University, 1962); and Bowman, "What Helps or Harms Promotability?" *Harvard Business Review* 42 (1964):6-26, 184-96.

4. Frederick D. Sturdivant and Roy D. Adler, "Executive Origins: Still a Gray Flannel World?" *Harvard Business Review* (November/December 1976), pp. 125-32.

5. See John P. Fernandez, *Black Managers in White Corporations* (New York: John Wiley & Sons, 1975), pp. 66-77; Richard R. America and Bernard E. Anderson, *Moving Ahead: Black Managers in American Business* (New York: McGraw-Hill, 1978), p. 41, used with permission of McGraw-Hill Book Company; and *Profile of a Woman Officer* (Heichrick and Struggles, 1979), pp. 1-8.

6. Fernandez, *Black Managers*, p. 143.

7. *Profile of a Woman Officer*, pp. 1-8.

8. Fernandez, *Black Managers*, pp. 141-54.

9. Rosabeth Moss Kanter, *Men and Women of the Corporation* (New York: Basic Books, 1977), pp. 236-40. Reprinted with permission.

10. Judith Caditz, *White Liberals in Transition* (New York: Spectrum, 1976), p. 63.

11. Betty Lehan Harragan, *Games Mother Never Taught You: Corporate Gamesmanship for Women* (New York: Warner, 1977), p. 27.

12. For a comparative analysis of the two studies, see Fernandez, *Black Managers*, pp. 123-40.

13. Eugene E. Jennings, *The Mobile Manager* (Ann Arbor: Bureau of Industrial Relations, Graduate School of Business Administration, University of Michigan, 1967), p. 52.

14. Fernandez, *Black Managers*, p. 136.

15. *Profile of a Woman Officer*, pp. 1-8.

16. Gerard Roche, "Much Ado about Mentors," *Harvard Business Review* (January/February 1979), pp. 14-28.

17. America and Anderson, *Moving Ahead*, pp. 55-56.

18. Margaret Hennig and Anne Jardim, *The Managerial Woman* (New York: Doubleday, 1976), p. 67.

19. See Robert Blauner, *Alienation and Freedom* (Chicago: University of Chicago Press, 1964); and Ely Chinoy, *Automobile Workers and the American Dream* (New York: Doubleday, 1955). Reprinted with permission.

20. Kanter, *Men and Women of the Corporation*, p. 146.

Chapter 6

1. Lois E. Olive et al., "Moving as Perceived by Executives and Their Families," *Journal of Occupational Medicine* 18:8 (August 1976):546-50.

2. See Margaret Hennig and Anne Jardim, *The Managerial Woman* (New York: Doubleday, 1976); Betty Lehan Harragan, *Games Mother Never Taught You: Corporate Gamesmanship for Women* (New York: Warner, 1977); and June Kronholz, "Women at Work: Management Practices Change to Reflect Role of Women Employees," *Wall Street Journal*, 3 September 1978.

3. From *Work in America: The Decade Ahead* ed. Clark Kerr and Jerome M. Rosow, (New York: Van Nostrand Reinhold, 1979), p. 13. Reprinted with permission.

4. Kronholz, "Women at Work," p. 1.

5. U.S. Commission on Civil Rights, *The State of Civil Rights: 1977: A Report of the United States Commission on Civil Rights* (Washington, D.C.: U.S. Government Printing Office, February 1978), pp. 16-21.

6. *The Federal Fair Housing Enforcement Effort: A Report of the U.S. Commission on Civil Rights,* (Washington, D.C.: U.S. Government Printing Office, 1979), pp. 1-235.

7. Ibid.

8. Olive et al. "Moving as Perceived by Executives," pp. 546-50.

9. Ibid.

Chapter 7

1. Chris Argyris, "A Few Words in Advance," in Alfred J. Marrow, ed., *The Failure of Success* (New York: American Management Association, 1972), pp. 3-4. Reprinted with permission.

2. Erich Fromm, *The Sane Society* (New York: Holt, Rinehart and Winston, 1955), pp. 141-42.

3. John B. Miner, "Twenty Years of Research on Role-Motivation Theory of Managerial Effectiveness," *Personnel Psychology* 31 (1978):739-59. Used with permission.

4. Eve Spangler, Marsha Gordon, and Ronald Pipkin, "Token Women: An Empirical Test of Kanter's Hypothesis," *AJS* 84 (1978):160-70.

5. Helen B. Lewis, *Psychic War in Men and Women* (New York: New York University Press, 1976), pp. 92-93.

6. Laurie Larwood and Marion M. Wood, *Women in Management,* (Lexington, Mass.: Lexington Books, D.C. Heath and Company, 1977), p. 100.

7. John P. Fernandez, *Black Managers in White Corporations* (New York: John Wiley & Sons, 1975), p. 164.

Chapter 8

1. Robert Blauner, *Alienation and Freedom* (Chicago: University of Chicago Press, 1964), pp. 15-34.

2. Ibid.

3. Robert D. Caplan and John R.P. French, Jr., "Organizational Stress and Industrial Strain," in Alfred J. Marrow, ed., *The Failure of Suc-*

cess (New York: American Management Association, 1972), pp. 49-50. Reprinted with permission.

4. Wilbert Moore, *The Conduct of the Corporation* (New York: Random House, 1962), pp. 151-66. Reprinted with permission.

5. Angus Campbell, P.E. Converse, and W.L. Rogers, *Quality of American Life* (New York: Russell Sage Foundation, 1976), p. 299.

6. Rosabeth Moss Kanter, "Work in a New America," *Daedalus* 107:1 (Winter 1978):47-78.

7. Charles N. Weaver, "What Workers Want from Their Jobs," *Personnel* (May/June 1976), pp. 48-54.

8. Douglas Bray, Richard J. Campbell, and Donald L. Grant, *The Management Recruit: Formative Years in Business* (New York: Wiley-Interscience, 1974), p. 78.

9. J.R. Hackman and E.E. Lawler, "Employee Reactions to Job Characteristics," *Journal of Applied Psychology* 55 (1971):259-86.

10. Richard O. Peterson and Bruce H. Duffany, "Job Enrichment and Redesign," in R.L. Craig, ed., *Training and Development Handbook,* 2nd ed. (New York: McGraw-Hill, 1976), p. 15. Used with the permission of McGraw-Hill Book Company.

10. Denis D. Umstot et al., "Goal Setting and Job Enrichment: An Integrated Approach to Job Design," *Academy of Management Review,* (October 1978), pp. 867-79.

12. Benson Rosen and Thomas H. Jerdee, "Influence of Sex-Role Stereotypes on Personnel Decision," *Journal of Applied Psychology* 59 (1974a):9-14.

13. Richard Balzar, *Clockwork* (Garden City, N.Y.: Doubleday, 1976), p. 326.

14. Pamela L. Steen, "Designing Compatible Work Systems," *Journal of the College and University Personnel Association* 28:3 (Summer 1977):43-46. Reprinted with permission.

15. Otis D. Duncan, Howard Schuman, and Beverly Duncan, *Social Change in a Metropolitan Community* (New York: Russell Sage Foundation, 1973), pp. 73-74.

16. Daniel Yankelovich, "The Meaning of Work," in J.M. Rosow, ed., *The Worker and the Job: Coping with Change* (Englewood Cliffs, N.J.: Prentice-Hall, 1974), pp. 19-48.

Chapter 9

1. Harry Levinson, "Thinking Ahead," *Harvard Business Review* (July/August 1976), pp. 30-46.

2. L. W. Porter, E.E. Lawler, and J.R. Hackman, *Behavior in Organizations* (New York: McGraw-Hill, 1975). Used with permission of McGraw-Hill Book Company.

3. Paul H. Thompson and Gene W. Dalton, "Performance Appraisal: Managers Reward," *Harvard Business Review* 48 (January/February 1970), pp. 149-57.

4. Levinson, "Thinking Ahead," pp. 30-46.

5. Gail Pheterson, Sara Kiesler, and Philip Goldberg, "Evaluation of Women as a Function of Their Sex Achievement and Personal History," *Journal of Personality and Social Psychology* 19 (1971):114-18.

6. W. Clay Hamner et al., "Race and Sex as Determinants of Ratings by Potential Employers in a Simulated Work Sampling Task," *Journal of Applied Psychology* 59:6 (1974):705-11.

7. Ibid.

8. Randall Schuller, "Male and Female Routes to Managerial Success," *Personnel Administrator* (February 1979), pp. 35-38.

9. Kay Deaux and Tim Emswiller, "Explanations of Successful Performance and Sex-Linked Tasks: What is Skill of the Males is Luck for the Female", *Journal of Personality* 29 (1974):80-85.

10. Ibid.

11. Ibid.

12. Mary Ellen Cline et al., "Evaluations of the Work of Men and Women as a Function of the Sex of the Judges and Type of Work," *Journal of Applied Social Psychology* 71 (1977):89-93.

13. Laurie Larwood and Marion M. Wood, *Women in Management* (Lexington, Mass.: Lexington Books, D.C. Heath and Company, 1977), p. 68.

14. A.P. Raia, "Goal Setting and Self-Control: An Empirical Study," *Journal of Management Studies* 21 (1965):34-53.

15. Daniel Yankelovich, "Work, Values, and the New Breed," in Clark Kerr and Jerome M. Rosow, eds., *Work in America: The Decade Ahead* (New York: Van Nostrand Reinhold, 1979), pp. 3-26.

16. Charles A. Hanson and Donna K. Hanson, "Motivation: Are the Old Theories Still True?" *Supervisory Management* (New York: AMA COM, a division of American Management Associations, June 1978) pp. 9-13.

17. Walter R. Nord and Douglass E. Durand, "What's Wrong with the Human Resources Approach to Management?" *Organizational Dynamics* (New York: AMA COM, a division of American Management Association, Winter 1978), pp. 13-18. Reprinted with permission.

Chapter 10

1. Frederick A. Harmon, "The Search for New Corporate Managers in a Shrinking Pool of Talent," *Pittsburgh Post Gazette,* 18 May 1979, p. 10.

2. Ibid.

3. Ibid.

4. See chapter 5 for a more-detailed discussion.

5. Daniel Bar-Tal and Leonard Saxe, "Physical Attractiveness and Its Relationship to Sex-Role Stereotyping," *Sex Roles* 2:2 (1976):123-33.

6. E.A. Shaw, "Differential Impact of Negative Stereotyping in Employee Selection," *Personnel Psychology* 25 (1972):333-38.

7. John P. Fernandez and Gene Kofke, "Racial and Sexual Bias Among College Students" (Unpublished study, Yale University, September-November 1975).

8. Harry Levinson, "Thinking Ahead," *Harvard Business Review* (July/August 1976), pp. 30-46.

9. Douglas W. Bray, (Lecture at Yale University, 2 October 1974).

10. Richard J. Klimonski and William J. Strickland, "Assessment Centers-Valid or Merely Prescient," *Personnel Psychology* 30 (1977):353-56. Used with permission.

11. Ibid.

12. Ibid.

13. Theodore Caplow, *The Sociology of Work* (New York: McGraw-Hill, 1954), pp. 71-72.

Chapter 11

1. George Thorton, "Differential Effects of Career Planning on Internals and Externals," *Personnel Psychology* 31 (1978):471-76. Used with permission.

2. John D. Walker and Thomas G. Gutteridge, "Career Planning Practices: An AMA Survey Report," *AMA COM* (New York: A division of the American Management Associations, 1978), pp. 1-40. Reprinted with permission.

3. Ibid.

4. Ibid.

5. Thorton, "Differential Effects," pp. 471-76.

6. Walker and Gutteridge, "Career Planning Practices," pp. 1-40.

7. Reinhart Bendix, *Work and Authority in Industry: Ideologies of Management in the Course of Industrialization* (New York: John Wiley & Sons, 1956).

8. Daniel Bell, *The End of Ideology* (New York: Collier, 1961), pp. 39-45.

9. Wilbert Moore, *The Conduct of the Corporation* (New York: Random House, 1962), pp. 3-22.

10. Jane Miller, "Who Is Responsible for Employee Career Planning?" *Personnel* (New York: AMA COM, a division of American Management Association, March/April 1978), pp. 1-19.

Chapter 12

1. Carol Hymowitz, "Sisterhood Inc.—Business is Booming for Those Who Help Women in Business, *Wall Street Journal,* 31 August 1979, pp. 1 and 7.

2. George Neeley's comments are from an analysis of data commissioned by the author in June 1979.

3. Betty Lehan Harragan, *Games Mother Never Taught You: Corporate Gamesmanship for Women* (New York: Warner, 1977), p. 35.

4. Laurie Larwood and Marion M. Wood, *Women in Management* (Lexington, Mass.: Lexington Books, D.C. Heath and Company, 1977), p. 71.

5. See for example, W.E. Abraham, *The Mind of Africa* (Chicago: University of Chicago Press, 1962); D. Forde, *African Worlds* (London: Oxford University Press, 1964); J. Jahn, *Muntu* (New York: Grove Press, 1961); and G.P. Murdock, *Africa: Its Peoples and Their Cultural History* (New York: McGraw-Hill, 1959).

6. Hymowitz, "Sisterhood Inc." pp. 1 and 7.

7. Pamela Steen's comments are from an analysis of data commissioned by the author in January 1980.

Chapter 13

1. Speech written by Lou O'Leary, vice-president, Employee Information, AT&T. Reprinted with permission.

Appendix

1. Gen. 9:25.

2. Barry N. Schwartz and Robert Disch, *White Racism* (New York: Dell, 1970), p. 6.

3. Winthrop D. Jordan, *White over Black: American Attitudes toward the Negro, 1550-1812* (Baltimore, Md.: Penguin Books, 1969).

4. Philip L. Berg, "Racism and the Puritan Mind," *Phylon* (March 1975), pp. 1-7.

5. Kenneth M. Stampp, *The Peculiar Institution: Slavery in the Ante-Bellum South* (New York: Vintage Books, 1956), p. 11.

6. Melvin Steinfield, *Cracks in the Melting Pot: Racism and Discrimination in American History* (Beverly Hills: Glencoe Press, 1970), p. 199.

7. Ibid, p. 200.

8. Ibid., p. 130.

9. Donald Keith Fellows, *A Mosaic of America's Ethnic Minorities* (New York: John Wiley & Sons, 1972), p. 137.

10. Marvin Harris, *Cannibals and Kings: The Origins of Cultures* (New York: Random House, 1977), p. 57.

11. Ibid.

12. Alleen Pace Nilsen et al., *Sexism and Language* (Urbana, Ill.: National Council of Teachers of English, 1977), p. 79. Copyright © 1977 by the National Council of Teachers of English. Reprinted by permission of the publisher and the author.

13. Ibid., pp. 82-83.

14. Ibid., p. 89.

15. Ibid., pp. 90-91.

16. Ibid., pp. 146-49.

17. Ibid., p. 104.

18. Ruth Benedict, *Patterns of Culture* Copyright renewed 1962 by Ruth Valentine (Boston: Houghton Mifflin, 1934), pp. 230-31. Reprinted by permission of Houghton Mifflin Publishers.

19. See footnotes 20, 21, and 22 for studies related to this subject.

20. J. Singh and A. Yancey, "Racial Attitudes in White, First Grade Children," *Journal of Educational Research* 67 (1974):370-72.

21. For an excellent review of racism and black mental health see Charles V. Willie et al., *Racism and Mental Health* (Pittsburgh: University of Pittsburgh Press, 1973).

22. M.E. Goodman, *Race Awareness in Young Children* (New York: Collier, 1964), pp. 36-46.

23. Helen B. Lewis, *Psychic War in Men and Women* (New York: New York University Press, 1976), p. 85.

24. Nilsen, *Sexism and Language,* pp. 30-31.

25. Ibid.

26. Ibid.

27. Judy H. Katz, *White Awareness: A Handbook for Anti-Racism Training* (Norman: University of Oklahoma Press, 1978), pp. 11-12. Reprinted with permission.

28. Ibid., p. 15.

29. James Harrison, "Warning: The Male Sex Role May Be Dangerous to Your Health." *Journal of Social Issues,* 34:1 (1978):68-69. Reprinted with permission.

30. Ibid., p. 65.

31. Ibid., p. 81.

32. Leonard Bloom, *The Social Psychology of Race Relations* (Cambridge, Mass.: Schenkman Publishing Company, 1972), p. 47.

33. See, for example, J. Grambs, eds., *Black Self-Concept—Implica-*

tions for Education and Social Science, (New York: McGraw-Hill, 1972); J. Killens, "The Black Psyche," in R. Gutherie, ed., *Being Black* (San Francisco: Canfield Press, 1970); X. Luther, "Awareness: The Key to Black Mental Health," *Journal of Black Psychology* 1 (1974):30-37; A. Thomas and S. Sillen, *Racism and Psychiatry* (New York: Brunner & Mazel, 1972); J. White, "Toward a Black Psychology," *Ebony* (September 1970), pp. 44, 45, 48-50, 52; C. Willie, B. Kramer, and B. Brown, eds., *Racism and Mental Health* (Pittsburgh: University of Pittsburgh Press, 1973); and S. Yette, *The Choice, The Issue of Black Survival in America* (New York: Berkeley Medallion, 1971).

34. Harrison, "Warning," p. 71.

35. Raymond E. Rainville and Edward McCormick, "Extent of Covert Racial Prejudice in Pro Football Announcers' Speech," *Journalism Quarterly* 54 (Spring 1977):20-26.

36. Kay Deaux and Tim Emswiller, "Explanations of Successful Performance on Sex-Linked Tasks: What is Skill of the Male is Luck for the Female," *Journal of Personality and Social Psychology* 29:1 (1974):80-85; and Rosen Benson and Thomas H. Jerdee, "Influence of Sex-Role Stereotypes on Personnel Decisions," *Journal of Applied Psychology* 59:1 (1974a):9-14.

37. Howell Raines, "Black Doctors Assert Race is Factor at Alabama Hospitals," *The New York Times,* 22 April 1979, p. 26.

38. John A. Feinblatt and Alice R. Gold, "Sex Roles and the Psychiatric Referral Process," *Sex Roles* 2:2 (1976):109-22.

39. Harold M. Baron, "The Web of Urban Racism," in Lewis L. Knowles et al., eds., *Institutional Racism in America* (Englewood Cliffs, N.J.: Prentice-Hall, 1969), pp. 142-43.

40. Robert Blauner, *Racial Oppression in America* (New York: Harper & Row, 1972), pp. 9-10.

41. Ibid.

42. See Robert Tsuchigane and Norton Dodge, *Economic Discrimination against Women in the United States* (Lexington, Mass.: D.C. Heath, 1974); and Helen S. Astin and Alan E. Bayer, "Discrimination in Academe," *Educational Record* 53:2 (Spring 1972):101-18.

43. Ibid.

44. Ibid.

45. Jeanne Spurlock, "Some Consequences of Racism for Children," in Charles V. Willis et al., *Racism and Mental Health* (Pittsburgh: University of Pittsburgh Press, 1973), p. 161.

46. Ibid.

Bibliography

Ainsworth, Leonard H. "Rigidity, Insecurity, and Stress." *Journal of Abnormal and Social Psychology* 56 (1958):67-74.

Alderfer, Clayton P. "Job Enlargement and the Organizational Context." *Personnel Psychology* 22 (1969):418-26.

Almquist, Elizabeth. *Minorities, Gender and Work.* Lexington, Mass.: Lexington Books, D.C. Heath and Company, 1979.

America, Richard F., and Anderson, Bernard E. *Moving Ahead: Black Managers in American Business.* New York: McGraw-Hill, 1978.

Applebaum, Steven H. "Changing Attitudes: A Path to the Management of Conflict." *The Personnel Administrator,* June 1974, pp. 23-25.

_____ . "Attitudes and Values: Concerns of Middle Managers." *Training and Development Journal,* October 1978, pp. 52-58.

Aquarius, Cass. "Corporate Tactics—Games People Play." *MBA,* October 1971, pp. 51-52.

Argyris, Chris. "T-Groups for Organizational Effectiveness." *Harvard Business Review* 42 (1964):60-74.

_____ . *Integrating the Individual and the Organization.* New York: John Wiley & Sons, 1964.

_____ . "A Few Words in Advance." In *The Failure of Success,* edited by Alfred J. Morrow. New York: American Management Association, 1972.

_____ . "Some Limits of Rational Man Organization Theory." *Public Administration Review,* May/June 1973, pp. 253-69.

Armstrong, Thomas P. "Job Content and Context Factors Related to Satisfaction for Different Occupational Levels." *Journal of Applied Psychology* 55 (1977):57-65.

Astin, Helen S., and Bayer, Alan E. "Discrimination in Academe." *Educational Record* 53:2 (Spring 1972):101-18.

Athanassiades, John C. "An Investigation of Some Communication Patterns of Female Subordinates in Hierarchial Organizations." *Human Relations* 27 (1974):195-209.

Balzar, Richard. *Clockwork* (Garden City, N.Y.: Doubleday, 1976).

Bankston, D.H., and Kragerer, R.L. "Communication and the Minority Employee." *Personnel Administrator,* June 1974, pp. 17-19.

Baron, Harold M. "The Web of Urban Racism." In *Institutional Racism in America,* edited by Louis L. Knowles and Kenneth Prewitts. Englewood Cliffs, N.J.: Prentice-Hall, 1969.

Bar-Tal, Daniel and Saxe, Leonard. "Physical Attractiveness and its Relationship to Sex-Role Stereotyping." *Sex Roles* 2:2 (1976):123-33.

Bartol, Kathryn M. "Male versus Female Leaders: The Effect of Leader Need for Dominance on Follower Satisfaction." *Academy of Management Journal* 17 (1974):225-33.

_____ . "The Effect of Male versus Female Leaders on Follower Satisfaction and Performance." *Journal of Business Research* 3 (1975):33-42.

Bell, Daniel. *The End of Ideology.* New York: Collier, 1961, pp. 39-45.

Bendix, Reinhard. *Work and Authority in Industry.* New York: John Wiley & Sons, 1956.

_____ and Lipset, Seymour M. *Class, Status, and Power.* Glencoe, N.Y.: Free Press, 1953.

_____ . *Social Mobility in an Industrial Society.* Berkeley and Los Angeles: University of California Press, 1962.

Benedict, Ruth. *Patterns of Culture.* Boston: Houghton Mifflin, 1934.

Benson, Rosen and Jerdee, Thomas H. "Influence of Sex-Role Stereotypes on Personnel Decisions." *Journal of Applied Psychology* 59:1 (1974a):9-14.

Berg, Ivar. *Education and Jobs: The Great Training Robbery.* Boston: Beacon, 1971.

Berg, Philip L. "Racism and the Puritan Mind." *Phylon* 36 (March 1975):1-7.

Blake, Robert R., and Mouton, Jane S. *The Managerial Grid.* Houston: Gulf, 1964.

Blauner, Robert. *Alienation and Freedom: The Factory Worker and His Industry.* Chicago: University of Chicago Press, 1964.

_____ . *Racial Oppression in America.* New York: Harper & Row, 1972.

Bloom, Leonard. *The Social Psychology of Race Relations.* Cambridge, Mass.: Schenkman, 1972.

Bonjean, Charles M.; Grady, Bruce D.; and Allen, William J.; Jr. "Social Mobility and Job Satisfaction: A Replication and Extension." *Social Forces* 46 (1967):492-501.

Bowin, Robert Bruce. "Middle Manager Mobility Patterns." *Personnel Journal,* December 1972, pp. 878-82.

Bowman, Garda W. The Image of a Promotable Person in Business Enterprise. Unpublished Ph.D. dissertation, New York University, 1962.

_____ . "What Helps or Harms Promotability?" *Harvard Business Review* 42 (1964):6-26, 184-96.

Boyd, Monica. "Oriental Immigration: The Experience of the Chinese, Japanese, and Filipino Population in the United States." *International Migration Review* 5 (Spring 1971):48-60.

Bray, Douglas W. "The Assessment Center Method of Appraising Management Potential." In *The Personnel Job in a Changing World,* edited by J.W. Blood. New York: American Management Association, 1964.

_____ . "The Assessment Center: Opportunities for Women." *Personnel* 48 (1971):30-34.

_____ and Campbell, Richard J. "Assessment Centers: An Aid in Management Selection." *Personnel Administration* 30 (1967):6-13.

_____ . "Selection of Salesmen by Means of an Assessment Center." *Journal of Applied Psychology* 52 (1968):36-41.

Bray, Douglas W. and Grant, Donald L. "Contributions of the Interview to Assessment of Management Potential." *Journal of Applied Psychology* 53 (1969):24-34.

Bray, Douglas W.; Campbell, Richard J.; and Grant, Donald L. *The Management Recruit: Formative Years in Business.* New York: Wiley—Interscience, 1974b.

Brewer, Weldon M. *Behind the Promises: Equal Employment Opportunity in the Federal Government.* Washington, D.C.: Public Interest Group, 1972.

Bruner, Dick. "Why White Collar Workers Can't be Organized." In *Man, Work and Society,* edited by S. Nosow and W.H. Form. New York: Basic Books, 1962, pp. 188-97.

Bryan, E. James. "Work Improvement and Job Enrichment: The Case of Cummins Engine Company." In *The Quality of Working Life,* edited by L.E. Davis and A.B. Cherns. New York: Free Press, 1975b, pp. 315-29.

Buckholz, Rogene A. "An Empirical Study of Contemporary Beliefs about Work in American Society." *Journal of Applied Psychology* 63:2 (1978):219-27.

Burger, Chester. *Survival in the Executive Jungle.* New York: Macmillan, 1964.

Burstein, Paul. "Legislation and the Income of Women and Nonwhites." *American Sociological Review* 44 (June 1979):367-91.

Campbell, Angus. *White Attitudes towards Black People.* Ann Arbor: University of Michigan, Institute for Social Research, 1971.

_____ ; Converse, P.E.; and Rogers, W.L. *Quality of American Life.* New York: Russell Sage Foundation, 1976.

Campbell, J.P., et al. *Managerial Behavior, Performance and Effectiveness.* New York: McGraw-Hill, 1970.

Campbell, R.J. Attitudes, Expectations, and Career Mobility. Unpublished article, New York, AT&T, 1973.

Caplan, Robert D., and French, John R.P., Jr. "Organizational Stress and Industrial Strain." In *The Failure of Success,* edited by Alfred J. Morrow. New York: American Management Association, 1972.

Caplow, Theodore. *The Sociology of Work.* New York: McGraw-Hill, 1954.

Carpenter, H.H. "Formal Organizational Structural Factors and Perceived Job Satisfaction of Classroom Teachers." *Administrative Science Quarterly* 16 (1971):460-65.

Carroll, Stephen J., Jr. "Beauty, Bias, and Business." *Personnel Administration*, March/April 1969, pp. 21-25.

Carzo, Rocco, Jr., and Yanouzas, John N. "Effects of Flat and Tall Organization Structure." *Administrative Science Quarterly* 14 (1969):178-91.

Chinoy, Ely. *Automobile Workers and the American Dream*. Garden City, N.Y.: Doubleday, 1955.

Clark, Kenneth B. "A Psychologist Looks at Discrimination Patterns." *MBA* 6 (1972):33-34.

Cline, Mary Ellen, et al. "Evaluations of the Work of Men and Women as a Function of the Sex of the Judges and Type of Work." *Journal of Applied Social Psychology* 71 (1977):89-93.

Coates, Charles H., and Pellegrin, Roland J. "Executives and Supervisors: A Situational Theory of Differential Mobility." *Social Forces* 35 (1956): 121-26.

Cohen, Stephen L. "Issues in the Selection of Minority Group Employees." *Human Resource Management,* Spring 1974, pp. 12-18.

Collins, Orvis. "Ethnic Behavior in Industry: Sponsorship and Rejection in a New England Factory." *American Journal of Sociology* 51 (1946):293-98.

Cooper, M.R., et al. "Changing Employees Values: Deepening Discontents?" *Harvard Business Review,* January/February 1979, pp. 117-25.

Corwin, Ronald; Taves, Marvin J.; and Eugene, Haas J. "Social Requirements for Occupational Success: Internalized Norms and Friendship." *Social Forces* 39 (1961):135-40.

Crewdson, John M. "Hispanics Angered as U.S. Bars Brutality Charges against Police." *The New York Times,* 10 July 1979.

Crochett, Harry J., Jr. "Psychological Origins of Mobility." In *Social Structure, Social Mobility and Economic Development,* edited by Neil J. Smelser and Seymour M. Lipset. Chicago: Aldine, 1965.

Crotty, Philip T., and Timmons, Jeffrey A. "Older Minorities—'Road-blocked' in the Organization." *Business Horizons,* June 1974, pp. 27-34.

Crowley, Joan E.; Levitan, Teresa E.; and Quinn, Robert P. "Seven Deadly Half-Truths About Women." *Psychology Today* 7 (1973):94-96.

Cussler, Margaret. *The Woman Executive*. New York: Harcourt Brace, 1958.

Dalton, Melville, "Conflicts between Staff and Line Managerial Officers." *American Sociological Review* 21 (1950): 342-51.

——— . "Informal Factors in Career Achievement." *American Journal of Sociology* 56 (1951):407-15.

——— . *Men Who Manage*. New York: John Wiley & Sons, 1959.

Davis, Keith. *Human Relations at Work*. New York: McGraw-Hill, 1967.

Davis, Louis E., and Cherns, Albert B., eds. *The Quality of Working Life*. New York: Free Press, 1975.

Deaux, Kay and Emswiller, Tim. "Explanations of Successful Performance on Sex-Linked Tasks: What is Skill of the Male is Luck for the Female." *Journal of Personality and Social Psychology* 29:1 (1974): 80-85.

Deloria, Vine, Jr. *Custer Died for Your Sins*. New York: Avon Books, 1970.

Dore, Ronald. *British Factory—Japanese Factory: The Origins of National Diversity in Industrial Relations*. Berkeley: University of California Press, 1973.

Drucker, Peter F. *The Practice of Management*. New York: Harper & Row, 1954.

_____ . *Managing for Results*. New York: Harper & Row, 1964.

Duncan, Otis D.; Schuman, Howard; and Duncan, Beverly. *Social Change in a Metropolitan Community*. New York: Russell Sage Foundation, 1973.

Ehrenreich, Barbara and English, Deidre. *Complaints and Disorders*. New York: Faculty Press, 1973.

Einstein, Kurt. "Screening Executives: The Guy Who Just Slipped By." *Management Review*, July 1972, pp. 26-32.

Elbing, Alvar O.; Gordon, Herman; and Gordon, John R. "Flexible Working Hours: It's About Time." *Harvard Business Review* 52 (January/February 1974):18-33.

Epstein, Cynthia. *Woman's Place*. Berkeley: University of California Press, 1970.

Featherman, David L., and Hauser, H. Robert M. "Sexual Inequalities and Socioeconomic Achievement in the United States, 1962-1973." *American Sociological Review* 41 (June 1976):462-83.

Feinblatt, John A., and Gold, Alice R. "Sex Roles and the Psychiatric Referral Process." *Sex Roles* 2:2 (1976):109-22.

Fellow, Donald Keith. *A Mosaic of America's Ethnic Minorities*. New York: John Wiley & Sons, 1972.

Fernandez, John P. *Black Managers in White Corporations*. New York: John Wiley & Sons, 1975.

Fong, Stanley L.M., and Peskin, H. "Sex Role Strain and Personality Adjustment of China-Born Students in America." *Journal of Abnormal Psychology* 74 (October 1969):563-67.

Ford, Robert N. *Motivation through the Work Itself*. New York: American Management Association, 1969.

_____ . "Job Enrichment Lessons from AT&T." *Harvard Business Review* 51 (1973):96-106.

Frank, Linda L., and Hackman, J. Richard. "A Failure of Job Enrichment: The Case of the Change that Wasn't." *Technical Report No. 8*

New Haven: Department of Administrative Sciences, Yale University, 1975.

Freeman, Evelyn S., and Fields, Charles L. *A Study of Black Male Professionals in Industry*. Washington, D.C.: U.S. Labor Department, 1972.

————. "Black Professionals: The Gap is Not Closing." *MBA* 6 (1972): 73-84(a).

Fromm, Erich. *The Sane Society*. New York: Holt, Rinehart and Winston, 1955.

Fujitomi, Irene and Wong, Diane. "The New Asian-American Woman." In *Asian Americans: Psychological Perspective*, edited by S. Sue and N. Wagner. Palo Alto, Calif.: Science and Behavior Books, 1973, pp. 236-48.

Fulmer, Robert M., and Fulmer, William E. "Providing Equal Opportunities for Promotion." *Personnel Journal*, July 1974, pp. 491-97.

Ginsburg, Sigmund G. "The Problem of the Burned Out Executive." *Personnel Journal*, August 1974, pp. 598-600.

Ginzberg, Eli and Yohalem, Alice M., eds. *Corporate Lib: Women's Challenge to Management*. Baltimore, Md.: Johns Hopkins University Press, 1973.

Goode, Kenneth G. "Query: Can the Afro American Be an Effective Executive?" *California Management Review*, Fall 1970, pp. 22-26.

Goodman, M.E. *Race Awareness in Young Children*. New York: Collier, 1964.

Goodman, Richard Alan. "A Hidden Issue in Minority Employment." *California Management Review*, Summer 1969, pp. 27-30.

Green, Barbara J. "Upgrading Black Women in the Supervisory Ranks." *Personnel*, November/December 1969, pp. 47-50.

Greenhaus, Jeffrey M., and Gavin, James F. "The Relationship between Expectancies and Job Behavior for White and Black Employees." *Personnel Psychology* 25 (1972):440-55.

Grier, William H., and Cobbs, Price M. *Black Rage*. New York: Basic Books, 1968.

Hackman, J.R., and Lawler, E.E. "Employee Reactions to Job Characteristics." *Journal of Applied Psychology* 55 (1971):259-86.

Hall, Douglass T., and Hale, Francine S. "Career Development: How Organizations Put Their Fingerprints on People." In *Careers in Organizations: Individual Planning and Organizational Development*, edited by Lee Dyer. Ithaca, N.Y.: New York State School of Industrial and Labor Relations, Cornell University, 1976.

Hamill, Katharine. "Women as Bosses." *Fortune*, June 1956, pp. 105-108.

Hamner, W. Clay, et al. "Race and Sex as Determinants of Ratings by Potential Employers in a Simulated Work Sampling Task." *Journal of Applied Psychology* 59:6 (1974):705-11.

Harmon, Frederick A. "The Search for New Corporate Managers in a Shrinking Pool of Talent." *Pittsburgh Post Gazette*, 18 May 1979, p. 10.

Harragan, Betty Lehan. *Games Mother Never Taught You: Corporate Gamesmanship for Women*. New York: Warner, 1977.

Harris, Marvin. *Cannibals and Kings: The Origins of Cultures*. New York: Random House, 1977.

Hennig, Margaret and Jardim, Anne. *The Managerial Woman*. Garden City, N.Y.: Doubleday, 1976.

Herzberg, Frederick. *Work and the Nature of Man*. Cleveland: World, 1966.

Hill, Raymond. "Interpersonal Values and Personal Development in Executives." *Human Resource Management*, Summer 1973, pp. 24-27.

Hughes, Charles L. *Goal Setting*. New York: American Management Association, 1965.

Hymowitz, Carol. "Sisterhood Inc.—Business is Booming for Those Who Help Women in Business." *Wall Street Journal*, 31 August 1979, pp. 1 and 7.

Jacobsen, R. Brooke. "Changes in the Chinese Family." *Social Science* 51 (Winter 1976):26-31.

Janeway, Elizabeth. *Man's World, Woman's Place*. New York: Dell, 1971.

Jennings, Eugene E. *An Anatomy of Leadership*. New York: McGraw-Hill, 1960.

_____ . *The Executive in Crisis*. New York: McGraw-Hill, 1965.

_____ . *The Mobile Manager*. Ann Arbor: Bureau of Industrial Relations, Graduate School of Business Administration, University of Michigan, 1967.

_____ . *Routes to the Executive Suite*. New York: McGraw-Hill, 1971.

Jobu, Robert M. "Earnings Differences of White and Ethnic Minorities: The Case of Asians, Americans, the Blacks and Chicanos." *Sociology and Social Research* 66:1 (October 1976):24-38.

Jordan, Winthrop D. *White over Black: American Attitudes toward the Negro 1550-1812*. Baltimore, Md.: Penguin Books, 1969.

Jung, Marshall and Homma-True, Reiko. "Characteristics of Contrasting Chinatowns: Philadelphia, Pennsylvania and Oakland, California." *Social Casework* #5 (March 1976):149-59.

Kanter, Rosabeth Moss. *Commitment and Community*. Cambridge, Mass.: Harvard University Press, 1972.

_____ . "The Impact of Hierarchial Structures on the Work Behavior of Women and Men." *Social Problems* 23 (1976):415-30.

_____ . "Some Effects of Proportion in Group Life Skewed Sex Ratios and Responses to Token Women." *American Journal of Sociology* 82 (1977):965-90.

————— . *Men and Women of the Corporation*. New York: Basic Books, 1977.

————— . "Work in a New America." *Daedalus* 107:1 (Winter 1978):47-78.

Kasl, Stanislav V. "Work and Mental Health." In *Work and the Quality of Life*, edited by James O'Toole. Cambridge, Mass.: MIT Press, 1974, pp. 171-96.

Katz, Judy H. *White Awareness: A Handbook for Anti-Racism Training*. Norman: University of Oklahoma Press, 1978.

Katzell, Raymond A., and Yankelovich, Daniel. *Work, Productivity and Job Satisfaction*. New York: Psychological Corporation, 1975.

Kaufman, Carl B. *Man Incorporate: The Individual and His Work in an Organized Society*. Rev. ed. Garden City, N.Y.: Doubleday Anchor, 1969.

Kay, Emanuel. "Middle Management." In *Work and the Quality of Life*, edited by James O'Toole. Cambridge, Mass.: MIT Press, 1974, pp. 106-30.

Keller, Suzanne. *Beyond the Ruling Class: Strategic Elites in Modern Society*. New York: Random House, 1953.

Kerr, Clark and Rosow, Jerome M., eds. *Work in America: The Decade Ahead*. New York: Van Nostrand Reinhold, 1979.

Klimonski, Richard J., and Strickland, William J. "Assessment Centers—Valid or Merely Prescient?" *Personnel Psychology* 30 (1977):353-56.

Knight, Michael. "Gains Affirm Indian Rights Demands." *The New York Times*, 9 July 1979, p. 10.

Korda, Michael. *Male Chauvinism: How It Works*. New York: Random House, 1973.

Kovel, Joel. *White Racism: A Psychohistory*. New York: Vintage Press, 1971.

Kronholz, June. "Women at Work: Management Practices Change To Reflect Role of Women Employees." *Wall Street Journal*, 3 September 1978, p. 1.

Laird, Donald A., with Laird, Eleanor C. *The Psychology of Supervising the Working Woman*. New York: McGraw-Hill, 1942.

Laws, Judith Long. "The Psychology of Tokenism: An Analysis." *Sex Roles* 1 (1975):51-67.

————— . "Work Aspirations in Women: False Leads and New Starts." *Signs: A Journal of Women in Culture and Society* 2 (1976):33-50.

Larwood, Laurie and Wood, Marion M. *Women in Management*. Lexington, Mass.: Lexington Books, D.C. Heath and Company, 1977.

Lerner, Gerda, ed. *Black Women in White America: A Documentary History*. New York: Vintage, 1973.

Levinson, Harry. "Thinking Ahead." *Harvard Business Review* (July/August 1976):30-46.

Lewis, Diane K. "The Black Family: Socialization and Sex Roles." *Phylon* 36:3 (September 1975):221-37.

Lewis, Helen B. *Psychic War in Men and Women.* New York: New York Univesity Press, 1976.

Litton, Robert Jay. *The Life of the Self: Toward a New Psychology.* New York: Simon and Schuster, 1976.

Maccoby, Eleanor Emmons and Jacklin, Carol Nagy. *The Psychology of Sex Differences.* Stanford, Calif.: Stanford University Press, 1974.

Makielski, S.J., Jr. *Beleagued Minorities: Cultural Politics in America.* San Francisco: W.H. Freeman, 1973.

Mann, Richard D. "A Review of the Relationship between Personality and Performance in Small Groups." *Psychological Bulletin* 56 (1959):241-70.

Marcus, Philip M., and House, James S. "Exchange between Superoirs and Subordinates in Large Organizations." *Administrative Science Quarterly* 18 (1973):209-22.

Marden, Charles F., and Meyer, Gladys. *Minorities in American Society,* New York: Van Nostrand Reinhold, 1973.

Marx, Gary. *Protest and Prejudice.* New York: Harper & Row, 1967.

McClelland, David. *The Achieving Society.* New York: Free Press, 1961.

Megaree, Edwin I. "Influence of Sex Roles on the Manifestation of Leadership." *Journal of Applied Psychology* 53 (1969):377-82.

Meier, Matt S., and Riviera, Feliciano. *The Chicanos: A History of Mexican Americans.* New York: Hill and Wang, 1972.

Miller, Jane. "Who Is Responsible for Employee Career Planning?" *Personnel.* March/April 1978, pp. 1-19.

Mills, C. Wright. *White Collar.* New York: Oxford University Press, 1951.
_____ . *The Sociological Imagination.* New York: Oxford University Press, 1959.

Miner, John B. "Twenty Years of Research on Role-Motivation Theory of Managerial Effectiveness." *Personnel Psychology* 31 (1978):739-59.

Mintzberg, Henry. *The Nature of Managerial Work.* New York: Harper & Row, 1973.

Mitchell, Juliet. *Woman's Estate.* New York: Pantheon Books, 1971.

Moore, Wilbert. *The Conduct of the Corporation.* New York: Random House, 1962.

Morgan, John S., and Van Dyke, Richard L. *White Collar Blacks: A Breakthrough?* New York: American Management Association, 1970.

Morrow, Alfred J., ed. *The Failure of Success.* New York: American Management Association, 1972.

Morse, Nancy. *Satisfaction in the White Collar Job.* (Ann Arbor: Survey Research Center, 1953.

_____, and Weiss, Robert S. "The Function and Meaning of Work and the Job." *American Sociological Review* 20 (1955):191-98.

Nason, Robert W. "The Dilemma of Black Mobility in Management: Discrimination Is Still a Problem." *Business Horizons*, August 1972, pp. 57-68.

Newcomer, Mable. *The Big Business Executive: The Factors that Made Him.* New York: Columbia University Press, 1955.

Nilsen, Alleen Pace. *Sexism and Language.* Urbana, Ill.: National Council of Teachers of English, 1977.

Nord, Walter R., and Durand, Douglass E. "What's Wrong with the Human Resources Approach to Management?" *Organizaional Dynamics* Winter 1978, pp. 13-18.

Olive, Loise E., et al. "Moving as Perceived by Executives and Their Families." *Journal of Occupational Medicine* 18:8 (August 1976):546-50.

Ornati, Oscar A., and Pisano, Anthony. "Affirmative Action: Why It Isn't Working." *Personnel Administrator*, September/October 1972, pp. 50-52.

Packard, Vance. *The Pyramid Climbers.* New York: McGraw-Hill, 1962.

Patz, Alan L. "Performance Appraisal: Useful But Still Resisted." *Harvard Business Review* 53 (May/June 1975), pp. 74-80.

Pelz, Donald C. "Influence: A Key to Effective Leadership in the First-Line Supervisor." *Personnel* 29 (1959):3-11.

Pennings, J.M. "Work-Value Systems of White Collar Workers." *Administrative Science Quarterly* 15 (1970):397-405.

Peterson, Richard O., and Duffany, Bruce H. "Job Enrichment and Redesign." In *Training and Development Handbook,* 2nd ed., edited by R.L. Craig. New York: McGraw-Hill, 1976.

Phelps, E.S. "The Statistical Theory of Racism and Sexism." *American Economic Review* 62 (1972):659-61.

Pheterson, Gail; Kiesler, Sara; and Goldberg, Philip. "Evaluation of Women as a Function of Their Sex Achievement and Personal History." *Journal of Personality and Social Psychology* 19 (D1971):114-18.

Porter, L.W., and Lawler, E.E. "The Effects of 'Tall' Versus 'Flat' Organization Structures on Managerial Satisfaction." *Personnel Psychology* 17 (1964):135-48.

Porter, L.W., Lawler, E.E., and Hackman, J.R., Jr. *Behavior in Organizations.* New York: McGraw-Hill, 1975.

Porter, Lyman W. "A Study of Perceived Need Satisfactions in Bottom and Middle Management Jobs." *Journal of Applied Psychology* 45 (1961):1-10.

_____. "Job Attitudes in Management. I. Perceived Deficiencies in Need Fulfillment as a Function of Job Level." *Journal of Applied Psychology* 46 (1962):375-84.

Poussaint, Alvin F. "The Negro American: His Self-Image and Integration." In *The Black Power Revolt,* edited by Floyd B. Barbour. Boston: Sargent, 1968.

Quinn, R.P.; Gordon, L.K.; and Tabor, J.M. *The Decision to Discriminate: A Study of Executive Selection.* Ann Arbor: Institute for Social Research, 1968.

Raia, A.P. "Goal Setting and Self-Control: An Empirical Study." *Journal of Management Studies* 21 (1965):34-53.

Raines, Howell. "Black Doctors Assert Race is Factor at Alabama Hospitals." *The New York Times,* 22 April 1979, p. 26.

Rainville, Raymond E., and McCormick, Edward. "Extent of Covert Racial Prejudice in Pro Football Announcers' Speech." *Journalism Quarterly* 54 (Spring 1977):70-76.

Reimers, David M., et al. *Natives and Strangers: Ethnic Groups and the Building of America.* New York: Oxford University Press, 1979.

Reitan, Harold T., and Shaw, Marvin E. "Group Membership, Sex-Composition of the Group, and Conformity Behavior." *Journal of Social Psychology* 64 (1964):45-51.

Ritzer, George. *Working: Conflict and Change.* Englewood Cliffs, N.J. Prentice-Hall, 1977.

Roche, Gerard. "Much Ado About Mentors." *Harvard Business Review* (January/February 1979), pp. 14-28.

Rosen, Benson and Jerdee, Thomas H. "Influence of Sex-Role Stereotypes on Personnel Decisions." *Journal of Applied Psychology* 59 (1974a):9-14.

_____ . "Sex Stereotyping in the Executive Suite." *Harvard Business Review* 52 (March/April 1974):45-58.

Rosenbloom, David H. "Equal Employment Opportunity: Another Strategy." *Personnel Administration and Public Personnel Review* 1 (1972):39-41.

Rosenfeld, Rachel A. "Women's Intergenerational Occupational Mobility." *American Sociological Review* 43 (February 1978):36-46.

Rothman, Sheila M. *Woman's Proper Place: A History of Changing Ideals and Practices, 1870 to the Present.* New York: Basic Books, 1978.

Ryan, Mary P. *Womanhood in America: From Colonial Times to the Present.* New York: New Viewpoints, 1975.

Ryan, William. *Blaming the Victim.* New York: Random House, 1971.

Schein, V.E. "The Relationship between Sex Role Stereotypes and Requisite Management Characteristics." *Journal of Applied Psychology* 57 (1973):95-100.

_____ . "Relationships between Sex Role Stereotypes and Requisite Management Characteristics among Female Managers." *Journal of Applied Psychology* 60 (1975):340-44.

Schoonover, Jean Way. "Why American Men Fear Women Executives." *Boston Globe,* 27 March 1974.

Schuller, Randall. "Male and Female Routes to Managerial Success." *Personnel Administrator,* February 1979, pp. 35-38.

Schwartz, Barry N., et al. *White Racism.* New York: Dell, 1970.

Seidenberg, Robert. *Corporate Wives—Corporate Casualties?* New York: AMACOM, 1973.

Shaw, E.A. "Differential Impact of Negative Stereotyping in Employee Selection." *Personnel Psychology* 25 (1972):333-38.

Silberman, Charles E. *Crisis in Black and White.* New York: Random House, 1964.

––––––. *Criminal Violence, Criminal Justice.* New York: Random House, 1978.

Sinclair, Upton. *The Jungle.* New York: New American Library, 1906.

Singh, J., and Yancey, A. "Racial Attitudes in White, First Grade Children." *Journal of Educational Research* 67 (1974):370-72.

Smuts, Robert W. *Women and Work in America.* New York: Columbia University Press, 1951.

Sowell, Thomas. *Race and Economics.* New York: David McKay, 1975.

"Special *Ebony* Poll: Survey Queries of 4,500 Black Elected Officials." *Ebony,* May 1979, pp. 183-85.

Stampp. Kenneth M. *The Peculiar Institution: Slavery in the Ante-Bellum South.* New York: Vintage Books, 1956.

Staples, Robert. *The Black Woman in America.* Chicago: Nelson-Hall, 1978.

Steen, Pamela L. "Designing Compatible Work Systems." *Journal of the College and University Personnel Association* 28:3 (Summer 1977):43-46.

Steiner, Stan. *La Roza: The Mexican Americans.* New York: Harper and Row, 1968.

Steinfield, Melvin. *Cracks in the Melting Pot: Racism and Discrimination in American History.* Beverly Hills: Glencoe Press, 1970.

Sturdivant, Frederick D., and Adler, Roy D. "Executive Origins: Still a Gray Flannel World?" *Harvard Business Review* (November/December 1976), pp. 125-32.

Suter, Larry and Mitler, Henry. "Income Differences between Men and Career Women." *American Journal of Sociology* 78 (January 1973):962-74.

Taylor, Shelley and Fiske, Susan T. "The Token in a Small Group: Research Findings and Theoretical Implications." In *Psychology and Politics, Collected Papers,* edited by J. Sweeney. New Haven: Yale University Press, 1976.

Taylor, Stuart A. "The Black Executive and the Corporation—A Difficult Fit" *MBA,* January 1972, pp. 91-102.

Theodore, Athena, ed. *The Professional Woman.* Cambridge, Mass. Schenkman, 1971.

Thompson, Paul H., and Dalton, Gene W. "Performance Appraisal: Managers Beware." *Harvard Business Review* 48 (January/February 1970):149-57.

Thorndike, R.L. *Personnel Selection.* New York: John Wiley & Sons, 1966.

Thorton, George. "Differential Effects of Career Planning on Internals and Externals." *Personnel Psychology* 31 (1978):471-76.

Tracy, Lane. "Postscript to the Peter Principle." *Harvard Business Review* 50 (July/August 1972):65-71.

Tsuchigane, Robert and Dodge, Norton. *Economic Discrimination against Women in the United States.* Lexington, Mass. D.C. Heath, 1974.

Umstot, Denis D., et al. "Goal Setting and Job Enrichment: An Integrated Approach to Job Design." *Academy of Management Review* October 1978, pp. 867-79.

U.S. Commission on Civil Rights, *The State of Civil Rights: 1977: A Report of the United States Commission on Civil Rights.* Washington, D.C.: U.S. Government Printing Office, February 1978, pp. 16-21.

Valentine, Charles A. *Black Studies and Anthropology: Scholarly and Political Interests in Afro-American Culture.* Reading, Mass.: Addison-Wesley, 1972.

Vroom, Victor H. *Work and Motivation.* New York: John Wiley & Sons, 1964.

Walker, John D., and Thomas G. Gutteridge. "Career Planning Practices: An AMA Survey Report." *AMA COM* (1978):1-40.

Wallace, Phyllis A., ed. *Equal Employment Opportunity and the AT&T Case.* Cambridge, Mass.: MIT Press, 1976.

Walton, Richard. "Innovative Restructuring of Work." In *The Worker and the Job,* edited by J.M. Rosow. Englewood Cliffs, N.J.: Prentice-Hall, 1974.

Warner, William L., and Abeggelen, James C. *Occupational Mobility in American Business and Industry.* Minneapolis: University of Minnesota Press, 1955.

_____. *Big Business Leaders in America.* New York: Harper & Row, 1963.

Weaver, Charles N. "Negro-White Differences in Job Satisfaction." *Business Horizons.* February 1974, pp. 67-72.

_____. "Sex Differences in Job Satisfaction." *Business Horizons.* June 1974, pp. 43-49.

_____. "What Workers Want from Their Jobs." *Personnel.* May/June 1976, pp. 48-54.

Welds, Kathryn. "It's a Question of Stereotypes vs. Reality, Limits vs. Potential." *Personnel Journal* June 1979, pp. 380-83.

White, Phyllis. National Committee Against Discrimination in Housing (NCDH). Telephone interview, 3 November 1977. The National Committee, under contract to the Department of Housing and Urban Development, conducted a 1977 study which unearthed evidence of pervasive, continuing housing discrimination. See NCDH. *Trends in Housing* (Fall 1977).

Wilensky, Harold. "Measures and Effects of Social Mobility." In *Social Structure and Mobility in Economic Development,* edited by Neil J. Smelser and Seymour M. Lipset. Chicago: Aldine, 1966.

Wilkinson, Doris Y., and Taylor, Ronald L. *The Black Male in America: Perspectives on His Status in Contemporary Society.* Chicago: Nelson-Hall, 1977.

Wilson, William Julius. *The Declining Significance of Race, Blacks and Changing American Institutions.* Chicago: University of Chicago Press, 1978.

Wong, William. "Chinese Americans Help U.S. Employees Bridge the Language Gap in China." *Wall Street Journal,* 3 July 1979, p. 30.

Work in America. Report of a special task force to the secretary of the Department of Health, Education, and Welfare. Cambridge, Mass. MIT Press, 1973.

Yankelovich, Daniel. "The Meaning of Work." In *The Worker and the Job: Coping with Change,* edited by Jerome M. Rosow. Englewood Cliffs, N.J.: Prentice-Hall, 1974, pp. 19-47.

————. "Work Values and the New Breed." In *Work in America: The Decade Ahead,* edited by Clark Kerr and Jerome M. Rosow. New York: Van Nostrand Reinhold, 1979.

Zaleznik, Abraham. "The Management of Disappointment." *Harvard Business Review* (November/December 1967), pp. 59-70.

Zanden, James Wilfred Vander. *American Minority Relations: The Sociology of Race and Ethnic Groups.* New York: Press Company, 1963.

Index

Ability: basic, 279; bosses' supervisory, 166-167; criteria, 88, 134, 137; development, 241-242; learning, 241; reward for, 3, 103

Acculturation, Afro-American, 76

Achievement: job, 170; levels of, 160; and motivation, 98; personal, 43

Administrative skills, 241, 279-280

Advancement: career, 109, 136; goals, 101-136; lack of, 13; of managers, 103-105; opportunities, 3, 134, 140, 298; rate of, 17, 111, 223; sponsorship effects on, 133-135

Affirmative Action Programs (AAP), 5, 8, 77, 96, 117-126, 262, 282. *See also* Equal Employment Opportunities (EEO)

Africa and Afro-Americans, 36, 76

Age: of bosses, 169; discrimination, 130; and education, 109-111; effects of, 13, 38, 43, 47, 92-94, 144, 225, 231, 245, 300; and job performance, 220; and promotions, 130-133

Aggressiveness, feelings of, 281, 314

Alcoholism, rate of, 23

Alder, Roy, 102-103

Alibarhou, Gloria Lindsy, 74, 77

Alibi, race and sex used as, 270, 277

Alienation: feelings of, 40, 158, 224; job, 183

Aliens, illegal, 33-34

Almquist, Elizabeth, 25, 34-36, 75-76

Ambiguity and ambition, 157, 280-281

America, Richard, 134

American Latino Community, 33

American Management Associations (AMA), 6

American Telephone and Telegraph Company (AT&T), 241, 292, 295

Anderson, Bernard, 134

Anglo: authority, 31; society, 31, 33

Anti-: blacks, 306; Chinese, 27; feminist movement, 74; Hispanics, 31; immigration laws, 26; Japanese, 28; Mexicans, 32; social behavior, 183, 191

Anxiety, feelings of, 158

Appraisal: management, 257; performance, 168, 185, 203-210

Appearance, personal, 201, 225, 232, 245, 281

Argyris, Chris, 157

Arizona, 32

Army language schools, U.S., 29

Asia and Asians, 9-10, 39-40, 50, 53, 61; cultures, 25, 233; male managers, 40, 172; men, 298; society, 78; women, 11, 47, 71, 73-76, 108, 116-117, 170, 196, 203-205, 211, 218, 232, 254, 268, 273

Asian-Americans: factor of, 20, 25, 29, 31, 40; as managers, 233

Aspirations, feelings of, 101-136

Assembly-line workers, 209

Assertiveness: feelings of, 158, 280; training for, 274-275

Attitudes and opinions, 6; conformist, 59; of cynicism, 113; getting-along-together, 157; job, 190; managerial, 7, 9, 270; negative, 43-45, 293-294; new-breed, 229-230; nonambivalent, 40; political, 102; prejudicial, 310; pro-integrationist, 125; racist, 19, 26, 43-47, 53, 176, 293, 309-310; relocation, 154; sexist, 71, 74, 77, 82, 98, 167, 270, 277, 280, 284, 286, 296, 309-310; stereotyped, 57; temporary work, 68; white-male, 82; women's, 215

Attractiveness, physical, 231

Authoritarianism, policy of, 8, 275, 280

Authority: Anglo, 31; assertion of, 3, 159, 229, 265; female, 273; traditional, 8, 300

Autonomy, 181, 186, 199, 221, 299; job, 193-195

About the Author

John P. Fernandez received the B.A. from Harvard University and the Ph.D. from the University of California, Berkeley. He was manager of education and development at American Telephone and Telegraph, and an assistant professor of sociology at Yale University. Dr. Fernandez served as operations manager for a large, multidepartment division of Bell of Pennsylvania, where he is currently division manager of labor relations for the Philadelphia area. His first book is titled *Black Managers in White Corporations*.